Shih Poo

Shih Poo Complete Owner's Manual

Shih Poo temperament, care, costs, feeding, health, grooming and training all included.

by

Elliott Lang

Table of Contents

Table of Contents

Table of Contents

Table of Contents

Table of Contents

Table of Contents

Foreword

When it comes time to find the perfect dog for your household, there are going to be many options that come to mind. There are many different dog breeds out there that are known to be good for one type of situation or another, but one crossbreed that is increasing in popularity and fame is the Shih Poo.

This small dog is a crossbreed with both poodle and Shih Tzu ancestry, and though it is primarily known for its size, there are many factors that make it a great pet.

Before purchasing a Shih Poo for your situation, there are quite a few things to learn. This is a very new type of dog, and without recognition from any of the major kennel clubs, there is not a great deal of consensus on what the standards for this crossbreed are. Having said that, some major kennel clubs do accept registration of crossbreed and mixed-breed dogs for performance events such as agility and obedience

To make sure that the Shih Poo is going to be a good fit for you, consider all of the factors that go into making the Shih Poo the dog it is before you decide to bring one home.

You will find several spelling of Shih Poo on the web and in books: Shih-poo, Shih poo, Shih-Poo, Shihpoo. I have opted for Shih Poo in this book.

Chapter 1) Learning About the Breed

Before you purchase any dog, you need to learn a little bit about the breed or breeds involved, and the Shih Poo is no exception. To ensure that you have a thorough grounding in everything that this crossbreed may throw at you, it is important to understand both of the parent breeds as well. After that, you can learn more about the Shih Poo and what traits it might express.

1) Poodles

Though poodles are very much associated with the wealthy, the truth is that poodles were originally working dogs. Their fluffy curly coats were designed to protect them in cold weather and cold water, and anyone who brings a poodle to a pond or a lake will quickly realize that this dog was born and bred for the water.

Poodles are among the most intelligent dog breeds in the world, and they are very accustomed to working closely with their owners on a variety of tasks. They have been used as retrievers for hundreds of years, and during World War II, they were one of the 32 dog breeds registered as war dogs by the United States Army.

Today, poodles are still retrievers for hunters, and thanks to their keen sense of smell, they are also used to hunt truffles, the most valuable mushrooms in the world.

A long history as a work dog has gifted the poodle with a sharp intellect and a certain amount of independence. Though this dog is highly trainable and extremely bright, it can be seen by people who are not ready for it as downright stubborn. They need to know that something is a good idea before they blindly follow orders, and they can ignore orders that they do not understand or want to follow.

The poodle's fur, which is frequently passed on to its Shih Poo descendants, is tightly curly, having a little more in common with human hair rather than standard dog fur. Because of the quality of the fur, the poodle is considered to be a very low-shedding, hypoallergenic dog. It is a good choice for people who only have minor allergies to animals, and this is another desirable trait that can be passed on to its offspring

Because of its attractive appearance and the sculptured quality of its fur, the poodle is often brought into homes as a companion animal. The truth is that though poodles do bind very tightly to their owners and they are loyal to a fault, they were not originally designed to be companions.

A household that wants to take in a poodle needs to be willing to give this dog plenty of exercise and plenty of stimulation, or the dog will end up being destructive. These are definitely instincts that a Shih Poo can inherit, so be aware of this fact.

There are three commonly recognized sizes for a poodle, including standard, miniature and toy. For the most part, the Shih Poos are bred from miniature and toy poodles, as part of the intent is to get a dog that is as small and as cute as possible.

2) Shih Tzus

Shih Tzus are one of the oldest dog breeds in the world; there is evidence that the breed might have been developed around 800 BCE. Its roots seem to go back to China, and it shares certain features with small dogs like the long-haired Chihuahua and the Papillion.

Despite their pampered appearance, the age of the breed actually puts it genetically very close to wolves. As you may guess from the name, the Shih Tzu breed was a favorite of Chinese royalty, who gave away these lovely dogs to their favorite ministers and politicians.

The Shih Tzu was such a favorite that it was forbidden to buy one. They could only ever be gifts, and receiving one was a very important sign of royal favor. European explorers mention these dogs when they write about China, but it wasn't until the early half of the twentieth century that the first Shih Tzus made their way to England and from there to the United States

The Shih Tzu is a small dog with long silky fur. Though it was bred primarily as a companion animal, it has a loud bark that occurs at the least provocation in untrained dogs.

Despite having a coat that is very different from that of the poodle, the Shih Tzu is also known to be a low-shedding, hypoallergenic dog, an excellent companion for someone with only mild allergies.

These dogs are alert and very loving, but they do need to be trained carefully. Like other small dog breeds, they can become snappish and easily frustrated if they are not given enough training and enough socialization when they are young.

Another thing that distinguishes the Shih Tzu is that it is quite a headstrong dog in some ways. People who like this breed enjoy its temperament, but those who are not used to it might end up being frustrated with a dog that is not as eager to please as say, a German shepherd or a Labrador.

A Shih Tzu is a fine companion animal once it is well trained and acclimated to its family.

3) Shih Poo History

Shih Poos are a relatively new crossbreed, and they did not gain much attention before 2005. There were certainly poodle/Shih Tzu crosses before that, but they were generally regarded as mutts. They tended to be accidents rather than the deliberate crossbreeding that is going on today.

They are occasionally called designer dogs or mutts, but in many cases, this is exactly how other breeds got their start. The only difference between the Shih Poo and other breeds that were developed within the last 200 years is that the Shih Poo is much newer.

At this point, the majority of Shih Poos available are first generation crosses between poodles and Shih Tzus, but as time goes on, it is apparent that we will see second generation crosses between a Shih Poo and a Shih Poo, resulting in a greater consensus on what the breed will end up looking like and what it means to be a member of this breed.

Shih Poos, like maltipoos, morkies, and other similar breeds have a certain appeal simply because of their size. The use of miniature poodles and Shih Tzus guarantees a small dog, and some breeders have continued that trend, creating dogs that are at the small end of the spectrum for the breed.

The practice of breeding smaller and smaller dogs is one that is quite controversial, and it is something that has led to certain fragility in the Shih Poo.

The Shih Poo is known for its cute appearance, and its round face and the kinky/curly fur that it receives from its poodle ancestry is something that makes it quite a charmer!

4) Shih Poo Breed Appearance

Now that you have a little more information about the two-parent breeds, it is time to learn more about the Shih Poo.

According to various breeders, a Shih Poo can be anywhere from 8 to 18 pounds, or 3.5 to 8 kilograms. This makes for a very small dog, with some breeders advertising dogs that are as small as possible. They are usually between 8 to 11 inches (20 to 27 centimeters) at the shoulder. They usually finish the bulk of their growth within their first year.

A healthy Shih Poo is a small dog with legs that are proportionate to the body, a round face and a willing temperament. Some dog experts believe that the larger a Shih Poo is, the healthier it is. Shih Poos are one crossbreed that has fallen prey to the trend for extremely small designer dogs, and the smaller specimens of the crossbreed often end up having more health problems.

It is important to understand, however, that when you are

purchasing a Shih Poo, there is no guarantee on what it will turn out to be like. Temperament and coat color and quality are discussed below.

5) Temperament

As you might guess by looking at the natures of the poodle and the Shih Tzu, the inherent nature of the Shih Poo is a bit of a mixed bag. These are two vibrantly different dogs, and the end result is a puppy that can end up having a bit of either lineage in its temperament.

Due to their size and their fragility, these dogs are best when they are merely kept as companion animals. They are invariably sweet -natured and curious, but they can also be quite excitable. Because of their Shih Tzu parentage, they can be prone to barking, and this is something that needs to be trained out of them as they grow and develop.

Shih Poos are very personable dogs, and they are relatively intelligent as well. Do not be surprised if you have a dose of the poodle's intelligence in their nature as well. This can make them a little stubborn when it comes to training, and in turn, it is something that can make training an essential part of your day!

They are loyal animals, and they have the ability to bond firmly to their owners. As a matter of fact, they can bond so firmly to their owners that they need to be socialized to other animals and people when they are young so that they do not get stressed out when dealing with these things as they get older.

6) Coats

Because there is no breed standards for the Shih Poo, the coat can have a variety of different textures and colors. There are no show standards for this dog, but generally, there will be a little bit of a wave to the coat, which is the natural result of crossing the Shih Tzu's silky fur with the curly fur of the poodle.

There is no standard color for Shih Poo coats, but there is a great demand for white Shih Poos and black Shih Poos especially. In addition to the dogs that are solid colored, you will also find that there are some dogs that have a speckled coat or ones with markings on their backs and their faces.

Some Shih Poos have fur that is as curly and dense as the poodle, while other Shih Poos have fur that is slightly more relaxed. Some Shih Poos have fur that is almost as smooth as that of their Shih Tzu parent, though there is generally a bit of texture to it.

The grooming needs of the Shih Poo are discussed later, but in general, this is a breed that does well with some attention paid to their fur on a regular basis. Many people take their Shih Poos to the groomer once every six weeks, while other people take them to the groomer more regularly than that.

7) Hypoallergenic or Not?

With two parent breeds that are considered to be hypoallergenic, it seems like a surety that the Shih Poo would be. This is generally true, but if you have severe allergies to dogs, it is important to understand a few things.

In the first place, when people are allergic to dogs, they are generally allergic to dander, the shed skin flakes from the dog, and saliva from the dog's mouth. They are not actually allergic to the dog's fur.

However, if the dog is a low-shedding breed, like the poodle and the Shih Tzu, the production of dander is usually reduced. This means that someone who has only a small allergy or who has become used to the dander produced by a certain animal will have a mild reaction or no reaction at all to a specific dog.

If you are someone who is allergic to dogs, it is worth spending some time with Shih Poos to figure out if you are allergic to them.

Remember that as you get more used to an animal, your allergy will tend to reduce over time. Allergies can further be reduced by medication and a thorough cleaning regimen that removes dander from the environment.

8) Understanding Crossbreeds

It is important to understand that the Shih Poo is a crossbreed. There is not yet a real standard for this dog, and when you choose one, you must be willing to take your chances.

People talk about hybrid vigor, but the truth is that with only a few generations to work with, it is impossible to see what is being reinforced and what is being bred out. It is just as easy to get a dog that has all the frailties of the parent breeds as it is to get one with all the benefits of the parent breeds.

Be aware of this before you purchase a Shih Poo!

Chapter 2) Shih Poo Myths

If you want to take good care of your Shih Poo, it is important to recognize and to disregard some of the myths that grow up around the breed. Being aware of these myths makes you a savvy owner, and they can help prevent harm or injury to your dog.

1) Myth: Shih Poos Love to Be Carried in Purses

Fact: No dog should be carried in a purse. Purses keep a dog off of its feet, giving it a feeling of being hung in the air and off balance. A purse that is carried too carelessly can result in the dog being swung into something that will hurt it. If you are worried about carrying your Shih Poo through crowds, either pick it up and hold it close to your body or carry it in a hard carrier where it will feel enclosed and safe.

2) Myth: Shih Poos Stay Small If You Feed Them Less

Fact: You should always feed your Shih Poo according to the directions given to you by your veterinarian. If anyone tells you to feed your Shih Poo less to keep it small and cute, they are advocating a form of animal abuse. Malnourished animals are small, but they are far from healthy or happy.

3) Myth: Shih Poos Are a Recognized Breed

Fact: Some unscrupulous breeders will tell you that Shih Poos are a recognized breed to inflate their worth. The truth is that while Shih Poos are recognized by the International Designer Canine Registry, more recognized organizations like the American Kennel Club and The Kennel Club of the UK do not see the Shih Poo as a real breed.

Though there are general guidelines for what this dog looks like, and though there are a few things that you can expect from the breed, the truth is that there are quite a few things that are not standardized at all.

4) Myth: Shih Poos Need No Exercise

Fact: Though Shih Poos do not need the same kind of exercise that, say, an Australian cattle dog or a Dalmatian does, still they require regular outings where they can stretch their legs. Take the time to make sure that your Shih Poo gets the right kind of exercise it needs. While you cannot expect a Shih Poo to go on long runs with you, a Shih Poo will always appreciate one or two brisk walks every day, and it will also enjoy plenty of play time with you.

5) Myth: Shih Poos Do Not Need to Be Trained

Fact: Shih Poos need to be trained just as much as any other dog. Because Shih Poos are so small, some people believe that they do not have to undergo the same kind of training that other dogs require. As a matter of fact, any dog can be dangerous, and any dog can be put down for biting.

Shih Poos are independently-minded, and thanks to their poodle ancestry, they can be quite clever. This means that they need to be well trained so that they will take your orders more readily.

One issue that many owners of small dogs run into is that people will automatically reach for your Shih Poo in a way that they will not reach for a breed that is perceived as more menacing. This means that whether you like it or not, there are always going to be people who reach for your dog unexpectedly or at a point where you are not watching them.

When this happens, your dog needs to be well-trained enough to avoid snapping at the person or biting them. It takes remarkably little to get a dog picked up and even put down for viciousness.

Good training for your Shih Poo is an essential part of ensuring that your dog stays safe no matter what is going on.

6) Myth: Shih Poos Always Come From One Poodle Parent and One Shih Tzu Parent.

Fact: There are more and more Shih Poos that are actually the offspring of two Shih Poos instead of being the offspring of a poodle or a Shih Tzu. This means that it is even more important to make sure that you know what the parents look like and to consider what conditions they were raised in.

Part of getting a dog means that you should be able to take care of it its entire life, and that means that you need to consider how that dog grows up. With a crossbreed like a Shih Poo, be willing to consider how you can learn more about its parentage.

There is no real advantage to looking for a Shih Poo born of two Shih Poo parents over a first generation cross except for perhaps having a better idea about what the puppy will look like as it gets older. In either case, it is still too early to get an idea of what the crossbreed will end up with as a standard.

Chapter 3) Should I Have a Shih Poo?

There is no doubt about it that Shih Poos are charming dogs, but the truth of the matter is that they are not dogs for everyone. Take a moment to learn more about this crossbreed and whether it is the one for you.

1) Genetic Uncertainty

Some people believe that when you cross the traits of two breeds, you will invariably get the best parts of both breeds. For example, there are many Shih Poos out there that have the poodle's intelligence and the Shih Tzu's cuddly nature. On the other hand, it is important to remember that you may also get a dog with a poodle's stubbornness and a Shih Tzu's tendency to bark!

Genetics is always a gamble, and because the Shih Poo is such a new breed, you will find that there is little information at the moment over what is being reinforced.

With standardized dog breeds, things like certain genetic issues and temperament problems have been bred out, while favorable traits have been selected for reinforcement. With a crossbreed that is as young as the Shih Poo, there has not yet been the opportunity to do so.

If you are someone who is a little nervous about knowing what they are going to get with their dog, it may be best for you to go with a purebred dog that has an established history and genetic inheritance. Choosing a Shih Poo is in many ways a gamble.

2) Kids and the Shih Poo

The Shih Poo, due to its size, seems to be a prime candidate for households with children, and this is true to a certain extent. While it is not as immediately threatening as a pit bull or a Dalmatian, Shih Poos, like every other dog, can deliver a painful bite if provoked.

These dogs are companion animals, but they can be a little high-strung if they are constantly confronted by children.

If you decide to bring a Shih Poo into a house with children in it, make sure that those children are older. A child that is around the age of ten and eleven can be trusted not to aggravate a dog, but one that is younger might provoke a bite or worse.

Another thing to keep in mind is that the Shih Poo is a relatively delicate animal. This is something that can turn into a fatal issue if the child plays too rough with the dog. In some cases, it might be best to get a larger dog that your children can roughhouse with safely.

This is not to say that a child and a Shih Poo cannot make great companions, but the idea does need to be approached with caution. Make sure that you are considering what your child is like and how much time you can spend teaching them to respect each other.

3) Homes

One of the big benefits of the Shih Poo when it comes to housing is that this is a small dog. It is a dog that fits well into apartment spaces, and provided it has enough space to get some exercise every day, it can be quite happy in a one bedroom apartment.

You do not need to dedicate large amounts of space to the Shih Poo, and if you are living in a smaller space, this can make it the ideal pet.

However, one thing to keep in mind is that when you are looking at the Shih Poo, you are looking at a dog that has a rather piercing bark. Most Shih Poos can be trained out of this issue, but there are always a few members of the crossbreed that cannot.

If your dog is always barking, it can mean some serious issues with you and your neighbors. A dog that barks whenever someone passes your apartment's door is a nuisance, and you may have the police called, or you may be evicted if it keeps up.

Shih Poos are usually ideal for apartment living if you are considering looking for a small dog, but consider the barking issue carefully.

4) Indoor Dogs

While Shih Poos can enjoy spending a fair amount of time outside, they are a little more vulnerable to the dangers out there than larger dogs are. For example, if you live in a rural area, there is always a chance that you have to worry about coyote packs, but if you happen to live in a rural area and own a Shih Poo, you need to be aware that eagles and other birds of prey can injure or even kill your dog.

This is not a dog that you can leave outside for long stretches of the day. It is meant to live inside and to be allowed out for exercise on a regular basis.

5) Companionship

The Shih Poo is without a doubt a companion animal. This means that it will want to be close with you and it will want to be around you. This is a serious issue if you are someone who works between eight and 10 hours a day and the dog ends up being left home alone a great deal.

While most people understand that people love dogs for the companionship that they provide, it is also important to remember that dogs love us for the same reason! A Shih Poo that is left on its own for hours and hours every day is an animal that will quickly grow restless and even destructive.

Remember that despite thousands of years of selective breeding, a Shih Poo is still an animal that is descended from a wolf. Wolves hunted in packs, and their survival was predicated on knowing where their family members were. In the modern era, dogs have replaced their packs with people, and if you leave a Shih Poo alone constantly, you will quickly find that it grows nervous, upset and even neurotic.

If you are someone who is quite busy but would still like to have a Shih Poo in your life, it is best for you to consider a doggy day care service or a private service that will bring someone over to your house to look after your dog. This is a serious thing to consider before you commit!

6) The Pros of Purchasing a Shih Poo

This is a charming breed, and there are a few things that will surely endear them to you.

1. Shih Poos Are Small

These dogs are small enough to fit into a standard one bedroom apartment, and they are quite content with that space as long as you take them out every day and let them run. They are more widely accepted into apartments than larger dogs.

2. Shih Poos Are Cute

With the adorably kinky fur that is a mix of the poodle's coat and the Shih Tzu's coat, a sweet face and adorably floppy ears, the Shih Poo is amazingly cute. They retain this look even as they age, oftentimes leading people to mistake them for puppies.

3. Shih Poos Can Be Long-Lived

As smaller dogs, Shih Poos can live quite lengthy lives compared to larger dogs. The general lifespan for a Shih Poo tends to be between 12 and 15 years, with some individuals living even longer. If you are someone who has a hard time with pets passing, this may be the right choice for you.

4. Shih Poos Are Loving

This is a crossbreed that is designed to be a companion animal, and with that in mind, it is amazingly loving. These dogs adore their people, and they are quite loyal. They want nothing more than to sit next to you and to keep you company.

7) The Cons of Purchasing a Shih Poo

Every breed and crossbreed has its downside, so make sure that you know what you are getting into!

1. Shih Poos Are Expensive

The price of Shih Poos are discussed later, but in general, remember that this is a designer dog brand that is growing in popularity. This means that they are expensive, and it is not uncommon to pay 1000 dollars or more for a Shih Poo.

2. Shih Poos Can Be Stubborn

Shih Poos can inherit a big dose of that poodle independence, and that means that they may need to be convinced to see things your way. Just because this dog is small does not necessarily mean that it is easy going, so be ready to do some serious obedience training if you are thinking about bringing this dog into your home.

3. No Breeding Standards

Because there is no breeding standard or conformation that a breeder needs to stick to, a Shih Poo can come in a wide range of body types, temperaments and coat qualities. You will not necessarily know what your puppy is going to grow up to look like, and you will find that this is something that can lead to problems later on down the line.

8) Male or Female?

When it comes to determining whether you want a male or female Shih Poo, one important thing to remember is that as long as a dog is well-trained and well socialized, there is actually very little difference between the two. Female Shih Poos tend to mature and develop faster than their male counterparts. This means that they tend to pick up their training a little faster than the males do. In addition, there is a general belief among people who own Shih Poos that the males are a little more outgoing, while the females are a little more serious.

However, this does not mean that you cannot have a boisterous female or a reserved male. The best way to be sure about a puppy's temperament is to observe its parents and to watch it closely while you play engage with it.

Getting to know a puppy before you adopt it is a great way to make sure that you are going to be getting the best dog that suits your needs.

Think about what kind of temperament that you need to see in your puppy and consider whether you need a male or a female.

9) Am I Home Enough?

Dogs need companionship, and a Shih Poo, even if it is small, is no different. An adult dog can be left on its own for up to four hours. Since Shih Poos are small though, they sometimes need to be taken out more often because their bladders are quite tiny.

In addition to that, dogs are pack animals, and your Shih Poo depends on you as its owner and as its family for emotional support. If you have ever been in a neighborhood or an apartment building with a dog that that will not stop barking, you know how frustrating that can be.

Dogs that are left alone for too long will become destructive and neurotic. Though your Shih Poo bears little resemblance to a wolf, the truth is that it needs its pack around it.

A Shih Poo is a wonderful companion animal, but you either need to be someone who is always willing to be there for it, or you need to be someone who is willing to find alternatives to giving it the care that it requires.

Some solutions include having a dog sitter, taking your Shih Poo to a doggy daycare or making sure to come home on your lunch break. These are all solutions that can work to keep your Shih Poo happy.

10) Are You Willing to Keep a Shih Poo Its Entire Life?

A Shih Poo is a fairly long-lived dog, all things considered. This means that you will need to consider how your life may look in 12 to 15 years, or more.

Most breeders and veterinarians recommend that you should only get a dog if you are willing to keep it for its entire life. For example, if you are planning a move to a different country, make sure that you will be in a position to take your Shih Poo with you when you move. Quarantine laws are things that can prevent you from having your dog with you.

Similarly, are you planning to move to another city? Moving with a dog is far from impossible, but if you are going to find it troublesome to drive with a dog in the car or to pay to have your dog shipped to the new location, you should hold off on getting your dog.

11) Is the Shih Poo an Escape Artist?

As clever as poodles are, it makes sense that a Shih Poo could have inherited that wit and will use it to make escapes! Shih Tzus are not known to be escape artists, but many people have found that Shih Poos can get away from them simply by virtue of being small enough to miss.

Any tiny opening in a fence will be an open door invitation to a curious Shih Poo who has caught a scent or simply has a zest for adventure. This is especially common when you are dealing with a puppy.

Early spaying or neutering of a Shih Poo puppy will go a long way toward helping to curb any wanderlust tendencies.

12) Yearly Cost

Although it is impossible to accurately estimate what the cost of owning a Shih Poo might be, there are some expenses to consider. Unexpected medical problems might arise or you may like to buy fancy clothes for your dog every week. Since you will be sharing your life with a dog, it's important to consider more than just the daily cost of feeding your Shih Poo.

Many people do not think about whether or not they can truly afford to care for a dog before they bring one home, and not being prepared can cause stress and problems later on.

Remember that being financially responsible for your Shih Poo is a large part of being a good guardian.

Beyond the initial investment of purchasing your Shih Poo puppy from a reputable breeder, for most guardians, owning a Shih Poo will include the costs associated with the following:

- food

- treats

- pee pads, poop bags, potty patches

- leashes and collars

- safety harnesses

- travel kennels or bags

- house training pens

- clothing

- toys

- beds

- grooming

- regular veterinary care

- obedience or dog whispering classes

- pet sitting, walking or boarding

- pet insurance

- yearly licensing

- unexpected emergencies

As you can see, depending upon where you shop, what type of food you feed your Shih Poo, what sort of veterinarian or grooming care you choose, whether or not you have pet insurance and what types of items you purchase for your Shih Poo's well-being, the yearly cost of owning a Shih Poo could be estimated at anywhere between $700 and $3,000 (£420 and £1,800). Other contributing factors that may have an effect on the overall yearly cost of owning a Shih Poo can include the region where you live, the accessibility of the items you need, your own lifestyle as well as your Shih Poo's age and individual needs.

13) Choosing Pet Insurance for Your Shih Poo

As mentioned above, insurance is something that is very important for the health of your new puppy. When considering medical insurance for their dog, owners must ask themselves if they can afford not to have it.

In light of all the expensive new treatments and medications that are now available for our dogs, an increasing number of guardians have decided to add pet insurance to their list of monthly expenses.

On the other hand, other people believe that placing money into a savings account, in case unforeseen medical treatments are required, makes more sense.

Pet insurance coverage can cost anywhere from $2,000 to $6,000 USD (£1201 to £3604) over an average lifespan, and unless your dog is involved in a serious accident, you may never need to pay out that much for treatment.

Whether you decide to start a savings account for your Shih Poo so that you will always have funds available for unforeseen health issues, or you decide to buy a health insurance plan, most of us dog lovers will go to any lengths to save the life of our beloved companions.

For those people who may not be independently wealthy, having some sort of pet insurance will provide peace of mind that could be much more preferable than the extra stress involved in going into debt, should you be faced with a substantial veterinarian bill.

Keep in mind that veterinary science has advanced in recent years, which means that veterinarians and our canine companions now have access to sophisticated, yet very costly diagnostic equipment.

Having access to advanced technological tools and procedures means that our dogs are now offered treatment options that were once only reserved for people. Now, some canine conditions that were once considered fatal are being treated at considerable costs ranging anywhere from $1,000 to $5,000 (£597 to £2,986), or more.

However, even in the face of rapidly increasing costs of caring for our dogs, owners who purchase pet insurance remain a small minority.

In an effort to increase the numbers of people buying pet insurance, insurers have teamed with the American Kennel Club and Petco Animal Supplies to offer the insurance. More than 1,600 companies, such as Office Depot and Google, now offer pet insurance coverage to their employees as an optional employee benefit.

Even though you might believe that pet insurance will be your savior anytime your dog needs a trip to the vet's office, you really need to be careful when considering an insurance plan, because there are many policies that contain small print that excludes certain ages, hereditary or chronic conditions.

Unfortunately, most people don't consider pet insurance when their pets are healthy because buying pet insurance means playing the odds, and unless your dog becomes seriously ill, you end up paying for something that may never happen.

However, just like automobile insurance, you can't buy it after you've had that accident.

Therefore, since many of us in today's uncertain economy could not afford to pay a high veterinarian bill, generally speaking, the alternative of paying monthly pet insurance premiums will provide peace of mind and provide better veterinarian care for our best friends.

The right policy can be an asset to the health care of your dog while having a significant impact on reducing the cost you might have to pay as a result of an emergency visit to your veterinarian's office.

Shop around, because as with all insurance policies, pet insurance policies will vary greatly between companies and the only way to know for sure exactly what sort of coverage you are buying is to have a copy of that policy in front of you so that you can clearly see what will be covered and what will not be covered.

Don't forget to carefully read the fine print to avoid any nasty surprises because the time to discover that a certain procedure will not be covered is not when you are in the middle of filing a claim.

There are several considerations to be aware of before choosing to purchase a pet insurance policy, including:

Is your dog required to undergo a physical exam?

Is there a waiting period before the policy becomes active?

What percentage of the bill does the insurance company pay — after the deductible?

Are payments limited or capped in any way?

Are there co-pays (costs to you up front)?

Does the plan cover pre-existing conditions?

Does the plan cover chronic or recurring medical problems?

Can you choose any vet or animal hospital to treat your pet?

Are prescription medications covered?

Are you covered when traveling with your pet?

Does the policy pay if your pet is being treated and then dies?

When you love your dog and worry that you may not have the funds to cover an emergency medical situation that could unexpectedly cost thousands, the right pet insurance policy will provide both peace of mind and better health care for your beloved fur friend.

14) Licensing

Many cities and jurisdictions around the world require that dogs be licensed.

Usually a dog license is an identifying tag that the dog will be required to wear on their collar. The tag will have an identifying number and a contact number for the registering organization, so that if someone finds a lost dog wearing a tag, the owner of the dog can be contacted.

Most dog tags are only valid for one year, and will need to be renewed annually at the beginning of every New Year. This involves paying a fee which can vary from jurisdiction to jurisdiction.

For instance, owners of dogs living in Beijing, China must pay a licensing fee of $600 (£360), while licensing for dogs living in Great Britain was abolished in 1987.

Ireland and Northern Ireland both require dogs to be licensed and in Germany dog ownership is taxed, rather than requiring licensing, with higher taxes being paid for breeds of dogs deemed to be "dangerous".

Most US states and municipalities have licensing laws in effect and Canadian, Australian and New Zealand dogs also must be licensed, with the yearly cost approximately $30 to $50 (£18 to £30) depending upon whether the dog is spayed or neutered.

15) Asking the Right Questions

When you are thinking about picking a Shih Poo puppy, or indeed any dog, it is essential for you to make sure that you have the space in your life for it. There are too many puppies abandoned every year because their owners do not know what they were taking on, so make sure that you do not contribute to this problem!

In order to be fair to ourselves, our family and the puppy we choose to share our lives with, we need to take a serious look at our life both as it is today and what we envision it being in the next ten to fifteen years. We must then ask ourselves a few important, personal questions, and honestly answer them, before making the commitment to a puppy, including:

(1) Do I have the time and patience necessary to devote to a puppy which will grow into a dog that needs a great deal of

attention, training and endless amounts of my devotion?

(2) Do I lead a physically active, medium or low intensity life? For instance, am I out jogging the streets daily or climbing mountains or would I rather spend my leisure time on the couch?

(3) Do I like to travel a lot? Perhaps a dog small enough to travel in the plane cabin with me is a consideration.

(4) Am I a neat freak? A non-shedding breed such as the Shih Poo would make more sense.

(5) Do I have a young, growing family that takes up all my spare time? A dog needs a lot of time and attention.

(6) Am I physically fit and healthy enough to be out there walking a dog two to three times a day, every day, rain or shine (and much more when it's just a puppy)?

(7) Can I afford the food costs and the veterinarian expenses that are part of being a conscientious dog guardian?

(8) Is the decision to bring a puppy into my life a family decision, or just for the children, who will quickly lose interest?

(9) What is the number one reason why I want a dog in my life?

Once you ask yourself these important questions and honestly answer them, you will have a much better understanding of the type of puppy that would be best suited for you and your family, and whether or not it should be a Shih Poo.

If you choose the wrong dog, you will inevitably end up with an unhappy dog which will lead to behavioral issues, which then will lead to an unhappy family. Please take the time to choose wisely.

Chapter 4) Choosing a Shih Poo

When you have decided to adopt a Shih Poo into your home, it is important for you to get the happiest, healthiest puppy possible. There's more to getting a healthy Shih Poo than simply finding someone with a litter. If you want to get the dog that is perfect for your family, there are a few things to keep in mind.

1) Paying the Price

If you want to purchase a Shih Poo puppy from a good breeder, you should be willing to invest a fair amount of money in it. For a good breeder who has worked extensively with the breed and who has paid a lot of attention to the dogs that produced the puppies, it is not unusually to pay anywhere from 800 to 1500 dollars for a Shih Poo or 480 to 900 English pounds.

This may sound like a large amount of money to pay for a puppy, but it at least tells you that you are dealing with a professional breeder. People who are giving away their puppies or who are only asking a hundred dollars or less have likely just ended up with an accidental litter.

A quality Shih Poo puppy from the breeder will be up to date on all of its shots, neutered or spayed, and have been tested for a host of inheritable genetic disorders. That, in addition to prenatal care, stud fees and puppy care fees adds up to a lot of money, and most good breeders really do not even start making a profit until they have established themselves.

If you are unable or unwilling to pay this price, it may be a good idea to look into a shelter or rescue option, or simply to choose a different breed of dog.

2) Avoiding Puppy Mills

The popularity of the Shih Poo has led to a lot of serious issues with puppy mills. A puppy mill is an operation that breeds a large number of puppies designated for the pet trade. They are typically only concerned about the bottom line, and because of that, the animals that are being bred suffer terribly. The end result produces puppies that are malnourished from the womb, poorly socialized, and often very nervous and traumatized when they are purchased.

Because the bottom line is on the puppies that can be sold, puppy mills tend to breed for quantity rather than quality. There is little to no attention paid to the fitness of either the sire or the dam, and the puppies are seldom tested for any of the genetic issues for which the breeds are prone.

Shih Poo puppies are popular, and because of that, they are frequently being bred by puppy mills and sent to pet stores. Most, if not all, pet stores get their animals from puppy mills, and this is a type of industry that many people are beginning to protest. The exceptions are pet stores that provide kenneling and adoption days for rescues, but this is something that is labeled and advertised very clearly.

Every time someone buys a puppy from a pet store, the store will order more from the puppy mill. As far as the pet store is concerned, the puppies are simply inventory, like bags of dog food, and when one item drops off of the inventory list, another is purchased to replace it. Puppy mill puppies are also sold at flea markets, on the side of the road, at the beach, through newspaper ads and through fancy websites and Internet classifieds.

The only way to put these shameful, commercial businesses out of business is by spreading the word and refusing to buy a puppy from a pet store, or any other advertising medium, unless you have first thoroughly checked them out by visiting the facility in person.

Always be wary if you answer an advertisement for a puppy for sale and the person selling offers to deliver the puppy to you, because this could easily be the first sign that you are about to be involved in an illegal puppy mill operation.

Educate yourself and spread the word to others about puppy mills, because this is the first step toward ensuring that you are never unknowingly involved in the suffering that is forced upon the breeding dogs and puppies trapped in a puppy mill operation.

When you are thinking about choosing a puppy, the best way to avoid puppy mill puppies is to actually visit the puppy's birthplace. A good breeder will always be happy to introduce you to at least the puppy's dam, and also to the puppy's sire if he is on the premises.

3) Considering Shelter Adoption or Rescues

There is also the possibility that you can pick up a Shih Poo from a shelter or a rescue. The regrettable fact is that these dogs are quite trendy, and as with the case of other breeds that get popular, they end up getting dumped when their owners get tired of them.

When you are considering shelter adoption, remember that you may still get a very young dog or even a puppy. Some shelters will charge just a hundred dollars for a puppy, and that means that its shots have been completed and it has been spayed or neutered.

If you are someone who has had some experience with dogs before, it may interest you to take on an older rescue dog. Older rescue Shih Poos often come with very sad stories in their pasts. They may have had owners who were negligent or abusive, or their families may have simply become unable to care for them.

Adopting an older shelter dog can come with its own unique challenges and joys. A dog from the shelter may have learned a lot of undesirable behaviors. Due to bad breeding or irresponsible care, they may have health problems that are not present when you choose a dog from a good breeder.

Do not simply choose a shelter dog because it is cheaper than getting a dog from a breeder. Shelter Shih Poos can turn their lives around and make exceptional pets, but it will take a lot of time and love on your part.

When you are interested in adopting a Shih Poo from a shelter, the best thing that you can do is to start calling the shelters and the rescues in your area. Let them know that you are someone who is interested in adopting a Shih Poo, and that you would like to be notified when they have them in.

Remember that as Shih Poos are a popular crossbreed at this point, it is very common for you to be placed on a waiting list. This is something that may mean a wait of several months or even a year.

You may also have better luck with organizations that rescue certain breeds. If you have a poodle or a Shih Tzu rescue nearby, there is a good chance that they may have a puppy or a dog for you.

While all dogs require good and consistent care, a Shih Poo that you adopt from the shelter needs more reassurance and understanding than most. It might be very shy around you, or it might have very strong reactions to certain types of people. For example, if the dog was abused by a large man, the dog might be very shy of or snappish with anyone fitting that category.

While it sounds like a lovely idea to bring a dog into your home to rehabilitate it, remember that it is far better to avoid the situation if you are not certain that you have the time, the energy and the patience for a shelter dog.

When you get a Shih Poo from the shelter, you do not necessarily know what kind of training it has had or what kind of life it has lead before you got it. It might have behavioral issues, it might have health issues that are not immediately apparent, and it might have serious fears that it never gets over.

When you adopt a Shih Poo from the shelter, look at the dog as it is. Make sure that you can deal with the animal as it is. You can generally expect some improvement, but sometimes, improvement is very slow and very minimal. Make sure that you know what you are getting in to!

4) Two Shih Poo Puppies or One?

The question of whether to buy one puppy or two is one that often occurs to people, but the short answer is that unless you are a dog training expert with a lot of time on your hands, it is invariably better to stick with just one puppy.

If you purchase two puppies, you are looking at twice the work and twice the mess. One puppy is enough of a handful for someone who doesn't know what they are getting in to, and two can make things pretty frustrating.

Also, there is the risk that the puppies will bond to each other instead of to you. This alone can make training very difficult, and training with two dogs, unless you have more than one person available all the time, can be trying enough as it is.

While there is nothing wrong with having two dogs in the house to keep each other company, you will find that it is a good idea to get one puppy first, and then to get a second puppy when the first one has spent four or five months with you. Depending on the situation that your breeder is in, they may even be able to sell you a second puppy from a litter with the same dam and sire.

Many people decide to get two puppies because they want their puppy to have someone to play with, and one of the reasons for this decision might be based on the fact that the person making this decision might not be the ideal candidate for having one puppy, let alone two.

For instance, if the reason you are considering two puppies is so that the one puppy will not be alone all day while you are at work, stop right there, because leaving one, two or a dozen puppies alone all day while you are at work is a terrible decision and you should NOT be considering any puppy at this stage of your life.

Another consideration when thinking about whether or not to get two puppies is that often when they grow up, there may be continual sibling rivalry as each puppy vies for your attention.

What often happens when the puppies mature is that they stop getting along with each other, and their relationship may deteriorate to the point where they no longer enjoy each other's company.

Further, when you have two puppies growing up together, one will always be the more dominant personality that will take over the other, and this could mean that neither puppy will fully develop their individual personalities.

Over all, it is far better to simply stick with one Shih Poo puppy. These puppies might be small, but as anyone can tell you, they can be quite mischievous and strong willed. Having just one puppy to worry about can make things a lot less of a problem as time goes on.

5) Is This Shih Poo Puppy Healthy?

Of course you will want to check if a puppy you are considering taking home is not just emotionally healthy, but also physically healthy.

First, ask to see veterinarian reports from the breeder to satisfy yourself that the puppy is as healthy as possible, and then once you make your decision to share your life with a particular puppy, make an appointment with your own veterinarian for a complete examination.

Before you get to this stage, however, there are a few general signs of good health to be aware of when choosing a healthy puppy from a litter, including the following:

Breathing: they will breathe quietly, without coughing or sneezing, and there will be no crusting or discharge around their nostrils;

Body: they will look round and well fed, with an obvious layer of fat over their rib cage;

Coat: they will have a soft, shiny coat with no dandruff, dullness, greasiness or bald spots;

Energy: a well-rested puppy should be alert and energetic;

Hearing: a puppy should react if you clap your hands behind their head;

Genitals: they will not have any sort of discharge visible in or around their genital or anal region;

Mobility: they will walk and run normally without wobbling, limping or seeming to be stiff or sore; and

Vision: they will have bright, clear eyes without crust or discharge and they should notice a ball rolling past within their field of vision.

6) Does Color Matter?

The question of whether the color of a dog matters is always a rather moot point. Except for some congenital disorders being carried by dogs who are albino, color does not carry any particular significance when it comes to a dog's general health or temperament. Remember that white dogs with dark eyes are not considered albinos for this case.

It is very easy to be attracted to the various colors found on Shih Poos, but at the end of the day, it is far more important to choose a puppy based on its health and its temperament rather than on its color.

There are no color standards for this breed, and because you will not be showing it, you will not need any specific color conformation at all.

The only thing to check on the coat is to make sure that the coat it is soft, shiny and has healthy appearance.

If you are planning to get two puppies, it might be worth your while to get puppies with two different coat colors, as it will help you tell them apart; especially when they are very young and you do not yet know their personalities.

7) Age of an Adopted Shih Poo

Generally speaking, no puppy, including a Shih Poo puppy, should be removed from their mother any earlier than 8 weeks of age and leaving them until they are 10 to 16 weeks of age is preferred. This will give them the time to learn important life skills from the mother dog, including eating solid food and grooming.

As well, leaving a puppy among their litter mates for a longer period of time will help to ensure that they learn socialization skills.

Removing a puppy from the mother and other siblings too early could mean that they will miss out on valuable skills, and may not socialize well with others.

For the first month of a puppy's life they will be on a mother's milk only diet. Once the puppy's teeth begin to appear, they will start to be weaned from mother's milk and by the age of 8 weeks should be completely weaned and eating just puppy food.

Removing a puppy from their mother any earlier than eight weeks could mean they are not fully weaned and they would be much more difficult to feed.

8) Picking a Specific Puppy

Although your breeder can often help you with selecting the right puppy for you and your family, you will likely be feeling especially drawn to one puppy over another.

Although there are other considerations, how you feel toward a particular puppy in a litter is also an important part of deciding which pup to bring home.

Beyond your feelings, considering other factors will help improve the odds of you having a positive guardianship experience with your new Shih Poo puppy.

For instance, being a little objective when evaluating each puppy in the litter will help you to make the right choice.

While some people become very emotional when choosing a puppy and will be attracted to those who display extremes in behavior because they want to "save" them, it is not particularly good advice to choose a puppy that may be very shy or frightened in the hope that they may grow into a happy, well-behaved dog.

Some people will delve even further into their emotional desires or needs to "save" or "rescue" and will choose a particular puppy because it has obvious health or behavioral issues and they want to provide it with a chance that they believe the puppy might not otherwise have.

While it is certainly wonderful that we humans have the capacity to raise and care for puppies that may be afflicted with health or behavior problems, it's important that these types of decisions are not undertaken lightly as such challenges can be a daunting undertaking.

While many minor behavioral problems can be modified with early training, it's important to be aware that the time and effort needed to do so will be difficult to predict.

Generally speaking, when choosing a puppy out of a litter, look for one that is friendly and outgoing, rather than one who is overly aggressive or fearful.

Taking note of a puppy's social skills, when they are still with their litter mates, will help you to choose the right puppy to take home. Puppies who demonstrate good social skills with their litter mates are much more likely to develop into easy going, happy adults who play well with other dogs.

In a social setting where all the puppies can be observed together, take notice:

During play, which puppies are comfortable both on top and on the bottom when play fighting and wresting with their litter mates. Which puppies seem to only like being on top? Puppies who don't mind being on the bottom or who appear to be fine with either position, will usually play well other dogs when they become adults.

If the puppies have toys to play with, observe which puppies try to keep the toys away from the other puppies and which puppies share. Those who want the toys to themselves may be more aggressive with other dogs or in play where toys are involved as they become older.

Which puppies seem to like the company of the other pups and which ones seem to be loners? Puppies who like the company of their litter mates are more likely to be interested in the company of other dogs as they mature, more than anti-social puppies.

It is important to pay attention to the reaction of puppies that get yelped at when they bite or roughhouse with another puppy. Puppies that ease up when another puppy yelps or cries are more likely to respond appropriately when they play too roughly as adults.

Also, check to see if the puppy you are interested in is sociable with people, because if they will not come to you, or display fear to strangers, this may be a problem when they become adults.

Further, always check if the puppy you are interested in is relaxed about being handled. If they are not, they may become difficult with adults and children during daily interactions, during grooming or visits to the veterinarian's office.

9) Bring the Whole Family

When you are interested in picking a puppy or an older dog, remember that it is a good idea to bring along everyone that the puppy will be living with. This might mean making more than one trip, but in general, this is a good idea. Not only does it let you see the breeder/rescuer's conditions, you can also learn a lot more about a puppy by visiting more than once.

Basically, what you want to do is to bring along all of the people that the puppy will be interacting with normally. A puppy that gets along well with everyone is going to be far better for a happy home than a puppy that bonds closely with one person and then shuns everyone else!

If you have younger children, it is worth it to watch how they handle the puppies closely. A child that you thought ready for puppy ownership may prove too rough or too careless when actually confronted with a dog.

In general, this is less important for puppies than it is for older dogs. Puppies can generally be trained to get used to just about anyone, while rescue dogs and older dogs might have some issues.

Because rescue dogs have often been abused or neglected, they often come with a number of negatively reinforced traits. In some cases, they are very afraid of people who share a certain set of traits with their abuser, or perhaps they are automatically nervous around children, if children have been careless with them in the past.

If a rescue dog is reacting very strongly to your presence or to the presence of someone in your home, it may be best to choose another animal.

Remember that you cannot save all of the dogs that need homes. Instead of choosing one that is a little riskier to care for, choose one that you know you will be able to get along with and make sure that you give it a great home.

Chapter 5) Finding a Great Shih Poo Breeder

There are many important advantages to having a good breeder. A good breeder is someone who is invested in the breed that they are working with, and they have guarantees for healthy puppies. Frequently, if you are unable to keep a puppy, they will make provisions to take the puppy back.

There is no universal registry available for Shih Poo breeders at this time. This is something that may change as time goes on and as people become more devoted to the breed, but at this point, there is a lot of information being traded through word of mouth.

Finding a good breeder in your area can take some time. You may need to travel to find a good breeder, but the results are far better than purchasing a dog from a pet shop or a backyard breeder.

1) Testimonials

Ask a Shih Poo breeder you are considering if they will provide you with testimonials from some of their previous clients. Be sure to contact those people to ask them about their experience with the breeder, and the health and temperament of their Shih Poo dog.

A good breeder has nothing to hide and will be more than happy to provide you with testimonials because their best recommendation is a happy customer.

Do you know anyone who has adopted a Shih Poo? If so, ask them where they got their dog. Would they recommend their breeder? Why or why not?

Simply take the time to make sure that your breeder is someone who is interested in providing you with the healthiest and happiest animal possible.

2) Making a Visit

Ask to visit the breeder's facilities. Depending on the breeder's scope, they may be operating a very small kennel, or they may simply be a professional breeder who only produces one or two litters a year in their home.

If a breeder does not want you to visit their facilities, there is something very wrong. If someone wants you to buy a puppy from them but they are unwilling to show you how that puppy grew up or what its mother's condition is, there is something very wrong. You should look for another place to get your companion.

When you visit the breeder's location, trust your instincts. Does the place look clean and well-kept? Do the animals on the property seem healthy and do they seem well-cared for? If you see animals that look morose, thin, or lethargic, it is worth reconsidering where you are getting your dog from!

A great breeder will sit down with you and make sure that you know what you are getting in to. The Shih Poo is not known to be a troublesome breed, but he or she will likely want to know what kind of home you have and whether you understand what the puppy needs. Someone who just wants you to hand over money for a puppy is not going to be someone who puts a lot of love into their business.

Remember that there is no such thing as spending too much time in selecting a good breeder. The right breeder is someone who works with you to ensure that you are getting the right dog for your home.

3) General Questions to Ask a Shih Poo Breeder

If you are spending several hundred dollars or pounds on a dog, it is your right to ask what you are getting. Be sure that you spend some time with the breeder to figure out what they are like and to learn more about what they consider important in the breed.

Get to know your breeder by asking them why they decided to breed Shih Poos and how long they have been breeding.

Ask if the breeder will permit you to visit their facility and will they give you a tour?

Ask if the breeder is familiar with, or worked closely with both parents of the Shih Poo puppy?

Ask how often the breeder allows the females and males to breed and reproduce?

Ask if the breeder will allow you to see the other dogs in the kennel. Notice whether the kennel is clean, well maintained and animal friendly.

Will the breeder permit you to see other adult dogs, or other puppies that the breeder owns, socialize together?

Pay attention to whether the breeder limits the amount of time that you are permitted to handle the Shih Poo puppies. A reputable breeder will be concerned for the safety and health of all their puppies and will only permit serious buyers to handle the puppies.

Check to find out if the breeder is recognized by your local, state or national breed organization.

4) Origins

Where did the breeder get their breeding stock? Some breeders look like they run great operations until you ask a little more closely and you realize that they got their breeding animals from a puppy mill or a pet shop!

When you are looking at Shih Poos, you are looking at crosses between poodles and Shih Tzus, or between two Shih Poos. There should be no other breeds involved, and if there are, they should not be called Shih Poos!

Ideally, a good Shih Poo breeder will only purchase from other breeders, whether they are thinking about poodles, Shih Tzus or Shih Poos. They will not introduce a rescue dog into their program when they have no knowledge of where it came from or what its genetics might be like.

5) Medical Questions

Every reputable breeder will certainly ensure that their Shih Poo puppies have received vaccinations and de-worming specific to the age of the puppies. Always ask the breeder what shots the puppy has received and when it was last de-wormed. Ask for the name of the breeder's veterinarian.

If you discover that the breeder has not carried out any of these procedures or they are unable to tell you when the last shots or de-worming was carried out, look elsewhere.

Also ask to see the breeder's veterinarian report on the health of the puppy you may be interested in purchasing, and if they cannot produce this report, look elsewhere.

6) Temperament Questions

You will want to choose a puppy with a friendly, easy going and congenial temperament and your breeder should be able to help you with your selection.

A good breeder will have noticed personality and temperament traits very early on in their Shih Poo puppies and should be able to provide a prospective purchaser with valuable insight concerning each puppy's unique personality.

Also ask the breeder about the temperament and personalities of the puppy's parents and if they have socialized the puppies.

Always be certain to ask if a Shih Poo puppy you are interested in has displayed any signs of aggression or fear, because if this is happening at such an early age, you may experience behavioral troubles when the puppy becomes older.

7) Guarantees

A reputable Shih Poo breeder will be interested in the lifelong health and well-being of all of their puppies and good breeders will want you to call them should a problem arise at any time during the life of your Shih Poo puppy.

As well, a good breeder will want you to return a puppy or dog to them, if for some reason you are unable to continue to care for it, rather than seeing the dog go to a shelter or rescue facility.

If the Shih Poo breeder you are considering does not offer this type of return policy, find one who does, because no ethical breeder would ever permit one of their puppies to end up in a shelter.

8) Return Contract

Reputable breeders offer return contracts. They do this to protect their reputation and to also make sure that a puppy they have sold that might display a genetic defect will not have the opportunity to breed and continue to spread the defect, which could weaken the entire breed.

Breeders also offer return contracts because purchasing a hybrid Shih Poo puppy from a breeder can be an expensive proposition, and if you find out that the puppy has a worrisome genetic defect, this could cost you a great deal with respect to unexpected veterinarian care. In such cases, most good breeders offer a return policy, and will be happy to give you another puppy.

9) Meet the Mother

Meeting the mother of your new Shih Poo puppy can tell you a great deal about what the temperament and demeanor of your puppy will likely be when they grow into adulthood. Some breeders also own the father, and you can meet both of them. The more you know about your new puppy's heritage, the more you know about what your own dog will be like when it is grown.

A Shih Poo puppy's personality or temperament will be a combination of what they experience in the early days of their environment, when they are in the breeder's care, and the genes inherited from both the poodle and the Shih Tzu parents.

Visiting the breeder several times, observing the parents, interacting with the puppies and asking plenty of questions will help you to get a true feeling for the sincerity of the breeder.

The early environment provided by the breeder and the parents of the puppies can have a formative impact on how your puppy will behave as an adult dog.

10) Do Your Research

The Internet can be a valuable resource when researching the reputation of a Shih Poo breeder. For instance, you will be able to post on most forums discussing breeders to quickly find out what you need to know from those who have firsthand experience.

Also, be prepared to answer questions the breeder may have for you, because a reputable breeder will want to ask a prospective purchaser their own questions, so that they can satisfy themselves that you are going to be a good caretaker for their puppy.

First, do your homework about the Shih Poo breed and then carry out as much research as possible about the specific breeder before making your initial visit to their facility.

The more information you have gathered about the Shih Poo hybrid, as well as the breeder, and the more information the breeder knows about you the more successful the match will be.

11) Where to Purchase a Puppy in the US

When wondering where to start your search for purchasing a Shih Poo puppy in the United States, there are several clubs and registries that will be good starting points, including:

American Canine Hybrid Club (ACHC) is a hybrid registry service established in 1969.

National Hybrid Registry (NHR) The NHR is a registry service for dogs from which both parents are verified to be pure bred dogs and eligible to be registered in the National Kennel Club.

International Designer Canine Registry® (IDCR) is the World's Premier Designer Dog Registry and is dedicated exclusively to providing certified registration and pedigree services for all designer breeds. The IDCR also provides a list of registered breeders.

12) Where to Purchase a Puppy in the UK

Little Rascals "takes great pride in being able to breed a varied range of pedigree and designer crossbreed puppies for sale to customers throughout Lincoln and the UK. As specialized licensed dog breeders we have almost 50 years experience in breeding, so you can be certain that a puppy from us has been given the best possible care and start in life."

www.littlerascalsuk.com

Designer Dogs - The Kennel Club is a registration and information service to help prospective owners find Kennel Club "assured breeders".

www.thekennelclub.org.uk

Chapter 6) Preparing for a Shih Poo

Part of taking great care of your Shih Poo puppy is making sure that your home is ready for it. However, getting your home and your household ready for your Shih Poo is more involved than you might think. Not only do you need to think about things like pet supplies, you should also consider your own habits as well. How can you make sure that your Shih Poo gets what it needs as soon as it comes home with you?

1) Basic Puppy Proofing

Most puppies will be a curious bundle of energy, which means that they will get into everything within their reach.

As a responsible puppy guardian, you will want to provide a safe environment for them, which means eliminating all sources of danger, similar to what you would do for a curious toddler.

Be aware that your Shih Poo puppy will want to touch, sniff, taste, investigate and closely inspect every electrical cord, every closet, every nook and cranny of your home and everything you may have left lying about on the floor.

Power cords can be found in just about every room in the home and to a teething puppy, these may look like irresistible, fun, chew toys. Make sure that you tuck all power cords securely out of your puppy's reach or enclose them inside a chew-proof PVC tube.

Kitchen: First of all, there are many human foods that can be harmful to dogs. Your kitchen should always be strictly off limits to your puppy any time you are preparing food. Calmly send them out of the kitchen any time you are in the kitchen, and they will quickly get the idea that this area is off limits to them.

Bathroom: Bathroom cupboards and drawers or the side of a bathtub where you may leave your shaving supplies can hold many dangers for a young and curious Shih Poo puppy.

Kleenex, cotton swabs, Q-tips, toilet paper, razors, pills, and soap left within your puppy's reach are an easy target that could result in an emergency visit to your veterinarian's office.

Family members need to put shampoos, soap, facial products, makeup and accessories out of reach or safely inside a cabinet or drawer.

Bedroom: If you don't keep your shoes, slippers and clothing safely behind doors, you may find that your puppy has claimed them for their new chew toys. Be vigilant about keeping everything in its safe place, including jewelry, hair ties, bills, coins, and other items small enough for them to swallow in containers or drawers, and secure any exposed cords or wires.

If you have children, make sure they understand that, especially while your puppy is going through their teething stage, that they must keep their rooms picked up and leave nothing on the floor that could cause a choking problem to the puppy.

Living Room: We humans often spend many hours in our cozy gathering places to watch movies or play games, and often the living areas of our homes will have many items that are very enticing for a curious and teething puppy, such as books, magazines, pillows, iPods, TV remotes and more.

You will want to keep your home free of excess clutter and remain vigilant about straightening up and putting things out of sight that could be tempting to your puppy.

Office: We humans often spend a great deal of time in our home offices, which means that our puppy will want to be there, too. They will be curious about all the items an office has to offer, including papers, books, magazines, and electrical cords.

Although your puppy might think that rubber bands or paper clips are fun to play with, allowing these items to be within your puppy's reach could end up being a fatal mistake if your puppy swallows them.

Plants: Plants are a very tempting target for your puppy's teeth, so you will want to keep them well out their reach. If you have floor plants, they will need to be moved to a shelf or counter or placed behind a closed door until your curious fur friend grows out of the habit of putting everything in their mouth. Also keep in mind that many common house plants are poisonous to dogs.

Garage and Yard: Obvious, as well as subtle, dangers could seriously harm or even kill a Shih Poo puppy. They are often found in the garage or yard. Some of these might include antifreeze, gasoline, fertilizers, rat and mice poison, snail and slug poison, weed killer, paint, cleaners and solvents, grass seed, bark mulch and various insecticides.

If you are storing any of these toxic substances in your garage or garden shed, make certain that you keep all such bottles, boxes, or containers inside a locked cabinet, or stored on high shelves that your puppy will not be able to reach. Even better, choose not to use toxic chemicals anywhere in your home or yard.

2) Puppy Supplies

Before bringing home your new Shih Poo for the first time, there will be a list of items you need to make sure you have on hand, including:

Food - Usually the puppy will remain on whatever food they have been fed at the breeder's for at least the first couple of weeks, until they are well-settled in their new home, so make sure you ask the breeder what brand to buy;

Food and Water Bowls - Make sure they are small enough for a young Shih Poo puppy to get into so that they can easily eat and drink. We suggest a durable stainless dining set that can later be used as travel bowls. For more information about great bowls, check the section below.

Kennel - When you buy your puppy's hard-sided kennel, make sure that you buy the size that will be appropriate for them when they are full grown. It must be large enough so that (when full grown) they can easily stand up and turn around inside it;

Martingale collar, 2 Leashes and Harness - Buy the harness and collar small enough to fit your puppy and buy new ones as they grow larger. You will be able to keep the same leashes as all you will ever need is a four foot (1.22 meters) leash made out of nylon webbing, with a light weight clip at the end (do not buy a leash that has a heavy clip on the end as it will be difficult for your tiny puppy to carry around);

Soft beds – Buy one or two beds for the puppies to sleep in when they are not in their kennel - get the beds large enough for a full grown Shih Poo;

Travel Bag - To get them used to traveling inside a carrier bag - get the bag large enough to fit them when they are full grown and take it with you when you pick up your puppy from the breeder;

Shampoo and Conditioner;

Finger tooth brush - This is a soft rubber cap that fits over the human's finger to get the puppy used to having their teeth regularly brushed;

Soft bristle brush and comb - For daily grooming;

Puppy nail scissors - For trimming their toenails;

Small blunt nosed grooming scissors - For trimming the hair around their eyes;

One or two soft toys - Or you can wait until they come home and let them pick their own toys from the store;

Puppy sized treats;

Poop bags;

Pee pads;

Bath towels;

Non-slip mat for the sink or tub.

Be sure to take your Shih Poo shopping list with you when you go to your local pet store or boutique, otherwise you may forget critical items. If you are getting your Shih Poo puppy from a shelter or a rescue, ask to see if they have a puppy starter pack that they can sell you. These starter packs typically contain everything you need at a fairly good discount.

3) What Bowl is Right for My Shih Poo Puppy?

Following is a brief description of the different categories and types of dog bowls that would be appropriate choices for your Shih Poo's particular needs.

Automatic Watering Bowls: are standard dog bowls (often made out of plastic) that are attached to a reservoir container which is designed to keep water constantly available to your dog as long as there is water remaining in the storage compartment.

Ceramic/Stoneware Bowls: a great choice for those who like options in personality, color and shape.

Elevated Bowls: raised dining table dog bowls are a tidy and classy choice that will make your dog's dinner time a more comfortable experience while getting the bowls off the floor.

No Skid Bowls: are for dogs that push their bowls across the floor when eating. A non-skid dog bowl will help keep the feed bowl where you put it.

No Tip Bowls: are designed to prevent the messy type of doggy eater from flipping over their dinner or water bowls.

Stainless Steel Bowls: are as close to indestructible as a bowl can be, plus they are sanitary and easy to clean, and water stays cooler for a longer period of time in a stainless bowl.

Wooden Bowls: for those people concerned about stylish home decor, wooden dog bowl dining stations are beautiful accessories unto themselves that can enhance your home decor.

Travel Bowls: a convenient, practical and handy addition to the traveling canine. Instead of a cloth bowl that is difficult to clean, consider a space-saving, collapsible dog bowl, made out of hygienic, renewable bamboo that comes in fun colors and different sizes, making it perfect for your travel bowl needs.

If you would like to learn more about all the many dog bowl choices available, visit DogBowlForYourDog.com, which is a comprehensive, one-stop website dedicated to explaining the ins and outs of every food bowl imaginable and helping you find the perfect bowl for all your Shih Poo's needs.

4) Picking Up Your Shih Poo

Before you go to the breeder's to pick up your new Shih Poo puppy, vacuum your floors and do a last minute check of every room to make sure that everything that could be a puppy hazard is carefully tucked away out of sight. There should be nothing that is left on the floor or low down on shelves where a curious puppy might get into trouble.

Close most of the doors inside your home, so that there are just one or two rooms that the puppy will have access to.

You have already been shopping and have everything you need, so get out a puppy pee pad and have it at the ready when you bring your new fur friend home.

Also have your soft bed(s) in an area where you will be spending most of your time and where they will be easily found by your puppy. If you have already purchased a soft toy, leave it in your puppy's soft bed, or take the toy with you when you go to pick up your puppy.

Take either your hard-sided kennel or your soft-sided travel bag with you when going to bring your new Shih Poo puppy home. Make sure that it is securely fastened to the seat of your vehicle with the seat belt system and lined with a puppy pee pad.

Even though you will be tempted to hold your new Shih Poo puppy in your lap on the drive home, this is a very dangerous place for them to be, in case of an accident.

Place them inside their kennel or bag, which will be lined with soft towels and perhaps even a warm, towel-wrapped hot water bottle, and close the door. If you have a friend who can drive for you, sit beside them in the back seat, and if they cry on the way home, remind them that they are not alone with your soft, soothing voice.

5) Your Shih Poo's First Night

Before bringing your new Shih Poo puppy inside your home, take them to the place where you want them to relieve themselves and try to wait it out long enough for them to at least go pee.

Then bring them inside your home and introduce them to the area where their food and water bowls will be kept, in case they are hungry or thirsty.

Let them wander around sniffing and checking out their new surroundings and gently encourage them to follow you wherever you go.

Show them where the puppy pee pad is located and place it near the door where you will exit to take them outside. Many pee pads are scented to encourage a puppy to pee, and if they do, happily praise them.

Show them where their hard-sided kennel is (in your bedroom) and put them inside with the door open while you sit on the floor in front and quietly encourage them to relax inside their kennel.

Depending on the time of day when you bring your new Shih Poo puppy home for the first time, practice this kennel exercise several times throughout the day, and if they will take a little treat each time you encourage them to go inside their kennel, this will help to further encourage the behavior of wanting to go inside.

After they have had their evening meal, take them outside approximately 20 minutes later to relieve themselves, and when they do, make sure you are very enthusiastic with your praise and perhaps even give a little treat.

So far your Shih Poo puppy has only been allowed in several rooms of your home; as you have kept the other doors closed, so keep it this way for the first few days.

Before it's time for bed, again take your puppy outside for a very short walk to the same place where they last relieved themselves and make sure that they go pee before bringing them back inside.

Before bed, prepare your Shih Poo puppy's hot water bottle and wrap it in a towel so that it will not be too hot for them, and place it inside their hard-sided kennel (in your bedroom).

Turn the lights down low and invite your puppy to go inside their kennel and if they seem interested, perhaps give them a soft toy to have inside with them. Let them walk into the kennel under their own steam and when they do, give them a little treat (if they are interested) and encourage them to snuggle down to sleep while you are sitting on the floor in front of the kennel.

Once they have settled down inside their kennel, close the door, go to your bed and turn all the lights off. It may help your puppy to sleep during their first night home, if you can play quiet, soothing music in the background.

If they start to cry or whine, stay calm and have compassion because this is the first time in their young life when they do not have the comfort of their mother or their litter mates. Do not let them out of their kennel. Simply reassure them with your calm voice that they are not alone until they fall asleep.

6) The First Week at Home

During the first week, you and your new Shih Poo puppy will be getting settled into their new routine, which will involve you getting used to your puppy's needs as they also get used to your usual schedule.

Be as consistent as possible with your waking and sleeping routine, getting up and going to bed at the same time each day, so that it will be easier for your puppy to get into the flow of their new life.

First thing in the morning, remove your puppy from their kennel and take them immediately outside to relieve themselves at the place where they last went pee.

At this time, if you are teaching them to ring a doorbell to go outside, let them ring the bell before you go out the door with them, whether you are carrying them, or whether they are walking out the door on their own.

During the first week, you may want to carry your puppy outside first thing in the morning as they may not be able to hold it for very long once waking up.

When you bring them back inside, you can let them follow you so they get used to their new leash and/or harness arrangement.

Be very careful not to drag your puppy if they stop or pull back on the leash. If they refuse to walk on the leash, just hold the tension toward you (without pulling) while encouraging them to walk toward you, until they start to move forward again.

Now it will be time for their first feed of the day, and after they have finished eating, keep an eye on the clock, because you will want to take them outside to relieve themselves in about 20 minutes.

When your puppy is not eating or napping, they will want to explore and have little play sessions with you. These times will help you bond with your puppy more and more each day.

As their new guardian, it will be your responsibility to keep a close eye on them throughout the day, so that you can notice when they need to relieve themselves and either take them to their pee pad or take them outside.

You will also need to make sure that they are eating and drinking enough throughout the day, so set regular feeding times at least three times a day.

Also set specific times in the day when you will take your puppy out for a little walk on leash and harness, so that they are not only going outside when they need to relieve themselves, but they are also learning to explore their new neighborhood with you beside them.

When your Shih Poo puppy is still very young, you will not want to walk for a long time as they will get tired easily, so keep your walks to no more than 15 or 20 minutes during your first week. If they seem tired or cold, pick them up and carry them home.

7) Continue as You Mean to Go On

In general, when you are thinking about how to treat your puppy, remember to simply treat it the way you will treat the dog it will become. Puppies get more lenience for not knowing the rules, but in general, they can be held to the same schedule and the same affection as adult dogs.

If you do not want a full-grown dog to sleep in your bed, do not allow the puppy to do so. If you do not want to have a dog that jumps up on you, do not allow the puppy to do that.

The first week or so is a critical time for you to get to know your puppy. In general, it is getting used to a brand new world for the first time, and this can be something that is quite distressing for it.

For the first time in its life, it is away from its mother and its siblings, and it will be very conscious of the fact that it needs to learn new rules and new ways of behavior.

Remember that you are replacing its family, and it will be taking its cues from you! Be firm, and even when it begs and cries, remember that you are doing something that will serve it far better in the long run.

A little bit of discipline in the beginning can save you a whole lot of retraining later on.

8) Timing

If at all possible, remember that your Shih Poo puppy should be brought into your home at a time when things are calm. This is why most breeders recommend against you bringing a puppy into your home when things are very busy or during a holiday.

Some people decide to bring Shih Poos into their homes around Christmas or as a birthday gift, and this is a bad idea. There is a lot of excitement centered on those holidays, and the result is that the puppy often gets overstimulated and overwhelmed. This does not make for a peaceful introduction to your home, and it can also create a situation where your new puppy ends up treated like just another toy or gift.

Adopting a puppy is a serious thing, so be willing to bring it into your home correctly.

The smoother the transition from the kennel to your home, the happier and more secure the puppy will be.

Many people take a few weeks off to get the Shih Poo puppy established in their home, and this can be quite beneficial. If you can work at home or if you have some vacation time, this is a good way to move forward. Simply remember that you need to ease the puppy into being alone slowly if at all possible.

A little bit of peace and quiet when you bring your puppy home is ideal. Remember that the Shih Poo puppy is nervous and scared, and it will need plenty of love and comfort.

Chapter 7) Common Mistakes to Avoid

Your new Shih Poo puppy is adorable, and the urge to spoil it while making it welcome in your home is going to be very strong. However, to make sure that the puppy gets off to a good start and that the puppy does not pick up any bad habits, make sure that you avoid these five most common mistakes. It is far easier to avoid bad habits than it is to break them, so simply be willing to pay attention to these damaging but common mistakes

1) Sleeping in Your Bed

Many of us humans make the mistake of allowing a crying puppy to sleep with them in their bed, and while this may help to calm and comfort a new puppy, it will set a dangerous precedent that can result in behavioral problems later in their life.

As well, a tiny Shih Poo puppy can easily be crushed by a sleeping human body.

As much as it may pull on your heart strings to hear your new Shih Poo puppy crying the first couple of nights in their kennel, a little tough love at the beginning will help them to learn to both love and respect you as their leader.

2) Picking Them Up at the Wrong Time

Never pick your puppy up if they display fear or growl at an object or person, because this will be rewarding them for unbalanced behavior.

Instead, your puppy needs to be gently corrected by you, with firm and calm energy so that they learn not to react with fear or aggression.

3) Playing Too Hard or Too Long

Many humans play too hard or allow their children to play too long with a young puppy. You need to remember that a young puppy tires very easily and especially during the critical growing phases of their young life, they need their rest.

4) Hand Play

Always discourage your Shih Poo puppy from chewing or biting your hands, or any part of your body for that matter. If you allow them to do this when they are puppies, they will want to continue to do so when they have strong jaws and adult teeth and this is not acceptable behavior for any breed of dog.

Do not get into the habit of playing the "hand" game, where you rough up the puppy and slide them across the floor with your hands, because this will teach your puppy that your hands are play things.

When your puppy is teething, they will naturally want to chew on everything within reach, and this will include you. As cute as you might think it is, this is not an acceptable behavior and you need to gently, but firmly, discourage the habit.

A light flick with a finger on the end of a puppy nose, combined with a firm "NO" when they are trying to bite human fingers will discourage them from this activity.

5) Distraction and Replacement

When your puppy tries to chew on your hand, foot, or your clothing, or anything else that is not fair game, you need to firmly and calmly tell them "No", and then distract them by replacing what they are not supposed to be chewing with their chew toy.

Make sure that you happily praise them every time they choose the toy to chew on.

If the puppy persists in chewing on you, remove yourself from the equation by getting up and walking away. If they are really persistent, put them inside their kennel with a favorite chew toy until they calm down.

Always praise your puppy when they stop inappropriate behavior so that they begin to understand what they can and cannot do.

6) Letting the Puppy Call the Shots

If your puppy wants your attention and you are doing something else, always finish what you are doing before you play with it. If your puppy thinks that it can demand your attention whenever it pleases, this is going to lead to a dog that is quite spoiled!

Exceptions should be made for puppies that are beginning to learn to be house broken and are indicating that they need to relieve themselves, but otherwise, you should be the one in charge.

Chapter 8) Everything You Need to Know About House Training

House training your Shih Poo is an essential part of training your puppy, and it is a process that should begin as soon as you get your puppy into your home. Shih Poos are known to be a little stubborn in this regard, and some Shih Poos have issues with house training even as adults. The key is that you should always be patient with your puppy. Never resort to smacking it when it has created a mess, or to shoving its nose in it. These are ineffective methods that will only frighten and alarm your puppy, leading to more accidents.

When it comes to house training, remember that patience is the key. Be firm with your puppy, and just accept the fact that there will be accidents.

1) Being Prepared

When it comes to house training, no matter what way you choose to do it, you must remember two things:

First, be patient. A puppy is going to mess up from time to time. These are very young dogs, and they are not perfect. They may misunderstand you, or they may be legitimately confused about what is going on.

This goes double if you have a rescue animal. Many rescue animals from abused situations have issues with housetraining. Perhaps they were harmed or injured for it in their previous home or perhaps they were encouraged to do things that you find unacceptable. When it comes to dogs like this, you must be patient as they need to unlearn bad habits even as they are learning good ones!

Second, remember that a dog's sense of smell is at least 2,000 times more sensitive than our human sense of smell.

As a result of your Shih Poo puppy's superior sense of smell, it will be very important to effectively remove all odors from house training accidents, because otherwise, your Shih Poo puppy will be attracted by the smell to the place where they may have had a previous accident, and will want to do their business there again and again.

While there are many products that are supposed to remove odors and stains, many of these are not very effective. You want a professional grade cleaner that will not just mask one odor with another. You want a product that will completely neutralize odors.

Consider going to RemoveUrineOdors.com and order yourself some "SUN" and/or "Max Enzyme" because these products contain professional-strength odor neutralizers and urine digesters that bind to and completely absorb odors on any type of surface.

2) Traditional Housetraining

House training, or "potty" training, is a critical first step in the education of any new puppy, and the first part of a successful process is training the human guardian.

When you bring home your new Shih Poo puppy, they will be relying upon your guidance to teach them what they need to learn.

When you provide your puppy with your consistent patience and understanding, they are capable of learning rules at a very early age, and house training is no different, especially since it's all about establishing a regular routine.

Potty training a new puppy takes time and patience — how much time depends entirely upon you.

Check in with yourself and make sure your energy remains consistently calm and patient and that you exercise plenty of compassion and understanding while you help your new puppy learn the new bathroom rules.

Shih Poo puppies and dogs flourish with routines, as do humans. Therefore, the first step is to establish a daily routine that will work well for both canine and human alike.

For instance, depending upon the age of your Shih Poo puppy, make a plan to take them out for a bathroom break every two hours and stick to it. While you are in the beginning stages of potty training, the more vigilant and consistent you are the quicker and more successful your results will be.

Generally speaking, while your puppy is still growing, a young puppy can hold it approximately one hour for every month of their age.

This means that if your 2-month-old puppy has been happily snoozing for a couple of hours, as soon as they wake up, they will need to go outside.

Some of the first indications or signs that your puppy needs to be taken outside to relieve themselves will be when you see them:

-sniffing around

-circling

-looking for the door

-whining, crying or barking

-acting agitated

It will be important to always take your Shih Poo puppy out first thing every morning, and immediately after they wake up from a nap as well as soon after they have finished eating a meal or having a big drink of water.

Also, your happy praise goes a long way toward encouraging and reinforcing future success when your Shih Poo puppy makes the right decisions. Let them know you are happy when they do their business in the right place.

Initially, treats can be a good way to reinforce how happy you are that your puppy is learning to relieve themselves in the right place. Slowly treats can be removed and replaced with your happy praise.

Next, now that you have a new puppy in your life, you will want to be flexible with respect to adapting your schedule to meet the requirements that will help to quickly teach your Shih Poo puppy their new bathroom routine.

This means not leaving your puppy alone for endless hours at a time because firstly, they are pack animals that need companionship and your direction at all times, plus long periods alone will result in the disruption of the potty training schedule you have worked hard to establish.

If you have no choice but to leave your puppy alone for many hours, make sure that you place them in a paper-lined room or pen where they can relieve themselves without destroying your favorite carpet.

Remember, your Shih Poo is a growing puppy with a bladder and bowels that they do not yet have complete control over and you will have a much happier time and better success if you simply train yourself to pay attention to when your young companion is showing signs of needing to relieve themselves.

3) Kennel Training

Kennel training, also known as crate training, is always a good idea for any puppy early in their education, because it can be utilized for many different situations, including being a very helpful tool for house training.

When purchasing a kennel for your Shih Poo puppy, always buy a kennel that will be the correct size for your Shih Poo puppy once they become adult size. The kennel will be the correct size if your full grown Shih Poo dog can stand up and easily turn around inside their kennel.

When you train your Shih Poo puppy to accept sleeping in their own kennel at nighttime, this will also help to accelerate their potty training, because no puppy or dog wants to relieve themselves where they sleep, which means that they will hold their bladder and bowels as long as they possibly can.

Always be kind and compassionate and remember that a puppy will be able to hold it approximately one hour for every month of their age.

Generally, a Shih Poo puppy that is three months old will be able to hold it for approximately three hours, unless they just ate a meal or had a big drink of water.

Be watchful and consistent so that you learn your Shih Poo puppy's body language, and when it's time for them to go outside. Presenting them with familiar scents, by taking them to the same spot in the yard or the same street corner, will help to remind and encourage them that they are outside to relieve themselves.

Use a voice cue to remind your puppy why they are outside, such as "go pee" and always remember to praise them every time they relieve themselves in the right place so that they quickly understand what you expect of them and will learn to "go" on cue.

3) Bell Training

A very easy way to introduce your new Shih Poo puppy to house training is to begin by teaching them how to ring a doorbell whenever they need to go outside.

Ringing a doorbell is not only a convenient alert system for both you and your Shih Poo puppy or dog, your visitors will be most impressed by how smart your Shih Poo is.

A further benefit of training your puppy to ring a bell is that you will not have to listen to your puppy or dog whining, barking or howling to be let out, and your door will not become scratched up from their nails.

Unless you prefer to purchase an already manufactured doggy doorbell or system, take a trip to your local novelty store and purchase a small bell that has a nice, loud ring.

Attach the bell to a piece of ribbon or string and hang it from a door handle or tape it to a door sill near the door where you will be taking your puppy out when they need to relieve themselves. The string will need to be long enough so that your Shih Poo puppy can easily reach the bell with their nose or a paw.

Next, each time you take your puppy out to the bathroom, say the word "Out", and use their paw or their nose to ring the bell. Praise them for this "trick" and immediately take them outside.

The only down side to teaching your Shih Poo puppy or dog to ring a bell when they want to go outside, is that even if they don't actually have to go out to relieve themselves, but just want to go outside because they are bored, you will still have to take them out every time they ring the bell.

There are many types and styles of "gotta go" commercially manufactured bells you could choose from, ranging from the elegant "Poochie Bells™" that hang from a doorknob, the simple "Tell Bell™" that sits on the floor, or various high tech door chime systems that function much like a doggy intercom system where they push a pad with their paw and it rings a bell.

Whatever doorbell system you choose for your Shih Poo puppy, once they are trained, this type of an alert system is an easy way to eliminate accidents in the home.

4) Using the Puppy Apartment System

While a similar concept and a more costly alternative, the Puppy Apartment™ is a step up from the exercise pen training system that makes the process of crate or pen training even easier on both humans and puppies.

The Puppy Apartment™ works well in a variety of situations, whether you're at home and unable to pay close attention to your Shih Poo puppy's needs, whether you must be away from the home for a few hours or during the evening when everyone is asleep. You don't particularly want to get up at 3:00 A.M. to take your Shih Poo puppy out to go pee. The Puppy Apartment™ is an innovation that is convenient for both puppy and human alike.

What makes this system so effective is the patent pending dividing wall with a door leading to the other side, all inside the pen. One side of the Puppy Apartment™ is where the puppy's bed is located and the other side (through the doorway), is the bathroom area that is lined with pee pads.

With the bathroom right next door, your Shih Poo puppy or dog can relieve themselves whenever they wish, without the need to alert family members to let them out.

This one bedroom, one bathroom system, which is a combination of the kennel/training pen, is a great alternative for helping to eliminate the stress of worrying about always keeping a watchful eye on your puppy or getting up in the night to take them outside every few hours to help them avoid making mistakes.

According to *"Modern Puppies"*...

> *"The Puppy Apartment™ takes the MESSY out of paper training, the ODORS AND HASSLES out of artificial grass training, MISSING THE MARK out of potty pad training and HAVING TO HOLD IT out of crate training. House training a puppy has never been faster or easier!*
>
> *The Puppy Apartment™ has taken all the benefits of the most popular potty training methods and combined them into one magical device and potty training system. This device and system has revolutionized how modern puppies are potty trained!"*

This product is manufactured in the United States, and it ships directly from the California supplier (Modern Puppies).

5) Exercise Pen Training

The exercise pen is a transition from kennel-only training and will be helpful for those times when you may have to leave your Shih Poo puppy for more hours than they can reasonably be expected to hold it.

During those times when you must be away from the home for several hours, it's time to introduce your Shih Poo puppy to an exercise pen. Exercise pens are usually constructed of wire sections that you can put together in whatever shape you desire. The pen needs to be large enough to hold your puppy's kennel on one half of the pen, while the other half will be lined with newspapers or pee pads.

Place your Shih Poo puppy's food and water dishes next to the kennel and leave the kennel door open, so they can wander in and out whenever they wish, to eat or drink or go to the papers if they need to relieve themselves.

Your puppy will be contained in a small area of your home while you are away and because they are already used to sleeping inside their kennel, they will not want to relieve themselves inside the area where they sleep. Therefore, your Shih Poo puppy will naturally go to the other half of the pen to relieve themselves on the newspapers or pee pads.

This method will help train your puppy to be quickly paper trained when you have to be away for a few hours.

The price of the Puppy Apartment™ begins at $138. USD (£83.37) and is only available online at Modern Puppies.

6) Should You Free Train?

If you would rather not confine your young Shih Poo puppy to one or two rooms in your home, and will be allowing them to freely range about your home anywhere they wish during the day, this is considered free training.

When free house training your Shih Poo puppy, you will need to closely watch your puppy's activities all day long so that you can be aware of the "signs" that will indicate when they need to go outside to relieve themselves.

For instance, circling and sniffing is a sure sign that they are looking for a place to do their business.

Never get upset or scold a puppy for having an accident inside the home, because this will result in teaching your puppy to be afraid of you. They will then only relieve themselves in secret places or when you're not watching.

If you catch your Shih Poo puppy making a mistake, all that is necessary is for you to calmly say "No", and quickly scoop them up and take them outside or to their indoor bathroom area. From your puppy's point of view, yelling or screaming when they make a potty mistake, is unstable energy being displayed by the person who is supposed to be their leader. This type of behavior will only teach your puppy to fear and disrespect you.

The Shih Poo is not a difficult puppy to housebreak and they will generally do very well when you start them off with "puppy pee pads". Move these pads closer and closer to the same door that you always use when taking them outside. This way they will quickly learn to associate going to this door when they need to relieve themselves.

When you pay close attention to your Shih Poo puppy's sleeping, eating, drinking and playing habits, you will quickly learn their body language so that you are able to predict when they might need to relieve themselves.

Your Shih Poo puppy will always need to relieve themselves first thing in the morning, as soon as they wake up from a nap, approximately 20 minutes after they finish eating a meal, after they have finished a play session, and of course, before they go to bed at night.

It's important to have compassion during this house training time in your young Shih Poo's life so that their education will be as stress-free as possible.

It's also important to be vigilant. Paying attention will minimize the opportunities your puppy may have for making a bathroom mistake in the first place, and the fewer mistakes they make, the sooner your Shih Poo puppy will be house trained.

7) Tips for Housetraining a Rescue Shih Poo

Sometimes, rescue Shih Poos have serious issues with house training. This is also an issue that can occur with puppy mill puppies that are never socialized correctly or given an option regarding where they should relieve themselves.

All of the methods above should work on a rescue dog, but there are a few things to keep in mind that can keep the process moving along.

First and foremost, do not lose your patience with your rescue dog. It does not know what it is doing wrong, and just because it gets the idea one day does not mean that it is going to get the idea the next day!

The more patient you can be with it, the better. Of course always remember that if you did not see it committing the deed, you cannot punish it. In fact, to prevent this, it is often recommended that you do not leave rescue dogs alone and unsupervised for a long period of time. The last thing that you want is to give it an association with its bodily functions and various places in your home.

Though it might seem contradictory, many rescue dogs grow to love kennel training in particular. This is something that can make a huge difference to a dog that has been cooped up for most of its life. You might think that it wants to roam, but the truth is that over all, it might need a place to retreat.

When you are dealing with a rescue dog that seems to forget about housetraining once in a while, just remember that this is a part of the process. There are some dogs that come out of wretched situations that do amazingly well, and there are some that remain nervous for years, if not their entire lives.

8) Checkups

Remember that if your dog has been housetrained for some time and it suddenly starts having accidents again, it may not be that your training has gone awry or been forgotten.

Dogs are among the most trainable animals in the world, and over all, they do not forget the things that they learn as very young puppies.

If your dog has suddenly forgotten a great deal of its training, take the time to take your dog to the veterinarian. A sudden loss of bowel or bladder control can mean that there is a serious issue at play regarding your dog's health.

9) Clean Up!

If you want your dog's house training to go faster, remember that you should clean up as soon as there is an accident. Use an enzymatic cleaner to get rid of all traces of the urine or feces.

A dog's nose is much stronger than a human's and if your dog can smell the mess, it might think that that is the place to make another one!

Chapter 9) Shih Poo Health Problems

One of the serious issues of choosing a Shih Poo is that there is not a great deal of information out there on the breed. There is no recognized list of disorders that will tell you what the problems of the breed are, and depending on the breeder you choose there may be more or less of these issues in play.

The Shih Poo is heir to some of the serious health issues that affect both poodles and Shih Tzus at the very least, and there are a few specific issues that should be recognized.

1) Problems With Teacup Dogs

While our human society seems completely enthralled with everything small, breeding ever smaller sized Shih Poos is not a particularly good idea for the dog, because in order to breed smaller, it means breeding runts with runts which generally produces weaker puppies with more health problems.

"Teacupism" is a term used to describe abnormally small, or "teacup" sized dogs, including the Shih Poo. Any dog weighing less than 4 pounds when fully grown is considered to be teacup sized.

"Teacupism" is a highly controversial breeding practice that is not encouraged by responsible breeders because it creates weak dogs with many health problems, including shortened lifespans.

Undersized Shih Poos will generally live a much shorter life because they are especially prone to health problems such as chronic diarrhea and vomiting.

Very small Shih Poos will be more sensitive to anesthesia and are much more difficult to operate on for spaying or neutering as their organs are so tiny.

As well, a very tiny Shih Poo can be more easily injured, sometimes even breaking their legs simply from jumping off of a chair.

2) Frailty

Many people do not realize how incredibly fragile a toy breed can be, and when breeders specifically shrink the size of a toy breed ever further, the dog becomes that much more fragile.

For instance, a human can seriously injure or kill a small Shih Poo by stepping on them or by accidentally sitting on them.

As well, a tiny but feisty little Shih Poo could easily injure or even die by fearlessly leaping out of your arms.

Further, many larger dogs with a high prey drive may think that such a small dog is a rodent, and they can quickly grab a small Shih Poo and kill them or break their neck with one quick shake.

Owning a very small toy breed, such as a teacup Shih Poo will mean that you must be constantly vigilant and keep your dog under close supervision, so that you are aware of everything that is happening and can avoid potentially harmful situations.

Very small Shih Poos with fearless temperaments need to be kept on a leash because they may place themselves into all sorts of circumstances whereby they could easily be injured if they are not under your complete control.

As well, a very small Shih Poo can easily be carried off by large birds of prey, such as hawks, eagles or owls.

A teacup sized Shih Poo will NOT be a suitable pet for young children, who may accidentally hurt them by squeezing too tightly, dropping them, or stepping on them. Children are usually loud, fast-moving, boisterous and oftentimes clumsy, which is a combination for danger around a small dog who might suffer all manner of injuries at the hands of a young child.

Finally, teacup sized dogs often feel overwhelmed simply because everything around them is so much larger. They may develop nervous habits, fear and stress that may manifest itself with constant trembling and/or defensive biting.

3) Tracheal Collapse

Tracheal collapse is an airway obstruction of the trachea, or "windpipe," sometimes also referred to as "reversed sneezing".

The trachea is a tube made up of sturdy rings of cartilage through which air is transported in and out of the dog's lungs. As air is squeezed through the windpipe during breathing, sometimes the tracheal rings collapse, which causes a coughing or honking sound.

Usually this coughing or honking is brought on by excitement over visiting a new dog or eating an especially tasty treat. As well, sometimes the symptoms may be provoked by irritants in the environment, such as vehicle exhaust, smoke or dust.

Further, symptoms can be exacerbated when exercising during hot or humid weather, and more so if the dog is overweight.

This genetic condition primarily affects toy breeds of both sexes, and while the symptoms of collapsing trachea can manifest at any age, on average, signs begin to appear after the dog reaches six to seven years of age.

Although treatment, which usually consists of cough suppressants and antibiotics, will not cure the condition, a study released in 1994 indicated that 71% of dogs treated showed a good long-term response.

In mild cases, a honking or coughing session will only last for a few seconds and can be assisted by gently rubbing the dog's nose or giving a quick squeeze around the rib cage to help relax the trachea and get the air flowing again.

In severe cases, surgery is recommended, which involves applying prosthetic rings to the outside of the trachea. The success rate of this tricky operation is reported to be in the 75% to 85% range.

4) Skin Issues

When it comes to common issues that plague Shih Poos, some of the biggest cited by owners relate to the dog's skin. From their poodle ancestry, Shih Poos oftentimes inherit skin that is meant to be submerged in the water on a regular basis. Over time, however, as poodles were bred more and more for their appearance, their skin became prone to certain issues, and some of those are known to have been inherited by Shih Poos.

For example, some Shih Poos have a condition known as Cushing's disease, which results in sensitive skin, irritation and hair loss. This issue is related to the endocrine system, and it can make your Shih Poo very prone to skin infections. Essentially, their hormones are sending their bodies incorrect messages regarding their metabolic function, and the result is a condition that can be quite uncomfortable for your dog. In very severe cases, surgery is recommended, but many Shih Poos can simply receive hormone therapy and be fine.

Another skin condition that is frequently seen on Shih Poos is called sebaceous adenitis, which involves an inflammation of the oil-producing glands on the Shih Poo's skin. It is a condition that is increasingly common among miniature poodles and therefore it is being passed on to Shih Poos as well. This condition often manifests with dry skin, red patches, itchiness and a general discomfort. When the condition continues long enough, it can result in hair loss. This is a chronic condition that will never go away, but the use of very mild shampoos and skin treatments can help a great deal.

5) Entropion

Shih Poos are prone to having rather sensitive eyes, and one of the exacerbating factors is a condition known as entropion. In this condition, the Shih Poo's eyelid curls back in on itself. As a result, the dog's eyelashes irritate the eye itself. In the short term, this causes irritation, redness and tears, but over time, this condition can lead to corneal ulcers, permanent vision loss and very severe pain.

This is something that can develop over an extended period of time, and that is why it is very important to check your dog's eyes on a very regular basis.

6) Hip Dysplasia: Possible Surgery

Hip dysplasia is a condition where the hip socket becomes malformed over time. Some giant breeds are very prone to this issue, but it is a condition that becomes very common among dogs that may be over-bred or bred carelessly.

This condition starts with a certain amount of pain and lameness, and over time, it can cause extremely painful arthritis and a near complete lack of mobility in your dog.

Make sure that your breeder tests for hip dysplasia in their dogs. Though this situation can be corrected to some extent by surgery, it is far better to get a dog that is healthy.

Chapter 10) Training Your Shih Poo

A Shih Poo is a lovely dog, but thanks to their poodle ancestry, they can be quite stubborn! Your Shih Poo puppy should start training as soon as it comes home. This does not mean that you need to start running it through a canine boot camp, but it does mean that it should get into the habit of following your commands.

Training your Shih Poo takes time, patience and a willingness to work with your puppy on a regular basis, so be willing to put in the time

In this section, we take a look at the stages your puppy will go through, and then we'll take you through the basic commands.

1) Early Days: Training Your Puppy

Most people believe that they need to take their puppy to puppy classes, and generally speaking, this is a good idea for any young Shih Poo (after they have had their vaccinations). It will help to get them socialized.

Beyond puppy classes for socializations reasons, hiring a professional dog whisperer for personalized private sessions to train the owners will be far more valuable than training situations where there are multiple dogs and humans together in one class. This can be very distracting for everyone concerned.

"Come", "Sit" and "Stay" will be the three most important words you will ever teach your Shih Poo puppy.

These three basic commands will ensure that your Shih Poo remains safe in almost every circumstance.

For instance, when your puppy correctly learns the "Come" command, you can always quickly bring them back to your side should danger approach.

When you teach your Shih Poo puppy the "Sit" and "Stay" commands you will further establish your leadership role. A puppy who understands that their human guardian is their leader will be a safe and happy follower.

One consideration that you have to make is finding a discipline sound. Choosing a discipline sound that will be used by every trainer will make it much easier for your puppy to learn what they can or cannot do. It will also be very useful when warning your puppy before they engage in unwanted behavior.

The best types of sounds are short and sharp so that you and your family members can quickly say them. The sound will immediately get the attention of your Shih Poo puppy, interrupting them when they are about to make a mistake.

It doesn't really matter what the sound is, so long as everyone in the family uses it consistently. A sound that is very effective for most puppies and dogs is a simple "UH" sound said sharply and with emphasis. It may be as simple as saying the word "no." Just make sure that everyone in the family agrees.

Most puppies and dogs respond immediately to this sound. If caught in the middle of doing something they are not supposed to be doing, they will quickly stop and give you their attention or back away from what they were doing.

The most important bonding exercise you will experience with your new Shih Poo puppy is when you go out for your daily walks together.

Far too many people ignore this critical time. It is not only important for your puppy's exercise, but also helps to fulfill their natural roaming urges. This is the time for them to learn discipline, as they follow, trust and respect you as their guardian and leader.

As soon as you bring your new puppy home you will want to teach them how to walk at your side while on leash and harness.

Every time your puppy needs to go to the bathroom, slip on their collar and snap on that leash.

At first your Shih Poo puppy may struggle or fight against having a harness around their body, because the sensation will be new to them. However, at the same time they will want to go with you, so exercise patience and encourage them to walk with you.

Be careful never to drag them, and if they pull backward and refuse to walk forward with you, simply stop for a moment. At this point, you must keep slight forward tension on the leash, until your Shih Poo puppy gives up and begins to move forward. Immediately reward them with your happy praise, and if they have a favorite treat, this can be an added incentive when teaching them to walk on their leash.

Always walk your puppy on your left side with the leash slack, so that they learn that walking with you is a relaxing experience. Keep the leash short enough so that they do not have enough slack to get in front of you.

If they begin to create tension in the leash by pulling forward or to the side, simply stop moving, get them back beside you, and start over.

Be patient and consistent with your puppy and very soon they will understand exactly where their walking position is and will walk easily beside you without any pulling or leash tension.

Remember that walking with a new puppy is an exciting experience for them as they will want to sniff everything and explore their new world, so give them lots of understanding. Don't expect them to be perfect all the time. Do not put a Shih Poo on a leash until it is at least 9 months old, as Shih Poos have fairly delicate necks as puppies. Some Shih Poo owners choose to keep them on a permanent harness.

2) Your Puppy's Adolescence

The adolescent period in a young Shih Poo's life, between the ages of 6 and 12 months, is the transitional stage of both physical and psychological development. Physically they are almost full grown in size, yet their minds are still developing and they are testing their boundaries and the limits that their human counterparts will endure.

This can be a dangerous time in a puppy's life because this is when they start to make decisions on their own which can lead to developing unwanted behaviors.

Learning how to make decisions on their own would be perfectly normal and desirable if your Shih Poo puppy was living in the wild, amongst a pack of dogs, because it would be necessary for their survival.

However, when living within a human environment, your puppy must always adhere to human rules. It will be up to their human guardians to continue their vigilant, watchful guidance in order to make sure that they do.

Many humans are lulled into a false sense of security when their new Shih Poo puppy reaches the age of approximately six months, because the puppy has been well socialized. They have been to puppy classes and long since been house trained.

The real truth is that the serious work is only now beginning and the humans and their new Shih Poo puppy could be in for a time of testing. This time can seriously challenge the relationship and leave the humans wondering if they made the right decision to share their home with a Shih Poo.

If the human side of the relationship is not prepared for this transitional time in their young Shih Poo's life, their patience may be seriously tried. The relationship of trust and respect that has been previously built can be damaged, sometimes irreparably.

While not all adolescent puppies will experience a noticeable adolescent period of craziness, because every puppy is different, most young dogs do commonly exhibit at least some of the usual adolescent behaviors, including reverting to previous puppy behaviors.

Some of these adolescent behaviors might include destructive chewing of objects they have previously shown no interest in, selective hearing or ignoring previously learned commands, displaying aggressive behavior, jumping on everyone, barking at everything that moves, or reverting to relieving themselves in the house, even though they were house trained months ago.

Keeping your cool and recognizing the sign of adolescence is the first step toward helping to make this transition period easier on your Shih Poo puppy and all family members.

The first step to take that can help keep raging hormones at bay, is to spay or neuter your Shih Poo puppy just prior to the onset of adolescence, at around five or six months of age.

While spaying or neutering a Shih Poo puppy will not eliminate the adolescent phase, it will certainly help. At the same time it will spare your puppy the added strain of both the physical and emotional changes that occur during sexual maturity.

As well, some female puppies will become extremely aggressive toward other dogs during a heat, and non-neutered males may become territorially aggressive and pick fights with other males.

Once your Shih Poo puppy has been spayed or neutered, you will want to become more active with your young dog, both mentally and physically. You can provide them with continued and more complex disciplined exercises.

This can be accomplished by enrolling your adolescent Shih Poo in dog whispering or more advanced training class. This will help them to continue their socialization skills while also developing their brain.

Even though it may be more difficult to train during this period, having the assistance of a professional and continuing the experience of ongoing socialization amongst other dogs of a similar size can be invaluable. This is the time when many young dogs begin to show signs of antisocial behavior with other dogs as well as unknown humans.

When your Shih Poo is provided with sufficient daily exercise and continued socialization that provides interest and expands their mind, they will be able to transition through the adolescent stage of their life much more seamlessly.

The adolescent period in a puppy's life is a time of boundless energy and you will need to find ways to safely allow them to release this energy every day.

Since most people cannot walk nearly fast enough to accommodate the needs of an energetic puppy, you will need to first walk your Shih Poo beside you on leash, and then find a safe place where they can run off leash, either chasing a ball or playing and running in an enclosed area with other similar sized dogs where you can always supervise.

When your puppy is going through what could be a belligerent and trying adolescence, when it seems that they have forgotten everything they may have learned so far, this is an especially good time to revisit the simple "Sit" command.

Now, to help re-establish your leadership role, you will want to ask your Shih Poo puppy to sit at every opportunity.

The simple act of "sitting" will help to calm an excited mind and will get your puppy's focus back on you.

3) Adult Training

When your Shih Poo is a full grown adult (approximately two years of age), now is the time that you can begin more complicated or advanced training sessions. They will enjoy it and when you have the desire and patience, there is no end to the tricks you can teach a willing Shih Poo.

For instance, you may wish to teach your adult Shih Poo more advanced tricks, such as how to dance, or the opposite paw shake or side roll over, which are more difficult than you might expect.

If you and your Shih Poo are really enjoying learning new tricks together, you might want to advance to teaching them the *"commando crawl"*, how to *"speak"* or to *"jump through the human hoop"*. All of these tricks are fun to teach and will exercise both your Shih Poo's body and mind.

As well, the more control you have over your Shih Poo, the easier it will be to teach them a fun sport, such as Agility.

The only restriction to how far you can go with training your adult Shih Poo will be your imagination and their personal ability or desire to perform.

4) Rewards

All that's necessary for effectively teaching your puppy their basic first command is a calm, consistent approach, combined with endless patience.

Most puppies are ready to begin training at about 10 to 12 weeks of age. However, be careful not to overdo it when they are less than six months of age as their attention span will be short.

Make your training sessions no more than 5 or 10 minutes, positive and pleasant with lots of praise and/or treats so that your puppy will be looking forward to their next session.

Some people believe that rewarding with treats is fine, while other people believe that you should avoid it entirely. The truth lay somewhere between.

In general, it is a good idea to use treats as a bonus. Give your puppy a treat when you feel like delighting them or when they have done an exceptional job, but limit it. After all, the ideal is that they are performing well for your praise and your approval, not for that tasty snack you have in your hand!

5) Are You Rewarding Unwanted Behavior?

Often people make the mistake of accidentally rewarding unwanted behaviors. It is very important to recognize that any attention paid to an out of control, adolescent puppy, even negative attention, is likely going to be exciting and rewarding for your puppy.

Therefore, when you engage with an out of control Shih Poo puppy you end up actually rewarding them, which will encourage them to continue more of this unwanted behavior.

Be aware that chasing after a puppy when they have taken something they are not supposed to have, picking them up when they are barking or showing aggression, pushing them off when they jump on you or other people, or yelling when they refuse to come when called, are all forms of attention that can actually be rewarding for most puppies.

As your Shih Poo's guardian, it will be your responsibility to provide structure for your puppy which will include finding acceptable and safe ways to allow your puppy to vent their energy without being destructive or harmful to others.

Activities that create or encourage an overly excited Shih Poo puppy, such as rough games of tug-o-war, or wild games of chase should be immediately curtailed. Your puppy will learn how to control their energy and play quietly and appropriately without jumping on everyone or engaging in barking or mouthy behavior.

Further, if your adolescent Shih Poo puppy displays excited energy simply from being petted by yourself, your family members or any visitors, you will need to teach everyone to ignore your puppy until they calm down. Otherwise, you will be teaching your Shih Poo puppy that humans mean excitement.

For instance, when you continue to engage with an overly excited puppy, you are rewarding them for out of control behavior and literally teaching them that when they see humans, you want them to display excited energy.

Worse, once your puppy has learned that humans are a source of excitement, you will then have to work very long and hard to reverse this behavior. Children are often a source of excitement that can cause an adolescent puppy to be extremely wound up. Do not allow your children to engage with an adolescent Shih Poo puppy unless you are there to supervise and teach the children appropriate and calm ways to interact with the puppy.

In order to keep everyone safe, it is very important that your Shih Poo puppy learn at an early age that children and adults are not sources of excitement.

You can help develop the minds of an adolescent Shih Poo and the minds of growing children at the same time by teaching children that your puppy needs structured walks. You can also show them how to play fetch, search, hide and seek, or how to teach the Shih Poo puppy simple tricks and obedience skills that will be fun and positive interaction for everyone.

6) Come

While most puppies are capable of learning commands and tricks, the first and most important command you need to teach your puppy is the recall, or "Come" command.

The hand signal for "Come" is your arms spread wide open. This is a command they can see from a great distance.

Begin the "Come" command inside your home. Go into a larger room, such as your living room area. Place your puppy in front of you and attach their leash to their collar, while you back away from them a few feet.

Say the command "Come" in an excited voice and hold your arms open wide. If they do not immediately come to you, gently give a tug on the leash so that they understand that they are supposed to move toward you. When they come to you praise them and give a treat they really enjoy.

After your puppy performs a "Come" command, almost every time inside your home, you can move them to a nearby park or quiet outside area. Here you will repeat the process.

You may want to purchase an extra-long line (25 or 50 feet) so that you are always attached to your Shih Poo puppy and can encourage them in the right direction should they become distracted.

7) Sit

The "Sit" and "Stay" commands are both easy commands to teach that will help to keep your Shih Poo puppy safe and out of danger in most every circumstance. Find a quiet time to teach these commands when your puppy is not overly tired.

Ask your puppy to "Sit". If they do not yet understand the command, show them what you mean by gently squeezing with your thumb and middle finger, the area across the back that joins with their back legs. Do not just push them down into a sit as this can cause damage to their back or joints. When they sit, give them a treat and praise them.

When you say the word "Sit", at the same time, show them the hand signal for this command, which is bending your arm at the elbow and raising your right hand, palm open facing upward, toward your shoulder.

8) Stay

Once your Shih Poo puppy can reliably "Sit", say the word "Stay" and hold your outstretched arm, palm open toward their head and back away a few steps.

If they try to follow, calmly say "No" and put them back into "Sit". Give a treat and then say again, "Stay" with the hand signal and back away a few steps.

Once your puppy is sitting and staying, you can then ask them to "Come". Don't forget to use the open arms hand signal for "Come." Show a little excitement with the "Come" command so that your puppy will always enjoy correctly responding and immediately returning to you.

Practice these three basic commands everywhere you go, and use the "Sit" command every time you go for a walk, before you open the door, after you are on the other side of the door, before you go down the stairs, once you are at the bottom of the stairs, and every time you stop when you are on your walk. Pretty soon you will have a puppy who automatically sits whenever you stop moving.

As your puppy gets older, and their attention span increases, you will be able to train for longer periods of time.

9) Shake a Paw

Who doesn't love a dog who knows how to shake a paw? This is one of the easiest tricks to teach your Shih Poo. Most dogs are naturally either right or left pawed. If you know which paw your dog favors, ask them to shake this paw.

Find a quiet place to practice, without noisy distractions or other pets, and stand or sit in front of your dog. Place them in the sitting position and have a treat in your left hand.

Say the command "Shake" while putting your right hand behind their left or right paw and pulling the paw gently toward yourself until you are holding their paw in your hand. Immediately praise them and give them the treat.

Most dogs will learn the "Shake" trick very quickly, and very soon, once you put out your hand, your Shih Poo will immediately lift their paw and put it into your hand, without your assistance or any verbal cue.

Practice every day until they are 100% reliable with this trick, and then it will be time to add another trick to their repertoire.

10) Roll Over

You will find that just like your Shih Poo is naturally either right or left pawed they will also naturally want to roll either to the right or the left side. Take advantage of this by asking your dog to roll to the side they naturally prefer. Sit with your dog on the floor and put them in a lie down position. Hold a treat in your hand and place it close to their nose without allowing them to grab it, and while they are in the lying position, move the treat to the right or left side of their head so that they have to roll over to get to it.

You will very quickly see which side they want to naturally roll to, and once you see this, move the treat to this side. Once they roll over to this side, immediately give them the treat and praise them.

You can say the verbal cue "Over" while you demonstrate the hand signal motion (moving your right hand in a circular motion) or moving the treat from one side of their head to the other with a half circle motion.

Once your Shih Poo can roll over every time you ask, it will be time to teach them another trick.

11) Sit Pretty

While this trick is a little more complicated, and most dogs pick up on it very quickly, remember that every dog is different so always exercise patience.

Find a quiet space with few distractions and sit or stand in front of your dog and ask them to "Sit".

Have a treat nearby (on a countertop or table) and when they sit, use both of your hands to lift up their front paws into the sitting pretty position, while saying the command "Sit Pretty". Help them balance in this position while you praise them and give them the treat.

Once your Shih Poo can do the balancing part of the trick quite easily without your help, sit or stand in front of your dog while asking them to "Sit Pretty" and hold the treat above their head, at the level their nose would be when they sit pretty.

If they attempt to stand on their back legs to get the treat, you may be holding the treat too high, which will encourage them to stand on their back legs to reach it. Go back to the first step and put them back into the "Sit" position and again lift their paws while their backside remains on the floor.

The hand signal for "Sit Pretty" is a straight arm held over your dog's head with a closed fist.

Make this a fun and entertaining time for your Shih Poo and practice a few times every day until they can "Sit Pretty" with a hand signal command every time you ask.

A young Shih Poo puppy should be able to easily learn these basic tricks before they are six months old and when you are patient and make your training sessions short and fun for your dog, they will be eager to learn more.

12) Training as a Bonding Experience

You will begin bonding with your Shih Poo puppy from the very first moment you bring them home from the breeders.

This is the time when your puppy will be the most distraught as they will no longer have the guidance, warmth and comfort of their mother or their other litter mates, and you will need to take on the role of being your new puppy's center of attention.

Be patient and kind with them as they are learning you are now their new center of the universe.

Your daily interaction with your puppy during play sessions and especially your disciplined exercises, including going for walks on leash, and teaching commands and tricks, will be the best bonding opportunities.

Do not make the mistake of thinking that "bonding" with your new puppy can only happen if you are playing or cuddling together, because the very best bonding happens when you are kindly teaching rules and boundaries.

Training forces you and the puppy to interact together in a way that has some very strict rules. Instead of coming across to your new puppy as mean or unreasonable, good training actually allows a puppy to feel more secure in its place.

Think of it this way. From the moment a puppy is born, it knows that its mother is in charge. As the puppy grows up a little, it fights with its brothers and sisters to learn more about who is bigger, stronger and tougher.

When it comes to your home, it knows nothing about how it is supposed to behave in relation to its new family. With the rules that you give, the puppy can once again figure out its place.

13) Never Give Up

Too often we get frustrated and give up on our dogs when they change from being the cute, cuddly and mostly obedient little puppy they once were, and become all kinds of trouble you never bargained for, as they grow into their adolescent stage.

Often times, it will be during the confusing adolescent stage of a dog's life that they find themselves abandoned and behind bars as their owners, who promised to love and protect them, leave their once loved fur friends at the local pound or SPCA.

First of all, not all dogs go through a crazy adolescent period, and secondly, even if they do, please read this section carefully. You can live through puppy adolescence and come out the other side relatively unscathed and a much more knowledgeable and patient guardian.

Congratulations are in order because you've been successful with potty training your young Shih Poo puppy and with teaching them to sleep in their own kennel at night. You've lived through the teething troubles, the chewing and the hand nipping and you no longer have to get up at 3:00 A.M. to let your puppy out to the bathroom.

As well, you've taught your Shih Poo puppy their first few basic commands, and socialized them with many other dogs, people and places. You should feel proud of your accomplishments and the leaps and bounds you and your puppy have accomplished together over the last several months.

Even though your adolescent puppy may be starting to act like a Tasmanian devil, and you may be having second thoughts, now is not the time to give up on them and yourself just because it may seem like someone switched your dog when you weren't looking.

Now is the time to remain consistent and persistent, know that you will eventually be able to enjoy the happy rewards of your puppy raising diligence.

Yes, it can be quite a shock when what used to be your well-behaved little darling who never chewed anything they weren't supposed to suddenly takes it into their head to rip the stuffing out of your $3,000 couch, or chew through a seat belt in your vehicle during the short 15 minutes you were shopping.

Even more disconcerting might be when the previously obedient and loving Shih Poo puppy who always listened to your directions suddenly appears to have gone deaf and cannot remember their name when you expect them to follow you inside the house. Instead, they take off running after a cat three blocks away.

And then, what happened to that quiet little puppy that never appeared to have a mean bone in their body, and now spends most of their time at the window barking and growling at everything and everyone passing by?

Welcome to the world of canine adolescence where it appears that your puppy has turned into some sort of monster and all your previous hard work was for naught.

Of course, this dramatic switch from being the world's best puppy into the monster you can no longer control is not true for all puppies, as every puppy is unique.

However, being prepared for the worst will help you weather any impending storm and get you both out the other side where you can enjoy an even closer relationship than you previously had.

The adolescent phase may be very subtle for your Shih Poo puppy or on the other hand, it may be so dramatic that you're starting to feel guilty every time you drive past the local SPCA or dog pound because thoughts of re-homing are running through your head.

If you are at the stage with your puppy that you are having great difficulties and wondering if you made the right decision to share your home with a dog, rest assured that puppy adolescence is a normal phase of their development. It can be managed and will definitely pass.

As well, if you are finding yourself totally overwhelmed, there are many professionals who can provide valuable assistance to help you through this stage of your Shih Poo puppy's development.

For most puppies, adolescence will begin between the ages of five and seven months. This is also the time that you need to be making an appointment at your veterinarian's office to have your puppy spayed or neutered.

Although neutering or spaying will not prevent adolescent behavior entirely, it can certainly reduce the intensity of it. During this period there are hormonal changes occurring that will affect your puppy's behavior.

While it's usually hormones that are the major cause of behavioral changes in your adolescent puppy, there are also physical changes occurring at the same time of which you may not be aware.

For instance, your puppy will be going through physical growth spurts which might be causing them some pain, as well as changes related to growth in their brain while your puppy's cerebral cortex becomes more involved in thinking for itself.

Usually, during this time of brain growth, a puppy will be trying to make independent choices, and may not yet be capable of making the right ones. This is why their behavior can appear to be quite erratic.

During the early adolescent period of brain development in your Shih Poo puppy, the signals sometimes get mixed up and rerouted. This can result in the perplexing responses you might notice, when for instance, you ask you puppy to sit and they stare dumbly at you, even though they learned this command months ago.

Don't worry because your previous training will return.

14) Exercise

Every dog is an athlete and therefore they need daily exercise to say fit and healthy. The energetic Shih Poo is no exception to this rule. Every Shih Poo will love going for walks with their guardian several times every day.

As well, taking your Shih Poo for a disciplined walk, where they are on leash and walking beside you without straining on the leash or trying to lead you, will reinforce that you are the boss and they are the follower.

Any type of disciplined exercise you can do with your Shih Poo will help to exercise both their body and their mind and will burn off daily energy reserves so that your Shih Poo will be a happy and contented lap dog.

If you find that your Shih Poo is being a pest by chewing inappropriate items around the home, being demanding of your time, or especially unruly when visitors come to call, this is likely because they are not being exercised often enough. They must be exercised enough to drain out their daily pent up energy.

A healthy, adult Shih Poo will thrive when being walked a few times each day and still has plenty of energy to play with you in the house or in the yard.

Chapter 11) Training with Hand Signals

Hand signal training is by far the most useful and efficient training method for every dog, including the Shih Poo.

This is because all too often we inundate our canine companions with a great deal of chatter and noise that they really do not understand. English is not their first language.

Contrary to what some humans might think, the first language of a Shih Poo, or any dog, is a combination of sensing energy and watching body language, which requires no spoken word or sound.

Therefore, when we take the time to teach our dog hand signals for all their basic commands, we are communicating with them at a level they instinctively understand, plus we are helping them to become great followers as they must watch us to understand what is required of them.

1) Come

When first teaching hand signals to your Shih Poo, always show the hand signal for the command at the same time you say the word. If they are totally ignoring the command, it will be time to incorporate a lunge line, which is a very long leash to help you teach the "Come" command. When using this command, you can kneel down or stay standing. Open your arms wide like you are hugging a very large tree. This hand signal can be seen from a long distance.

Simply attach a 20 foot line to their collar and let them sniff about in a large yard or at your neighborhood park.

At your leisure, firmly ask them to "Come" and show the hand signal. If they do not immediately come to you, give a firm tug with the lunge line, so that they understand what you are asking of them.

If they still do not "Come" toward you, simply reel them in until they are in front of you. Then let them wander about again, until you are ready to ask them to "Come".

Repeat this process until your Shih Poo responds correctly at least 80% of the time. You can also reinforce the command by giving a treat when they come back to you when asked. Always ask them to "Sit" when they return to you.

2) Sit

Sit: right arm (palm open facing upward) parallel to the floor, and then raise your arm, while bent at the elbow toward your shoulder. Sit is a very simple, yet extremely valuable command for all puppies and dogs.

If your dog is not sitting on command, try holding a treat above and slightly behind their head, so that when they look up for it they may automatically sit to see it.

Slowly remove the treats as a reward and replace the treat with a "life reward", such as a chest rub or a "thumbs up" signal and your smile.

If your Shih Poo is not particularly treat motivated, lift up and slightly back on the leash when asking them to sit (stand in front of them), and if they still are having difficulties, reach down with your free hand, place it across your dog's back at the place where the back legs join the hip and gently squeeze.

Do NOT simply push down on your dog's back to force their hind legs to collapse under them as this pressure could harm their spine or leg joints.

3) Stay

Stay: right armed fully extended toward your dog's head, palm open, hand bent up at the wrist.

Once your Shih Poo is in the "Sit" position, ask them to "Stay" with both the verbal cue and the hand signal.

If you are right-handed, use your right arm and hand for the signal, and if you are left-handed, use your left arm and hand for the signal. Using your dominant hand will be much more effective because your strongest energy emanates from the palm of your dominant hand.

While your dog is sitting and staying, slowly back away from them. If they move from their position, calmly put them back into sit and ask them to "Stay" again, using both the verbal cue and the hand signal.

Continue to practice this until your dog understands that you want them to stay sitting and not move toward you.

With all commands, when your Shih Poo is just learning, be patient and always reward them with a treat and your happy praise for a job well done.

Chapter 12) Daily Feeding and Care

One important part of caring for a Shih Poo is making sure that it gets the right nutrition throughout its life. You cannot feed a Shih Poo the same amount you would feed a German Shepherd, and you certainly cannot feed a Shih Poo puppy the same as you would feed an adult dog.

Learn a little bit more about how you can ensure that your puppy gets the best nutrition around!

1) Why Do Dogs Eat as They Do?

When you are looking to choose the best food for your Shih Poo, it is a good idea for you to consider why they need the food that they do. Dogs are omnivores that are descended from wolves, but a quick glance at your own Shih Poo will tell you that it will not be chasing down deer anytime soon! Getting to know the parts of your dog's body that are integral to what it eats is a helpful way for you to understand why your dog has the needs that it does.

The first part of your dog you will want to take a good look at when considering what to feed them, will be their teeth.

For example, take a look at your dog's teeth. Unlike humans, who are equipped with wide, flat molars for grinding grains, vegetables and other plant-based materials, canine teeth are all pointed because they are designed to rip, shred and tear into animal meat and bone.

Another obvious consideration when choosing an appropriate food source for our fur friends is the fact that every canine is born equipped with powerful jaws and neck muscles. These are for the specific purpose of being able to pull down and tear apart their hunted prey.

The structure of the jaw of every canine is such that it opens widely to hold large pieces of meat and bone, while the mechanics of a dog's jaw permits only vertical (up and down) movement that is designed for crushing.

A dog's digestive tract is short and simple and designed to move their natural choice of food (hide, meat and bone) quickly through their systems. Vegetables and plant matter require more time to break down in the gastrointestinal tract, which in turn, requires a more complex digestive system than the canine body is equipped with.

The canine digestive system is simply unable to break down vegetable matter, which is why whole vegetables look pretty much the same going into your dog as they do coming out the other end.

Given the choice, most dogs would never choose to eat plants, vegetables and fruits over meat. Although we continue to feed them a kibble-based diet that contains high amounts of vegetables and grains and low amounts of meat.

Plus, in order to get our dogs to eat fruits, vegetables and grains we usually have to flavor the food with meat or meat by-products.

How much healthier and long lived might our beloved fur friends be if we chose to feed them whole, unprocessed, species-appropriate food? Instead, we largely ignore nature's design for our canine companions,

2) Feeding Puppies

For growing puppies, a general rule of thumb is to feed 10% of the puppy's present body weight or between 2% and 3% of their projected adult weight each day.

Keep in mind that high energy puppies will require extra protein to help them grow and develop into healthy adult dogs, especially during their first two years of life.

There are now many foods on the market that are formulated for all stages of a dog's life (including the puppy stage). Whether you choose one of these foods or a food specially formulated for puppies, they will need to be fed smaller meals more frequently throughout the day (3 or 4 times), until they are at least one year of age.

NOTE: choose quality sources of meat protein for healthy puppies and dogs, including beef, buffalo, chicken, duck, fish, hare, lamb, ostrich, pork, rabbit, turkey, venison, or any other source of wild meaty protein.

3) Feeding Adults

An adult dog will generally need to be fed 2 to 3% of their body weight each day. Read the labels and avoid foods that contain a high amount of grains and other fillers. Choose foods that list high quality meat protein as the main ingredient.

Grated Parmesan cheese sprinkled on a Shih Poo's dinner will help to stop picky eaters from ignoring their food.

4) Choosing the Right Food

In order to choose the right food for your Shih Poo, first, it's important to understand the canine physiology and what Mother Nature intended when she created our fur friends.

More than 230 years ago, in 1785, the English Sportsman's dictionary described the best diet for a dog's health in an article entitled "Dog". It described the best food for dogs to be something called "Greaves", saying that it was "the sediment of melted tallow. It was often made into cakes for dogs' food. In Scotland and parts of the US it is called cracklings."

From the meager beginning of the first commercially made dog food has sprung a massively lucrative and vastly confusing industry. It has only recently begun to evolve beyond those early days of feeding our dogs the dregs of human leftovers because it was cheap and convenient for us.

Even today, the majority of dog food choices have far more to do with being convenient for people to serve than it does with being a diet truly designed to be a well-balanced, healthy food choice for a canine.

The dog food industry is big business and as such, because there are now almost limitless choices, there is much confusion and endless debate when it comes to answering the question, "What is the best food for my dog?"

Educating yourself by talking to experts and reading everything you can find on the subject, plus taking into consideration several relevant factors, will help to answer the dog food question.

For instance, where you live may dictate what sorts of foods you have access to. Other factors to consider will include the particular requirements of your dog, such as their age, energy and activity levels.

Next will be expense, time and quality. While we all want to give our dogs the best food possible, many people lead very busy lives and cannot, for instance, prepare their own dog food. But they still want to feed a high quality diet that fits within their budget.

However, perhaps most important when choosing an appropriate diet for our dogs, is learning to be more observant of Mother Nature's design and taking a closer look at our dog's teeth, jaws and digestive tract.

While humans are herbivores who derive energy from eating plants, our canine companions are carnivores, which means they derive their energy and nutrient requirements from eating a diet consisting mainly or exclusively of flesh or animal tissues (i.e. meat).

There are people out there who say that they can raise their dogs on a vegetarian or even a vegan diet, but there is no reputable veterinarian that will approve of such a plan. Though dogs are not obligate carnivores like cats are, they are descended from wolves that needed to hunt and kill prey to survive.

The truth is that though a dog can survive for a surprisingly long time without meat, it is only doing that: surviving. They may wolf down the vegetarian or vegan food that they are given, but that is because they are literally starving and malnourished.

A dog that is fed on a vegetarian or vegan diet will have far less energy than it should, and it will also have health problems, often evidenced by dry eyes, a brittle coat, loose teeth and discolored gums.

If you are ever in doubt about what to feed your Shih Poo or what it needs at this stage in its development, remember that you can always consult your veterinarian. There are times when your dog might need soft food to deal with a stomach issue, or there may be a time when you have to watch your dog's diet very carefully. No matter what the reason, always pay close attention to what your dog consumes!

With many hundreds of dog food brands to choose from, it's no wonder we are confused about what to feed our dogs to help them live long and healthy lives.

The following are some suggestions and questions that may help you choose a dog food company that you can feel comfortable with:

- How long they have been in business?

- Is dog food their main industry?

- Are they dedicated to their brand?

- Are they easily accessible?

- If you contact them, do they honestly answer your questions?

- Research the Company's Safety Standard.

- Look for pet food companies that set higher standards.

- Read the ingredients - where did they come from?

- Are the ingredients something you would eat?

- Are the ingredients farmed locally?

- Was it cooked in a kitchen using standards you would trust?

- Is the company certified under human food or organic guidelines?

Whatever you decide to feed your Shih Poo, keep in mind that, just as too much wheat, other grains and other fillers in our human diet have detrimental effects on our health, the same can be very true for our best fur friends.

Our dogs are also suffering from many of the same life threatening diseases that are rampant in our human society as a direct result of consuming a diet high in genetically altered, impure, processed and packaged foods.

5) Understanding Kibble

While many canine guardians are starting to take a closer look at the food choices they are making for their furry companions, there is no mistaking that the convenience and relative economy of dry dog food kibble continues to be the most popular pet food choice for most dog friendly humans. The industry began in the 1940's

Now, almost 75 years later, the massive pet food industry offers up a confusingly large number of choices with hundreds of different manufacturers and brand names lining the shelves of veterinarian offices, grocery stores and pet food aisles.

While feeding a high quality bagged kibble diet that has been flavored to appeal to dogs and supplemented with vegetables and fruits to appeal to humans, may keep most every Shih Poo companion happy and healthy, you will need to decide whether this is the best diet for them.

6) Considering the Raw Diet

While some of us believe we are killing ourselves as well as our dogs with processed foods, others believe that there are dangers in feeding raw foods.

Those who are advocates of raw feeding believe that the ideal diet for their dog is one which would be very similar to what a dog living in the wild would have access to. These canine guardians are often opposed to feeding their dog any sort of commercially manufactured pet foods, because they consider them to be poor substitutes.

On the other hand, those opposed to feeding their dogs a raw or biologically appropriate raw food diet, believe that the risks associated with food-borne illnesses during the handling and feeding of raw meats outweigh the purported benefits.

Interestingly, even though the United States Food and Drug Administration (FDA) states that they do not advocate a raw diet for dogs, they do advise that for those who wish to take this route, following basic hygiene guidelines for handling raw meat can minimize any associated risks.

Further, high pressure pasteurization (HPP), which is high pressure, water-based technology for killing bacterial, is USDA-approved for use on organic and natural food products, and is being utilized by many commercial raw pet food manufacturers.

Raw meats purchased at your local grocery store contain a much higher level of acceptable bacteria than raw food produced for dogs, because the meat purchased for human consumption is meant to be cooked, which will kill any bacteria that might be present.

This means that canine guardians feeding their dogs a raw food diet can be quite certain that commercially prepared raw foods sold in pet stores will be safer than raw meats purchased in grocery stores.

Many guardians of high energy, working breed dogs will agree that their dogs thrive on a raw or BARF (Biologically Appropriate Raw Food) diet and strongly believe that the potential benefits of feeding a raw dog food diet are many, including:

-healthy, shiny coats

-decreased shedding

-fewer allergy problems

-healthier skin

-cleaner teeth

-fresher breath

-higher energy levels

-improved digestion

-smaller stools

-strengthened immune system

-increased mobility in arthritic pets

-general increase or improvement in overall health

All dogs, whether working breed or lap dogs are amazing athletes in their own right, therefore every dog deserves to be fed the best food available.

A raw diet is a direct evolution of what dogs ate before they became our domesticated pets and we turned toward commercially prepared, easy-to-serve dry dog food that required no special storage or preparation.

The BARF diet is all about feeding our dogs what they are designed to eat by returning them to their evolutionary diet.

When considering the health of your Shih Poo, it is certainly worth remembering that just as too much wheat and processed foods in our human diet is having detrimental effects on our health, the same can be very true for our best fur friends who are also suffering from many of the same life threatening diseases that are rampant in our society today.

Dehydrated Dehydrogenated dog food comes in both raw and cooked forms and these foods are usually air dried to reduce moisture to the level where bacterial growths are inhibited.

The appearance of de-hydrated dog food is very similar to dry kibble and the typical feeding methods include adding warm water before serving, which makes this type of diet both healthy for our dogs and convenient for us to serve.

Dehydrated recipes are made from minimally processed fresh whole foods to create a healthy and nutritionally balanced meal that will meet or exceed the dietary requirements for healthy canines.

Dehydrating removes only the moisture from the fresh ingredients which usually means that because the food has not already been cooked at a high temperature and more of the overall nutrition is retained.

A de-hydrated diet is a convenient way to feed your dog a nutritious diet because all you have to do is add warm water, and wait five minutes while the food re-hydrates so your Shih Poo can enjoy a warm meal.

7) Treats

Since the creation of the first dog treat over 150 years ago the myriad of choices available on every pet store, feed store and grocery store shelf almost outnumbers those looking forward to eating them.

Today's treats are not just for making us guilty owners feel better because it makes us happy to give our fur friends something they really like, today's treats are designed to improve our dog's health.

Some give treats to their dogs, just because, others use treats for training purposes, others for health, while still others treat for a combination of reasons.

Whatever reason you choose to give treats to your Shih Poo, keep in mind that if we treat our dogs too often throughout the day, we may create a picky eater who will no longer want to eat their regular meals.

As well, if the treats we are giving are high calorie, we may be putting our dog's health in jeopardy by allowing them to become overweight.

8) Treats to Avoid

Rawhide: Rawhide is soaked in an ash/lye solution to remove every particle of meat, fat and hair and then further soaked in bleach to remove remaining traces of the ash/lye solution. Now that the product is no longer food, it no longer has to comply with food regulations.

While the hide is still wet it is shaped into rawhide chews, and upon drying, it shrinks to approximately 1/4 of its original size.

Further, arsenic based products are often used as preservatives, and antibiotics and insecticides are added to kill bacteria that also fight against good bacteria in your dog's intestines.

The collagen fibers in the rawhide make it very tough and long lasting which makes this chew a popular choice for humans to give to their dogs. It satisfies the dog's natural urge to chew while providing many hours of quiet entertainment.

Sadly, when a dog chews a rawhide treat, they ingest many harsh chemicals and when your dog swallows a piece of rawhide, it can swell up to four times its size inside your dog's stomach. This can cause anything from mild to severe gastric blockages that could become life threatening and require surgery.

Pigs' Ears: These treats are actually the ears of pigs, and while most dogs will eagerly devour them, they are extremely high in fat, which can cause stomach upsets, vomiting and diarrhea for many dogs. Pigs' ears are often processed and preserved with unhealthy chemicals that discerning dog guardians will not want to feed their dogs. While pig ears are generally not considered to be a healthy treat choice for any dog, they should be especially avoided for any dog that may be at risk of being overweight.

Hoof Treats: Many people give cow, horse and pig hooves to their dogs as treats because they consider them to be "natural".

The truth is that after processing these "treats" retain little, if any, of their "natural" qualities. Hoof treats are processed with preservatives, including insecticides, lead, bleach, arsenic-based products, and antibiotics to kill bacteria, that can also harm the good bacteria in your dog's intestines. If all bacteria is not killed in these meat based products before feeding them to your dog, your pet could also suffer from Salmonella poisoning.

Hooves can also cause chipping or breaking of your dog's teeth as well as perforation or blockages in your dog's intestines.

9) Healthy Treats

Hard Treats

There are so many choices of hard or crunchy treats available. As there are so many varieties of shapes, sizes and flavors, you may have a difficult time choosing. If your Shih Poo will eat them, hard treats will help to keep their teeth cleaner.

Whatever your choice, read the labels and make sure that the ingredients are high quality and appropriately sized for your Shih Poo friend.

Soft Treats

Soft, chewy treats are also available in a wide variety of flavors, shapes and sizes for all the different needs of our fur friends and are often used for training purposes as they have a stronger smell.

Often smaller dogs, such as the Shih Poo, prefer the soft, chewy treats over the hard crunchy ones.

Dental Treats

Dental treats or chews are designed with the specific purpose of helping your Shih Poo to maintain healthy teeth and gums. They usually require intensive chewing and are often shaped with high ridges and bumps to exercise the jaw and massage gums while removing plaque build-up near the gum line.

Freeze-Dried and Jerky Treats

Freeze-dried and jerky treats offer a tasty morsel most dogs find irresistible as they are usually made of simple, meaty ingredients, such as liver, poultry and seafood. These treats are usually light weight and easy to carry around, which means they can also be great as training treats.

Human Food Treats

You will want to be very careful when feeding human foods to dogs as treats, because many of our foods contain additives and ingredients that could be toxic and harmful.

Be certain to choose simple, fresh foods with minimal or no processing, such as lean meat, poultry or seafood, and even if your Shih Poo will eat anything put in front of them, be aware that many common human foods, such as grapes, raisins, onions and chocolate are poisonous to dogs.

10) Training Treats

While any sort of treat can be used as an extra incentive during training sessions, soft treats are often used for training purposes because of their stronger smell and smaller sizes.

Yes, we humans love to treat our dogs, whether for helping to teach the new puppy to go pee outside, teaching the adolescent dog new commands, for trick training, for general good behavior, or for no reason at all, other than that they just gave us the "look".

Make sure the treats you choose are high quality, so that you can help to keep your Shih Poo both happy and healthy, and generally, the treats you feed should not make up more than approximately 10% of their daily food intake.

11) Understanding Allergies

Though we have talked about allergies before in this book, it is only in relation to how humans can be allergic to dogs. Now it is important for you as a dog owner to understand that dogs can be allergic to things just like humans can be!

When it comes to allergies in dogs, the thing to consider is their food. When a human eats something that they are allergic to, whether it is oysters, chocolate or cheese, there is usually a common reaction. The person might find themselves vomiting or feeling generally unwell.

The same is true for dogs, and if a dog is forced to eat something that it is allergic to, it will make itself quite sick. Remember that just because a dog is allergic to something does not mean that it will stay away from it. Dogs do not understand that food that they eat in morning might make them sick in the evening, especially if that discomfort is minimal and the damage is cumulative rather than immediate.

Just like humans, dogs have can have mild and strong allergies. Symptoms of a food allergy in dogs include a general malaise, a loss of fur, loose teeth, an intestinal upset in the form of diarrhea, vomiting or dehydration.

One of the most common culprits when it comes to allergies in dogs is corn. Remember to look for a high-quality food for your dog that uses as little grain as possible!

If you are worried that your dog has an allergy, switch out the food and see if the symptoms improve. If the symptoms persist, take your dog to the veterinarian for a thorough checkup.

The reason why so many dogs suffer from allergies is that this condition, though serious, is not fatal. Your dog will not die from its allergies, but the truth is that its life enjoyment is curtailed, and a great deal of the intestinal discomfort and damage can lead to your dog's life being shorter over all.

If you want your dog to enjoy a long and happy life, be willing to consider what it takes to get any possible allergies dealt with once and for all!

Chapter 13) Grooming Your Shih Poo

Given the fact that your Shih Poo may need have one of several different coat types, it stands to reason that a variety of factors need to be understood before you decide what sort of grooming regimen is right for your puppy. Remember that a well-groomed Shih Poo puppy is a happy Shih Poo puppy, so take some time to learn more about this simple procedure.

1) Why Is Grooming Necessary?

It is important to remember that animal fur, even when it comes in such a wide range of textures as the fur of a Shih Poo puppy, is something that is quite different from human hair. A wolf's fur does not require grooming because it is designed to care for itself, but with dogs like poodles and Shih Tzus, which were bred for interesting fur qualities, some more care is needed.

If your Shih Poo does not receive regular grooming, mats, which are dense hair tangles, can form. These mats can sometimes be worked out with your fingers, but more frequently, they will need to be teased out or cut out. If left unattended, mats can grow to the point where they take over your dog's coat. Mats encourage the growth of bacteria and skin infections, and over time, they contribute greatly to skin issues in your dog. They also provide a serious risk of parasites, and they are also the cause of bad odor on your animal.

2) Some Tools to Consider

The right tools for grooming your Shih Poo will depend greatly on the type of fur that it has. Below you will find a list of general grooming tools of a kind that most groomers will have in their kit. If you are uncertain about how to use them, always feel free to ask a groomer for more information regarding how to keep your Shih Poo's fur in good order between sessions.

A bristle brush with its clusters of tightly-packed bristles will remove loose hair, dirt and debris while gently stimulating the skin, improving circulation and adding shine to the coat.

A pin brush usually has an oval head with wire bristles that are individually spaced and embedded into a flexible rubber pad.

Most guardians prefer pin brushes with rubber tips as these help to prevent a wire from accidentally piercing a dog's sensitive skin.

A pin brush is more normally used following a thorough bristle brushing to lift and fluff the hair at the end of a grooming session.

A slicker brush has short, thin, wire bristles arranged closely together and anchored to a flat, often rectangular, surface that's attached to a handle.

A slicker brush is an ideal grooming tool for helping to remove mats and tangles from a Shih Poo's coat. Slicker brushes are often used as a finishing brush after the use of a pin brush to smooth the dog's coat and create a shiny finish.

Mat splitters, as the name suggests, are tools for splitting apart matted hair, and they come in three different types, including the letter opener style, the safety razor style and the curved blade style.

All of these tools are used to split matted fur into smaller, lengthwise pieces, with minimal discomfort to the dog, so that you or your groomer can untangle or shave the area with a clipper.

Combs are very useful for getting down to the base of any tangles in a dog's coat and working them loose before they develop into painful mats.

Most metal combs have a combination of widely spaced and narrow-spaced teeth and are designed so that if you run into a tangle, you can switch to the wider spaced teeth while you work it out, without pulling and irritating your dog.

Some combs have rotating teeth which makes the process of

removing tangles from your Shih Poo's coat much easier on them without the pain of pulling and snagging.

Flea combs, as the name suggests, are designed for the specific purpose of removing fleas from a dog's coat.

A flea comb is usually small in size for maneuvering in tight spaces, and may be made of plastic or metal with the teeth of the comb placed very close together, to trap hiding fleas.

As well, you will want to keep a good quality pair of small scissors in your Shih Poo grooming box, even if you do not want to do the full grooming process yourself, so that you can regularly trim around your Shih Poo's eyes between full grooming sessions.

If you are planning to groom your Shih Poo yourself, you will need to invest in good quality scissors of several lengths that can cost anywhere between \$30 and \$200 each (£18 and £119) or more.

3) Dog Hygiene Products

Just like humans, Shih Poos require specific products to get clean. Shih Poos are delicate dogs, and you must always be sure that the products that you use for their fur does not hurt them or irritate their skin.

For example, NEVER make the mistake of using human shampoo or conditioner for bathing your Shih Poo because dogs have a different pH balance than humans. Shampoo for humans has a pH balance of 5.5, whereas shampoo formulated for our canine companions has an almost neutral pH balance of 7.5.

Any shampoo with a lower pH balance will be harmful to your dog because it will be too harshly acidic for their coat and skin, which can create skin problems.

Always purchase a shampoo for your dog that is specially formulated to be gentle and moisturizing on your Shih Poo's coat and skin, that will not strip the natural oils, and which will nourish your dog's coat to give it a healthy shine.

As a general rule, always read the instructions provided on the shampoo bottle, and avoid shampoos containing insecticides or harsh chemicals.

If your Shih Poo is suffering from an infestation of fleas, you may want to bathe them with shampoo containing pyrethrum (a botanical extract found in small, white daisies) or a shampoo containing citrus oil.

While many people use a conditioner after we shampoo our own hair, a large number of us canine guardians forget to use a conditioner on our own dog's coat after bathing.

Even if the bathing process is one that you wish to complete as quickly as possible, you will want to reconsider this little oversight because, just as conditioning our human hair improves its condition, the same is true for our dog's coat.

Conditioning your Shih Poo's coat will not only make it look and feel better, conditioning will also add additional benefits, including:

-preventing the escape of natural oils and moisture;

-keeping the coat cleaner for a longer period of time;

-repairing a coat that has become damaged or dry;

-restoring a soft, silky feel;

-a conditioned coat will dry more quickly;

-protection from the heat of the dryer and breakage from tangles during toweling, combing or brushing;

Spend the extra two minutes to condition your Shih Poo's coat after bathing because the benefits of doing so will be appreciated by both you and your dog. The dog will have an overall healthy coat and skin with a natural shine.

There are many de-tangling products you can purchase which will make the job of combing and removing mats much easier on both you and your Shih Poo, especially if you have opted to let their hair grow longer.

De-tangling products work by making the hair slippery, and while some de-tanglers work well when used full strength, you may prefer a lighter, spray-in product.

As well, there are silicone products and grooming powders or you can even use corn starch to effectively lubricate the hair to help with removing mats and tangles before bathing.

You will always want to avoid causing any pain when trimming your Shih Poo's toenails, because you don't want to destroy their trust in you while regularly performing this task.

However, accidents do happen, therefore if you accidentally cut into the vein in the toenail, know that you will cause your dog pain, and the toenail will bleed.

Therefore, it is always a good idea to keep some styptic powder (often called "Kwik Stop") in your grooming kit. Dip a moistened finger into the powder and apply it immediately to the end of the bleeding nail.

The quickest way to stop a nail from bleeding is to immediately apply styptic powder and firm pressure for a few seconds.

If you do not have styptic powder or a styptic pencil available, there are several home remedies that can help stop the bleeding, including a mixture of baking soda and corn starch, or simply cornstarch alone. Also, a cold, wet teabag or rubbing with scent-free soap can also be effective. These home remedies will not be as instantly effective as styptic powder.

Ear powders, which can be purchased at any pet store, are designed to help keep your dog's ears dry while at the same time inhibiting the growth of bacteria that can lead to infections.

Your local pet store will offer a wide variety of ear cleaning creams, drops, oils, rinses, solutions and wipes specially formulated for cleaning your dog's ears.

As well, there are also many home remedies that will just as efficiently clean your dog's ears.

Because a dog's ears are a very sensitive area, always read the labels before purchasing products and avoid any solutions that list alcohol as the main ingredient.

4) Home Remedy Hygiene Solutions

Sometimes, the items that you need to take care of your dog can be found right in your own medicine cabinet or kitchen

For example, witch hazel is a natural anti-inflammatory that works well to cleanse and protect against infection while encouraging faster healing of minor skin traumas.

A 50:50 solution of organic apple cider vinegar and purified water has been used as an external folk medicine for decades. This mixture is a gentle and effective solution that kills germs while naturally healing.

A 50:50 solution of hydrogen peroxide and purified water is useful for cleansing wounds and dissolving ear wax.

Whatever product you decide to use for cleaning your dog's ears, always be careful about what you put into your dog's ears and thoroughly dry them after cleaning.

Similarly, remember that cornstarch doubles for styptic powder in a pinch.

If your Shih Poo is white, you may notice staining around the dog's eyes, a condition known as tear staining. To return your Shih Poo's fur back to its bright white, create a solution that is half baking soda and half lemon can be applied to the stains and then brushed out after it is dry.

5) Brushing

The cornerstone of your dog's regular grooming regimen is brushing. When you brush your dog, you use a specific kind of brush to remove shed fur, allowing your dog's fur to remain free of debris. By brushing your dog on a daily basis, you can prevent mats from forming on your dog's coat.

Finding the right kind of brush for your Shih Poo's fur is something that requires a close look at your dog's coat. If your Shih Poo's coat matches its poodle ancestry, meaning that it is very dense, curly and thick, the right brush is going to be a wire-pin brush, which usually involves short metal tines with balls of plastic at the end of each tine.

If your dog has the very smooth and sleek fur of the Shih Tzu, you will find that it does very well with a soft bristle brush or the wire pin brush, assuming the tines are set fairly closely together.

A bristle brush is an excellent tool for most coat types, and if you are uncertain, this is the type to use. A veterinarian or a groomer can tell you more precisely what brush is ideal for your dog's coat.

Some dogs are very leery about the idea of grooming and brushing, but the best way to get them used to it is to start them young. Sit with the brush on your lap, and invite your puppy to come over and sit close to you. When it does so, praise it, and pet it. Let it sniff the brush and get used to it. That might be all that you do that day.

The next day, try touching the brush to the Shih Poo puppy. From there, you can slowly start to introduce the concept of grooming. Some people feed their Shih Poos treats as this process continues so that they always associate something good with the experience.

If your dog remains afraid of the brush, think about picking up a mitt. A grooming mitt has a nubby surface that is intended to catch loose hair from the dog's body and remove it. This can be a good way to ease your dog towards brushing and general grooming without traumatizing it.

Remember to be patient but persistent. Not only does brushing keep your dog looking good, it will also help your dog look great.

6) Bathing

The question on how often you should bathe your Shih Poo is one that comes up quite often. Over-bathing can make leave your dog with skin that is raw or inflamed, while under-bathing results in a companion animal that can be quite malodorous.

When it comes to Shih Poos, one standard to stick to is give your dog a bath once every six weeks and to see how it reacts. If you notice too much reddening in the skin or if the dog seems oversensitive, back it off a bit. When in doubt, always ask your veterinarian or your groomer.

Bathing your Shih Poo is actually quite easy, especially if you are starting with a puppy. The more comfortable your dog is with being handled, the easier a time it is going to have with being bathed.

Before you start a bath, make sure that you pick any debris out of the Shih Poos coat. Give the Shih Poo a thorough brushing to remove all of the dead hair, which will make the bath far simpler and far more pleasant.

A slight spray of leave-in conditioner is something that can make a huge difference when are getting your dog's coat smooth before a bath.

If your sink is large enough, you can easily bathe a Shih Poo in your sink. To protect the chrome or enamel, simply put a rubber bathmat down inside the sink so that your dog does not lose its grip on the floor and panic. Gather your supplies, which should include a dog-safe shampoo, a conditioner recommended by your groomer, a sponge and some dry towels.

Ideally, your sink will have a detachable head, allowing you to spray your Shih Poo down, but if it does not, simply get a small cup that will allow you to pour water over your dog's head. Make sure that the faucet is as a comfortably warm temperature for you and turn it on. Fill the sink with about four inches of water.

Place your dog in the sink and start wetting down its fur thoroughly, getting the water all the way to your dog's skin. When you get to your dog's head, use a soft sponge to wet the fur on the head and face instead of a sprayer or a cup. Most dogs do not like having water dropped on their heads as this can make them panic.

Apply shampoo as indicated on the bottle instructions by beginning at the head and working your way down the back. Be careful not to get shampoo in the eyes, nose, mouth or ears. Comb the shampoo lather through your dog's hair with your fingers, making sure you don't miss the areas under the legs and tail. After allowing the shampoo to remain in your dog's coat for a couple of minutes, thoroughly rinse your Shih Poo's coat, right down to the skin with clean, lukewarm water using the spray attachment, cup or pitcher.

Pull the plug and allow the water to drain from the sink. Comb through your dog's coat with your fingers to make sure all the shampoo residue has been rinsed away.

Be very careful to get all of the shampoo out of your dog's coat, as shampoo left in the dog's fur and next to the skin can irritate it.

After the shampoo is out, simply squeeze the Shih Poo's coat gently with your hands until most of the water is out.

Apply conditioner as indicated on the bottle instructions and work the conditioner throughout your Shih Poo's coat. Leave the conditioner in your dog's coat for two minutes and then thoroughly rinse the conditioner out of your dog's coat with warm water, unless the conditioner you are using is a "leave-in", no-rinse formula.

Remove your Shih Poo from the water, wrapping it immediately in dry towels so it doesn't get cold and use the towels to gently squeeze out extra water. If your Shih Poo has longer hair, be especially careful not to be too rough as you towel it dry, as this can cause breakage and hair loss. A Shih Poo with a very short cut does not need this kind of consideration.

Remember to dry your Shih Poo carefully and completely, as it may be very prone to chills and to respiratory infections. A hair dryer set to the lowest setting can help your Shih Poo dry faster, but if you do not own one, a thorough towel-drying and then keeping the Shih Poo in a warm room until it is completely dry will be enough.

7) Tooth-brushing

Cleaning your Shih Poo's teeth is a good way to ensure that it stays healthy its entire life. Dogs have tooth issues just like humans do, but unlike humans, it will never occur to your Shih Poo to pick up a toothbrush and some toothpaste! That is where good owners come in, and that means that this is a process that you need to look in to.

When it comes time to brush a dog's teeth, this is where many guardians fail miserably, using the excuse that "my dog doesn't like it". Whether they like it or not is not the issue, because in order to keep your Shih Poo healthy, they must have healthy teeth and the only way to ensure this is to brush their teeth every day.

The many canine toothpastes on the market are usually flavored with beef or chicken in an attempt to appeal to the dog's taste buds, while others may be infused with mint or some other breath freshening ingredient in an attempt to appeal to humans by improving the dog's breath.

Honestly, your dog is not going to be begging for you to brush his or her teeth no matter how tasty the paste might be, therefore, effectiveness, in the shortest period of time, will be more of a deciding factor than whether or not your dog prefers the taste of the toothpaste.

Some dog toothpastes contain baking soda, which is the same mild abrasive found in many human pastes, and it is designed to gently scrub the teeth. However, just how much time you will have to spend scrubbing your dog's teeth, before they've had enough, may be too minimal to make these pastes very effective. Other types of canine toothpastes are formulated with enzymes that are designed to work chemically by breaking down tartar or plaque in the dog's mouth. These pastes do not need to be washed off your dog's teeth and are safe for them to swallow. Whether or not they remain on the dog's teeth long enough to do any good might be debatable.

If you have run out of toothpaste, one solution can be found in your medicine cabinet. Old-fashioned hydrogen peroxide cleans while killing germs and keeping teeth white. Just dip your dog's toothbrush in a capful of hydrogen peroxide, shake off the excess, and brush their teeth. There will such a small amount in your dog's mouth that you don't need to worry about them swallowing it.

Slowly introduce your Shih Poo to teeth brushing early on in their young life so that they will not fear it.

Begin with a finger cap toothbrush when they are young puppies, and then move to a soft bristled toothbrush, or even an electric brush, as all you have to do is hold it against the teeth while the brush does all the work.

Sometimes with a manual brush, you may brush too hard and cause the gums to bleed. If you need help keeping your dog's mouth open while you do a quick brush or scrape, get yourself a piece of hard material (rubber or leather) that they can bite down on, so that they cannot fully close their mouth while you work on their teeth.

Never use human toothpaste or mouthwash on your dog's teeth because dogs cannot spit and human toothpaste that contains toxic fluoride will be swallowed. There are many flavored dog toothpastes available at the pet store or veterinarian's office.

Also, it's a good idea to get your dog used to the idea of occasionally having their teeth scraped or scaled; especially the back molars which tend to build up plaque. Be very careful if you are doing this yourself because the tools are sharp.

Slowly introduce the manual or electric toothbrush to your Shih Poo. When you go slowly, they will get used to the buzzing of the electric brush which will do a superior job of cleaning their teeth.

First, let them see the electric brush, then let them hear it buzzing, and before you put it in their mouth, let them feel the buzzing sensation on their body, while you move it slowly toward their head and muzzle.

When your Shih Poo will allow you to touch their muzzle while the brush is turned on, the next step is to brush a couple of teeth at a time until they get used to having them all brushed at the same time.

Whether you let the electric toothbrush do the work for you or you are using a manual toothbrush, make certain that you brush in a circular motion with the bristles of the brush angled so that they get underneath the gum line to help prevent gum disease and loose teeth.

Despite what most dog owners might put up with as normal, it is not normal for your dog to have smelly dog breath or canine halitosis. Bad breath is the first sign of an unhealthy mouth, which could involve gum disease or tooth decay.

Keep your dog's teeth sparkling white and their breath fresh by using old-fashioned hydrogen as your doggy toothpaste (hydrogen peroxide is what's in the human whitening toothpaste). There will be such a small amount on the brush that it will not harm your dog, and will kill any bacteria in your dog's mouth.

Help prevent tooth plaque and doggy halitosis by feeding your dog natural, hard bones at least once a month, which will also help to remove tartar while polishing and keeping their teeth white.

Feed large, bones so there is no danger of swallowing, and do NOT boil the bones first because this makes the bone soft (which defeats the purpose of removing plaque), and could cause it to splinter into smaller pieces that could create a choking hazard for your dog.

Shih Poos, which have short muzzles and smaller jaws, tend to have more issues with periodontal disease than other breeds. Make sure to feed your Shih Poo with a daily dental chew or hard biscuit to help to remove tartar while exercising jaws and massaging gums. Some dental chews contain natural breath freshening cinnamon, cloves or chlorophyll

Coconut oil also helps to prevent smelly dog breath while giving your dog's digestive, immune and metabolic functions a boost at the same time. Dogs often love the taste, so add a 1/2 tsp to your Shih Poo's dinner and their breath will soon be much sweeter.

Keep your Shih Poo's mouth comfortable and healthy by getting into the habit of brushing their teeth every night before bedtime.

The use of a tooth scraper once or twice a month can help to remove plaque buildup. Most accumulation will be found on the outside of the teeth and on the back molars, near the gum line. Go slowly and carefully because these tools are sharp and only do this when your dog is calm and relaxed, a little bit at a time.

8) Trimming Nails

Allowing your Shih Poo to have long, untrimmed nails can result in various health hazards including infections or an irregular and uncomfortable gait that can result in damage to their skeleton.

Although most dogs do not particular enjoy the process of having their nails trimmed, and most humans find the exercise to be a little scary, regular nail trimming is a very important grooming practice that should never be overlooked.

In order to keep your Shih Poo' toenails in good condition and the proper length, you will need to purchase a nail trimmer that is specifically meant for dog nails. Do not use the trimmers that are designed for humans, and make sure that the trimmers that you use are sharp and in good shape.

When your Shih Poo is a small puppy, handle its paws often so that it will not be nervous about having its nails trimmed. Take a close look at the nail itself. The only part you want to cut is translucent; where the claw is opaque, that is where it is attached to the paw. Do your best to trim the nail close to this point without hurting your puppy's paw.

Use the trimmer to cut away the hard part of the nail. Work quickly so that the dog does not have a chance to get fidgety, but not so quickly that you nick its flesh.

If you do, have a container of styptic powder or cornstarch nearby and dip the bleeding paw into the powder. This closes up the wound right away. If you do nick your Shih Poo, you may wish to simply let the nail trim go for a while and continue another day.

Further, if you want your dog's nails to be smooth, without the sharp edges clipping alone can create, you will also want to invest in a toenail file or a special, slow speed, rotary trimmer (Dremel™), designed especially for dog nails.

Some dogs will prefer the rotary trimmer to the squeezing sensation of the nail clipper. Never use a regular Dremel™ tool on a dog's toenails as it will be too high speed and will burn your dog's toenails. Only use a slow speed Dremel™, Model 7300-PT Pet Nail Grooming Tool.

If you are worried about handling this task yourself, it is something that can be passed on to a groomer.

9) Ear Care

There are many ear cleaning creams, drops, oils, rinses, solutions and wipes formulated for cleaning your dog's ears that you can purchase from your local pet store or veterinarian's office.

Alternately, you may prefer to use a home remedy that will just as efficiently clean your Shih Poo's ears, such as witch hazel or a 50:50 mixture of hydrogen peroxide and purified water.

If you are going to make your own ear cleaning solution, find a bottle with a nozzle, measure your solution, properly dilute and mix into the bottle, and use your preparation to saturate a cloth to wipe out the visible part of your dog's ears. Always make sure the ears are totally dried after cleaning.

This is especially important for your Shih Poo, which has floppy drop ears. Shih Poo ears are often prone to infection and inflammation because the ear flaps keep the ear moist and humid, so be sure to check your dog's ears on a regular basis.

10) Eye Care

Every dog should have their eyes regularly wiped with a warm, damp cloth to remove buildup of daily secretions in the corners of the eyes. The Shih Poo does not have the same kind of tear staining issues the way that a Maltese might, but its eyes can still look quite crusted and irritated.

The secretions from the Shih Poo's eyes can be unattractive and uncomfortable for the dog as the hair becomes glued together.

If this build up is not removed every day, it can quickly become a cause of bacterial yeast growth that can lead to eye infections.

When you take a moment every day to gently wipe your dog's eyes with a warm, moist cloth, and keep the hair trimmed away from their eyes, you will help to keep your dog's eyes comfortable and infection free.

11) Professional Grooming

If you decide that you are not interesting in buying all the equipment or if you are worried that you will not be able to do a completely safe or attractive job, you will want to locate a trusted professional service to do this for you.

The best way to find a groomer is to ask others who they use and whether they are happy with the results.

If you have decided to keep your Shih Poo's fur clipped short in a puppy cut, you will need to take them for a full grooming session approximately every 6 to 8 weeks.

An average price for professionally grooming a small Shih Poo will usually start around $40 (£24) and could be considerably more depending upon whether the salon is also bathing and trimming nails.

Find a groomer who is used to handling Shih Poos and who has worked with coat textures similar to the one on your dog. Ask them for references, and ask to see pictures of jobs that they have done before. This is something that will help you ensure that your dog ends up healthy and happy.

Remember that some dogs love grooming and some dogs hate it, but at the end of the day, it needs to get done! Sometimes a good professional groomer can do something to ensure that your Shih Poo stays happy while it is being groomed.

For example, some Shih Poo groomers will make house calls. Instead of traveling out to a space that might make your Shih Poo nervous or upset, the groomer will come to your home instead. This can be a great thing if your Shih Poo came from an abusive or neglectful condition and is a little wary around people in general.

12) Should I Clip My Shih Poo's Fur?

Remember that dog grooming is a skilled trade. It requires practice, training and professional investment. It is one thing to remove a mat, quite another to hold your dog safely still while you groom it.

If you have decided to learn how to clip your Shih Poo's hair yourself, rather than taking them to a professional grooming salon, you will need to purchase all the tools necessary and learn how to properly use them.

The first step will be learning which blades to use in your electric clipper in order to get the length of cut you desire.

The "blade cut" refers to the length of the dog's hair that will remain after cutting against the natural length of the hair.

As an example, if the blade cut indicates 1/4" (0.6 cm) the length of your Shih Poo's hair after cutting will be 1/4" (0.6 cm) if you cut with the natural growth of their hair, or it will be 1/8" (0.3 cm) if you cut against the direction of the hair growth.

Even if you decide to leave the full grooming to the professionals, in between grooming sessions you will still need to have a brush, a comb, a small pair of scissors and a pair of nail clippers on hand, so that you can keep the hair clipped away from your Shih

Poo's eyes, knots and tangles out of their coat and their nails trimmed short.

A good quality clipper for a Shih Poo, such as an "Andis", "Wahl" or "Oster" professional electric clipper will cost between $100 and $300 (£60 and £180) or more.

At the end of the day, it is usually worth it to allow a professional to take care of your Shih Poo. Not only will they be able to groom your dog efficiently and safely, you will discover that they can give your Shih Poo any number of interesting clips and cuts.

13) My Shih Poo Doesn't Like to Be Groomed!

Do not allow yourself to get caught in the "my dog doesn't like it" trap which is an excuse many owners will use to avoid regular grooming sessions.

When you allow your dog to dictate whether they will permit a grooming session, you are setting a dangerous precedent that could lead to lifetime of trauma for both you and your Shih Poo.

When people neglect daily grooming routines, many dogs develop a heightened sensitivity, especially with regard to having their legs and feet held, touched, brushed or clipped and will do anything they can to avoid the process when you need to groom them.

Make a pact with yourself right from the first day you bring your puppy home, never to neglect a regular grooming routine and not to avoid sensitive areas, such as trimming toenails, just because your dog may not particular "like" it.

Chapter 14) Socializing Your Shih Poo

People like to laugh about small dogs like Shih Poos having Napoleon complexes, but the truth of the matter is that a poorly socialized Shih Poo is a danger to itself and to the other dogs and the people around it.

A little bit of time spent socializing your puppy is something that can pay off a lot as your pet grows and encounters other animals and people.

1) With Other Dogs and Pets

Generally speaking, the majority of an adult dog's habits and behavioral traits will be formed between the ages of birth and one year of age. This is why it will be very important to introduce your Shih Poo puppy to a wide variety and types of locations, sights, sounds and smells during this formative period in their young life.

Your Shih Poo puppy will learn how to behave, in all these various circumstances, by following your lead, feeling your energy and watching how you react in every situation.

For instance, never accidentally reward your Shih Poo puppy for displaying fear or growling at another dog or person by picking them up.

Picking up a Shih Poo puppy or dog at this time, when they are displaying unbalanced energy, actually turns out to be a reward for them, and you will be teaching them to continue with this type of behavior.

As well, picking up a puppy literally places them in a top dog position, where they are higher and more dominant than the person or dog they just growled at.

The correct action to take in such a situation is to gently correct your Shih Poo puppy, with a firm, yet calm energy by distracting them with a "no", so that they learn to let you deal with the situation on their behalf. If you allow a fearful puppy to deal with situations that unnerve them all by themselves, they may learn to react with fear or aggression to unfamiliar circumstances and you will have created a problem that could escalate into something quite serious as they grow older.

The same is true of situations where a young puppy may feel the need to protect themselves from a bigger or older dog that may come charging in for a sniff.

It is the guardian's responsibility to protect the puppy so that they do not think they must react with fear or aggression to protect itself.

Once your Shih Poo puppy has received all their vaccinations, you can take them out to public dog parks and various locations where many dogs are found.

Before allowing them to interact with other dogs or puppies, take them for a disciplined walk on leash so that they will be a little tired and less likely to immediately pounce on all other dogs.

Keep your puppy on leash and close beside you, because most puppies are a bundle of out-of-control energy, and you need to protect them while teaching them how far they can go before getting themselves into trouble with adult dogs who may not appreciate their excited playfulness.

Keep a close watch on your Shih Poo puppy to make sure they are not being overwhelmed by too many other dogs, or getting overly excited and stressed because it is your job to protect your puppy.

If your puppy shows any signs of aggression or domination toward another puppy, dog or person, you must immediately step in and calmly discipline them. By doing nothing, you will be allowing them to get into situations that could become serious behavioral issues as they grow in age and size.

No matter the age or size of your puppy, allowing them to display aggression or domination over another dog or person is never a laughing matter and this type of behavior must be immediately curtailed.

2) With Other People

Take your puppy everywhere with you and introduce them to many different people of all ages, sizes and ethnicities. Most people will automatically be drawn to you when they see you have a puppy because few people can resist a cute puppy.

Most people will come to you and want to interact with your puppy and if they ask if they can hold your puppy, this is also a good way to socialize your puppy and show them that humans are friendly.

Do not let others (especially children) play roughly with your puppy or squeal at them in a high pitched voice because this can be very frightening for a young puppy. As well, you do not want to teach your puppy that humans are a source of excitement.

Be especially careful when introducing your puppy to young children who may accidentally hurt your puppy, because you don't want them to become fearful of children as this could lead to aggression later on in life.

Explain to children that your Shih Poo puppy is very young and that they must be calm and gentle when playing or interacting in any way.

3) Within Different Environments

It can be a big mistake not to take the time to introduce your Shih Poo puppy to a wide variety of different environments because when they are not comfortable with different sights and sounds, this could cause them possible trauma later in their adult life.

Be creative and take your puppy everywhere you can imagine when they are young. This insures that they are comfortable, no matter where they travel, whether you stroll down a busy city sidewalk or walk along a deserted seashore.

Don't make the mistake of only taking your Shih Poo puppy into areas where you live and will always travel because they need to also be comfortable visiting areas you might not often visit, such as noisy construction sites or airports.

Your puppy needs to see all sorts of sights, sounds and situations so that they will not become fearful should they need to travel with you to any of these areas.

Your Shih Poo puppy will take its cues from you, which means that when you are calm and in control of every situation, they will learn to be the same.

For instance, put your puppy in their Sherpa bag and take them to the airport where they can watch people and hear planes landing and taking off, take them to a local park where they can see a baseball game, or take them to the local zoo or farm and let them get a close up look at horses, pigs and ducks.

When you take your Shih Poo puppy everywhere you will be teaching them to be a calm and well-balanced member of your family in every situation.

A good idea is to introduce your dog to new sounds by playing music of those sounds e.g. in a car or in the house and pretend everything is perfectly normal when the sounds are being played. If you do this when the dog is still very young, it is likely he won't care about "strange" noises.

A few examples of noises you could get your dog used to:

airplanes, firework, the sound of a hoover, hot air balloon, crying children, a meowing cat, kids playing in the park, cars driving on the road, car hooters, a bicycle bell, thunder, etc....

There are CD's available online with all these sort of sounds recorded on for you to play in presence of your dog. Just search for it online.

4. Acclimatization Is Key

Overall, what you will quickly realize is that your Shih Poo will always do better if it becomes used to seeing people, animals and situations to which they are not accustomed.

A Shih Poo is naturally a dog that is very curious about the world around it, and as a result, it may start out coming on a little too strong. That, combined with the barking habit, can give your puppy a handful of bad habits before you know what happened!

It's not enough to take your Shih Poo for a walk in a new neighborhood only on occasion. It is also not enough to introduce it to only a few new people when you first get it.

Slow, steady and often wins the race, so be willing to make sure that your Shih Poo gets a lot of exposure to the world that you live in.

4) Behavior With Children and Pets

Prospective Shih Poo owners with children need to keep in mind that while the Shih Poo is an energetic and entertaining little dog, it is also a toy breed, which means that it can be somewhat fragile.

Play sessions with young children should be supervised to ensure that the Shih Poo is not roughly treated, that it does not get too tightly squeezed, stepped on, dropped or somehow become accidentally injured.

As well, the Shih Poo can become snappish with younger children who do not respect the dog's boundaries, therefore, caution and supervision when introducing small or overly excited children needs to be exercised so that the Shih Poo does not feel that it needs to protect itself.

When introducing a Shih Poo to larger dogs, a guardian will need to be aware that the fearless little Shih Poo will often not know their place or be at all intimidated by the larger dog. If it is allowed to be protective of its owner or family members, it may charge and bark at a larger dog.

This type of jealous or protective behavior must never be permitted because the tiny Shih Poo is at a distinct disadvantage should a larger dog decide to fight back.

The Shih Poo can be a vocal watch dog who will bark when they hear a new person entering the home. However, they will usually become quickly social and friendly as soon as they realize that the person is a friend.

Chapter 15) Medical Care & Safety

Looking after your Shih Poo's health is not always something that you can do on your own. You should take your Shih Poo in for veterinary visits at least once a year, in addition to any visits your veterinarian requires.

1) Choosing a Veterinarian

A consideration to keep in mind when choosing a veterinarian clinic will be that some clinics specialize in caring for smaller pets, and some specialize in larger animal care, while still others have a wide ranging area of expertise and will care for all animals, including reptiles.

Choosing a clinic will be a personal decision, however, since the Shih Poo is considered a small or "toy" breed of dog, your dog's needs may be better served by choosing a clinic that specializes in smaller pets.

Choosing a good veterinary clinic will be very similar to choosing the right health care clinic or doctor for your own personal health because you want to ensure that your Shih Poo puppy receives the quality care they deserve.

Start your search by asking other dog owners where they take their fur friends and whether they are happy with the service they receive.

If you don't know anyone to ask, visit the local pet store in your area and it will be able to provide you with references and local listings of pet care clinics.

Next, check online, because a good pet clinic will have an active website up and running that will list details of all the services they provide along with an overview of all staff members, their education and qualifications.

Once you've narrowed your search, it's time to personally visit the clinics you may be interested in, as this will be a good opportunity for you to visually inspect the facility, interact with the staff and meet the veterinarians face to face.

Of course, it's not just you who needs to feel comfortable with the clinic chosen and those working there. Your puppy needs to feel comfortable, too, and this is where visiting a clinic and interacting with the staff and veterinarians will show you their experience and expertise in handling your puppy.

If your puppy is comfortable with them, then you will be much more likely to trust that they will be providing the best care for your puppy. The puppy will need to receive all their vaccinations and eventually be spayed or neutered.

It's also a good idea to take your puppy into your chosen clinic several times before they actually need to be there, so that they are not fearful of the new smells and unfamiliar surroundings.

2) Neutering and Spaying

While it can sometimes be difficult to find the definitive answer about when is the best time to neuter or spay your young Shih Poo, because there are varying opinions on this topic, one thing that most veterinarians do agree on is that earlier spaying or neutering, between 4 and 6 months of age, is a better choice than waiting. Spaying or neutering surgeries are carried out under general anesthesia.

More dogs are being neutered at younger ages, so speak with your veterinarian and ask for their recommendations regarding the right age to spay or neuter your Shih Poo.

Intact (non-neutered) males and females are more likely to display aggression related to sexual behavior than are neutered animals. Fighting among males is less common after neutering.

The intensity of other types of aggression, such as irritable aggression in females will be totally eliminated by spaying.

While neutering or spaying is not a treatment for aggression, it can certainly help to minimize the severity and escalation of aggressiveness and is often the first step toward resolving an aggressive behavior problem. Performed by a licensed veterinarian surgeon, neutering is a surgical procedure that renders a male dog unable to reproduce.

In males, the surgery is also referred to as *"castration"* because the procedure entails the removal of the young dog's testicles. When the testicles are removed, what is left behind is an empty scrotal sac (which used to contain the puppy's testicles) and this empty sac will soon shrink in size until it is no longer noticeable. Neutering male Shih Poo puppies before they are six months of age can help to ensure that they will be less likely to suffer from obesity as they grow older. Neutering can also mean that a male Shih Poo will be less likely to have the urge to wander.

Further, waiting until a male Shih Poo is older than six months before having them neutered could mean that they will experience the effects of raging testosterone that will drive them to escape their yards by any means necessary to search out females to mate with.

Non-neutered males also tend to spray or mark territory far more, both inside and outside the home, and during this time can start to display aggressive tendencies toward other dogs as well as people.

In female puppies, sterilization, referred to as *"spaying"* is a surgical procedure carried out by a licensed veterinarian, to prevent the female dog from becoming pregnant and to stop regular heat cycles.

The sterilization procedure is much more involved for a female puppy (than for a male) as it requires the removal of both ovaries and the uterus by incision into the puppy's abdominal cavity. The uterus is also removed during this surgery, to prevent the possibility of it becoming infected later on in life.

Preferably, female Shih Poo puppies should be spayed before their very first estrus or heat cycle. Females in heat often appear more agitated and irritable, while sleeping and eating less and some may become extremely aggressive towards other dogs. Spaying female puppies before their first heat pattern can eliminate these hormonal stressors and reduce the opportunity of mammary glandular tumors. Early spaying also protects against various other potential concerns, such as uterine infections.

Many dog owners often become needlessly worried that a neutered or spayed dog will lose their vigor. Rest assured that a dog's personality or energy level will not be modified by neutering, and in fact, many unfavorable qualities resulting from hormonal impact may resolve after surgery.

Your Shih Poo will certainly not come to be less caring or cheerful, and neither will it resent you because you are not denying your dog any essential encounters. You will, however, be acting as an accountable, informed, and caring Shih Poo owner.

Further, there is little evidence to suggest that the nature of a female Shih Poo will improve after having a litter of puppies.

It is important that you do not place your own psychological needs or concerns onto your Shih Poo puppy, because there is no gain to be had from permitting sexual activity in either male or female canines.

It is not *"abnormal"* or *"mean"* to manage a puppy's reproductive activity by having them sterilized. Rather, it is unkind not to neuter or spay a dog and there are many benefits of having this procedure carried out

A neutered or spayed Shih Poo is less likely to wander. Castrated male dogs have the tendency to patrol smaller sized outdoor areas and are less likely to participate in territorial conflicts with perceived opponents.

NOTE: a Shih Poo that has actually already had successful escapes from the yard may continue to wander after they are spayed or neutered.

An unsterilized dog may urinate or defecate inside the home or in other undesirable areas in an attempt to stake territorial claims, relieve anxiety, or advertise their available reproductive status.

While neutering or spaying a Shih Poo puppy after they have

already begun to inappropriately eliminate or mark territory to announce their sexual availability to other dogs, will reduce the more powerful urine odor as well as eliminate the hormonal factors, once this habit has begun, the undesirable behavior may continue to persist after neutering or spaying.

While metabolic changes that occur after spaying or neutering can cause some Shih Poo puppies to gain weight, often the real culprit for any weight gain is the human who feels guilty for subjecting their puppy to any kind of pain and therefore, they attempt to alleviate their guilt by feeding more treats or meals to their Shih Poo companion.

If you are concerned about weight gain after neutering or spaying a Shih Poo puppy, simply adjust their food and treat consumption, as needed.

It is a very simply process to change your Shih Poo's food intake according to their physical demands and how they look, and if your Shih Poo puppy's daily exercise and level of activity has not changed after they have been spayed or neutered, there will likely be no change in food management necessary

3) Why Vaccinate a Puppy?

Puppies are vaccinated by a veterinarian to provide them with protection against four common and serious diseases. Vaccination against these common set of diseases is referred to as *"DAPP"*, which stands for **D**istemper, **R**etrovirus, **P**arainfluenza and **P**arvo Virus.

Approximate one week after your Shih Poo puppy has completed all three sets of these primary vaccinations; they will be fully protected from those specific diseases. Then, most veterinarians will recommend a once a year vaccination for the next year or two.

It has now become common practice to vaccinate adult dogs every three years, and if your veterinarian is insisting on a yearly vaccination for your Shih Poo puppy, you need to ask them why, because to do otherwise is considered by most professionals to be *"over vaccinating"*.

4) Distemper

Canine distemper is a contagious and serious viral illness for which there is currently no known cure.

This deadly virus, which is spread either through the air or by direct or indirect contact with a dog that is already infected, or distemper-carrying wildlife, including ferrets, raccoons, foxes, skunks and wolves, is a relative of the measles virus which affects humans.

Canine distemper is sometimes also called "hard pad disease" because some strains of the distemper virus actually cause thickening of the pads on a dog's feet, which can also affect the end of a dog's nose.

In dogs or animals with weak immune systems, death may result two to five weeks after the initial infection.

Early symptoms of distemper include fever, loss of appetite, and mild eye inflammation that may only last a day or two. Symptoms become more serious and noticeable as the disease progresses.

A puppy or dog that survives the distemper virus will usually continue to experience symptoms or signs of the disease throughout their remaining lifespan, including *"hard pad disease"* as well as *"enamel hypoplasia"*, which is damage to the enamel of the puppy's teeth that are not yet formed or that have not yet pushed through the gums. Enamel hypoplasia is caused by the distemper virus, killing the cells that manufacture tooth enamel. Adenovirus is a virus that causes infectious canine hepatitis, which can range in severity from very mild to very serious, and sometimes can cause death.

Symptoms can include coughing, loss of appetite, increased thirst and urination, tiredness, runny eyes and nose, vomiting, bruising or bleeding under the skin, swelling of the head, neck and trunk, fluid accumulation in the abdomen area, jaundice (yellow tinge to the skin), a bluish clouding of the cornea of the eye (called "hepatitis blue eye") and seizures.

There is no specific treatment for infectious canine hepatitis; therefore, treatment of this disease is focused on managing symptoms while the virus runs its course. Hospitalization and intravenous fluid therapy may be required in severe cases.

5) Canine Parainfluenza Virus (CPiV)

The canine par influenza virus originally affected only horses. It is also referred to as *"canine influenza virus"*, *"greyhound disease"* and *"race flu"*, and is easily spread through the air or by coming into contact with respiratory secretions.

This disease is believed to have adapted to become contagious to dogs and is easily spread from dog to dog, causing symptoms which may become fatal.

While the more frequent occurrences of this respiratory infection are seen in areas with high dog populations, such as race tracks, boarding kennels and pet stores, this virus is highly contagious to any dog or puppy, at any age.

Symptoms can include a dry, hacking cough, difficulty breathing, wheezing, runny nose and eyes, sneezing, fever, loss of appetite, tiredness, depression and possible pneumonia.

In cases where only a cough exists, tests will be required to determine whether the cause of the cough is the par influenza virus or the less serious *"kennel cough"*.

While many dogs can naturally recover from this virus, they will remain contagious, and for this reason, in order to prevent the spread to other animals, aggressive treatment of the virus with antibiotics and antiviral drugs will be the general course of action.

In more severe cases, a cough suppressant may be prescribed, as well as intravenous fluids to help prevent secondary bacterial infection.

6) Canine Parvovirus (CPV)

Canine parvovirus is a highly contagious viral illness affecting puppies and dogs. Parvovirus also affects other canine species including foxes, coyotes and wolves.

There are two forms of this virus (1) the more common intestinal form, and (2) the less common cardiac form, which can cause death in young puppies.

Symptoms of the intestinal form of parvovirus include vomiting, bloody diarrhea, weight loss, and lack of appetite, while the less common cardiac form attacks the heart muscle.

Early vaccination in young puppies has radically reduced the incidence of canine parvovirus infection, which is easily transmitted either by direct contact with an infected dog, or indirectly, by sniffing an infected dog's feces.

The virus can also be brought into a dog's environment on the bottom of human shoes that may have stepped on infected feces, and there is evidence that this hardy virus can live in ground soil for up to a year.

Recovery from parvovirus requires both aggressive and early treatment. With proper treatment, death rates are relatively low (between 5 and 20%), although chances of survival for puppies are much lower than older dogs, and in all instances, there is no guarantee of survival.

Treatment of parvovirus requires hospitalization where intravenous fluids and nutrients are administered to help combat dehydration. As well, antibiotics will be given to counteract secondary bacterial infections, and as necessary, medications to control nausea and vomiting may also be given.

Without prompt and proper treatment, dogs that have severe parvovirus infections can die within 48 to 72 hours.

7) Rabies Vaccinations

Rabies is a viral disease transmitted in the saliva of an infected animal, usually through a bite. The virus travels to the brain along the nerves and once symptoms develop, death is almost certainly inevitable, usually following a prolonged period of suffering.

If you plan to travel out of state or across country borders, you will need to make sure that your Shih Poo has an up to date Rabies Vaccination Certificate (NASPHV form 51) indicating they have been inoculated against rabies. Rabies vaccinations for dogs are also compulsory in most countries in mainland Europe, as is permanent identification and registration of dogs through the use of a Pet Passport.

Those living in a country that is rabies free (UK, Eire) are not required to vaccinate their dogs against rabies, unless they intend to travel.

8) Leishmaniasis

Leishmaniasis is caused by a parasite and is transmitted by a bite from a sand fly. There is no definitive answer for effectively combating Leishmaniasis, especially since one vaccine will not prevent the known multiple species.

In areas where the known cause is a sand-fly, deltamethrin collars (containing a neurotoxic insecticide) worn by the dogs has been proven to be 86% effective.

There are two types of Leishmaniasis: (1) a skin reaction causing hair loss, lesions and ulcerative dermatitis, and (2) a more severe, abdominal organ reaction, which is also known as black fever. When the disease affects organs of the abdominal cavity the symptoms include:

- loss of appetite
- diarrhea
- severe weight loss
- exercise intolerance

- vomiting

- nose bleed

- tarry feces

- fever

- pain in the joints

- excessive thirst and urination

- inflammation of the muscles

Leishmaniasis spreads throughout the body to most organs, with kidney failure being the most common cause of death. Virtually all infected dogs develop this system wide disease and as much as 90% of those infected will also display skin reactions.

Affected dogs in the US are frequently found to have acquired this infection in another country.

Notably this disease is regularly found in the Middle East, the area around the Mediterranean basin, Portugal, Spain, Africa, South and Central America, southern Mexico and the US (regular cases reported in Oklahoma and Ohio), where it is found in 20 to 40% of the dog population.

There have also been a few reported cases in Switzerland, northern France and the Netherlands.

NOTE: Leishmaniasis is a *"zoonotic"* infection, which is a contagious disease that can be spread between animals and humans. Organisms residing in the Leishmaniasis lesions can be transmitted to humans.

Treatment in dogs is often difficult with relapses and Leishmaniasis poses a significant risk to the health of your dog, especially if you travel to the Mediterranean.

9) Lyme's Disease

This is one of the most common tick-borne diseases in the world, which is transmitted by Borrelia bacteria found in the deer or sheep tick. Lyme's disease, also called *"borreliosis"*, can affect both humans and dogs and this disease can be fatal.

The Borrelia bacteria that causes Lyme's disease, is transmitted by slow-feeding, hard-shelled deer or sheep ticks, and the tick usually has to be attached to the dog for a minimum of 18 hours before the infection is transmitted.

Symptoms of this disease in a young or adult dog include:

- recurrent lameness from joint inflammation
- lack of appetite
- depression
- stiff walk with arched back
- sensitivity to touch
- swollen lymph nodes
- fever
- damage to the kidney
- rare heart or nervous system complications

While Lyme's disease has been reported in dogs throughout the United States and Europe, it is most prevalent in the upper Midwestern states, the Atlantic seaboard, and the Pacific coastal states.

In order to properly diagnose and treat Lyme's disease, blood tests will be required, and if the tests are positive, oral antibiotics will be prescribed to treat the conditions.

Prevention is the key to keeping this disease under control because dogs that have had Lyme disease before are still able to get the disease again.

There is a vaccine for Lyme disease and dogs living in areas that have easy access to these ticks should be vaccinated yearly.

10) Rocky Mountain Spotted Fever (RMSF)

This tick-transmitted disease is very often seen in dogs in the East, Midwest, and plains region of the US, and the organisms causing RMSF are transmitted by both the American dog tick and the Rocky Mountain spotted fever tick, which must be attached to the dog for a minimum of five hours in order to transmit the disease. Common symptoms of RMSF include:

- fever

- reduced appetite

- depression

- pain in the joints

- lameness

- vomiting

- diarrhea

Some dogs affected with RMSF may develop heart abnormalities, pneumonia, kidney failure, liver damage, or even neurological signs, such as seizures or stumbling gait.

Blood testing will be required to diagnose this disease after which oral antibiotics will be given to treat the infection for approximately two weeks.

Dogs that can clear the organism from their systems will recover and thereafter remain immune to future infection.

11) Ehrlichiosis

This is another tick disease transmitted by both the brown dog tick and the Lone Star Tick. Ehrlichiosis has been reported in every state in the US, as well as worldwide.

Common symptoms include:

- depression
- reduced appetite
- fever
- stiff and painful joints
- bruising

Signs of infection typically occur less than a month after a tick bite and last for approximately four weeks. There is no vaccine available.

Blood tests may be needed to test for antibodies and treatment requires antibiotics for up to four weeks in order to completely clear the organism.

After a dog has been previously infected, they may develop antibodies to the organism, but will not be immune to reinfection.

Dogs living in areas of the country where this tick disease is commonly found may be prescribed low doses of antibiotics during tick season.

12) Anaplasmosis

Deer ticks and western black-legged ticks are carriers of the bacteria that transmit canine anaplasmosis.

However, there is another form of anaplasmosis (caused by different bacteria) that is carried by the brown dog tick. Because the deer tick also carries other diseases, some animals may be at risk for developing more than one tick-borne disease at the same time.

Signs of anaplasmosis are similar to ehrlichiosis and include painful joints, diarrhea, fever, and vomiting as well as possible nervous system disorders.

A dog will usually begin to show signs of anaplasmosis within a couple of weeks after infection and diagnosis will require blood and urine testing, and sometimes other specialized laboratory tests.

Treatment is with oral antibiotics for up to 30 days, depending on how severe the infection may be. When this disease is quickly treated, most dogs will recover completely, however, subsequent immunity is not guaranteed, which means that a dog may be infected again if exposed. Tick Paralysis is caused when ticks secrete a toxin that affects the nervous system. Affected dogs show signs of weakness and limpness approximately one week after being first bitten by ticks.

Symptoms usual begin with a change in pitch of the dog's usual bark, which will become softer, and weakness in the rear legs that eventually involves all four legs, which is then followed by the dog showing difficulty breathing and swallowing. If the condition is not diagnosed and treated, death can occur.

Treatment involves locating and removing the tick and treatment with tick anti-serum.

13) Retained Primary Teeth

Often times a young dog will not naturally lose their puppy or baby teeth, especially those with small jaws, like the Shih Poo, without intervention from a licensed veterinarian.

Therefore, keep a close watch on your puppy's teeth around the age of 6 or 7 months of age to make certain that the baby teeth have fallen out and that the adult teeth have space to grown in.

If your Shih Poo puppy has not naturally lost their baby teeth, they will need to be pulled, in order to allow room for the adult teeth to grow in, and the best time to do this will be at the same time they visit the veterinarian's office to be spayed or neutered.

Smaller dogs, like the Shih Poo, have a smaller jaw, which can result in more problems with teeth overcrowding.

An overcrowded mouth can cause teeth to grow unevenly or crooked and food and plaque to build up, which will eventually result in bacterial growth on the surface of the teeth, causing bad breath, gum and dental disease.

14) Periodontal Disease

Please be aware that 80% of three year old dogs suffer from periodontal disease and bad breath because their guardians do not look after their dog's teeth.

What makes this shocking statistic even worse is that it is entirely possible to prevent canine gum disease and bad breath.

The pain associated with periodontal disease will make your dog's life miserable, as it will be painful for them to eat and the associated bacteria can infect many parts of the dog's body, including the heart, kidney, liver and brain, all of which they will have to suffer in silence.

If your Shih Poo has bad breath, this could be the first sign of gum disease caused by plaque build-up on the teeth.

As well, if your Shih Poo is drooling excessively, this may be a symptom secondary to dental disease. Your dog may be experiencing pain or the salivary glands may be reacting to inflammation from excessive bacteria in the mouth. Hypoglycemia or low blood sugar is usually seen in very young puppies (5-16 weeks of age) and is a result of a puppy not eating regular meals throughout the day.

Very small Shih Poo puppies may be especially prone to hypoglycemia because their insufficient muscle mass makes it difficult for them to store glucose and regulate blood sugar.

Symptoms of hypoglycemia include drowsiness, listlessness, a glassy-eyed look, and shaky or uncoordinated movement when walking because the brain relies upon sugar to function properly.

The gums of a Shih Poo puppy suffering from low blood sugar will appear very pale or grey in color and once the gums have become pale the puppy may require force feeding and injection of fluids as they may also be dehydrated. In extreme cases of hypoglycemia, the puppy may have a seizure or go into a coma.

A Shih Poo puppy or dog displaying any of these symptoms should be immediately given sugar in the form of corn syrup or honey and emergency veterinary treatment in order to avoid permanent brain damage or even death.

Sometimes a young Shih Poo puppy can get very busy playing and will forget to eat, which can result in a sudden drop in blood sugar.

If you are not paying attention to how much your Shih Poo is eating, and even if you are, it is a good idea to keep on hand a tube of high calorie paste that can be used in an emergency to get blood sugar quickly back to normal levels.

15) Luxating Patella

This slipping or floating kneecap condition is a common defect seen in many smaller breeds, including the Shih Poo, and may also be caused by accidentally falling or jumping from a height. Usually the condition will present itself between the ages of 4 and 6 months.

Often you will see a dog with this problem appear to be skipping down the road as they occasionally lift one leg as the kneecap slips out of the patellar groove and the leg locks up. In more severe cases, surgery may be the recommended treatment option to correct this condition.

16) Canine Coronavirus

While this highly contagious intestinal disease, which is spread through the feces of contaminated dogs, was first discovered in Germany during 1971 when there was an outbreak in sentry dogs, it is now found worldwide.

This virus can be destroyed by most commonly available disinfectants, and symptoms include

- diarrhea
- vomiting
- weight loss or anorexia

While deaths from this disease are rare, and treatment generally requires only medication to relieve the diarrhea, dogs that are more severely affected may require intravenous fluids to combat dehydration.

There is a vaccine available which is usually given to puppies that are more susceptible at a young age, and to show dogs that have a higher risk of exposure to the disease.

17) Leptosporosis

This is a disease that occurs throughout the world that can affect many different kinds of animals, including dogs.

The disease is always present in the environment which makes it easy for any dog to pick up. This is because it is found in rats, and wildlife, as well as domestic livestock.

Veterinarians see more cases in the late summer and fall – probably because that is when pets and wildlife are out and about, and more cases also occur after heavy rainfalls.

The disease is most common in mild or tropical climates around the world, and in the US or Canada, it is more common in states or provinces that have heavy rainfall.

Cold winter conditions lower the risk because leptospira do not tolerate the freezing and thawing of near-zero temperatures. They are killed rapidly by drying, but they persist in standing water, dampness, mud and alkaline conditions.

Most of the infected wild animals and domestic animals that spread leptospirosis do not appear ill.

The leptospira take up residence in the kidneys of infected animals, which can include rats, mice, skunks, and raccoons and when these animals void urine, they contaminate their environment with living leptospira.

While dogs usually become infected by sniffing this urine or by wading, swimming or drinking contaminated water, and this is how the disease passes from animal to animal, the leptospira can also enter through a bite wound or by dogs eating infected material.

18) Additional Vaccinations

Depending upon where you and your Shih Poo live, your veterinarian may suggest additional vaccinations to help combat diseases that may be more common in your area.

For example, Rocky Mountain Spotted Fever and Lyme Disease are both specific vaccinations that are very location-specific. If you and your dog are very much based in urban areas, there is a chance that your veterinarian will not recommend them.

19) When Is a Puppy Vaccinated?

The first vaccination needle is normally given to a puppy around six to eight weeks of age, which means that generally it will be the responsibility of the Shih Poo breeder to ensure that the puppy's first shots have been received before their new owner takes them home.

Then it will be the new Shih Poo puppy's guardians that will be responsible for ensuring that the next two sets of shots, which are usually given three to four weeks after each other, are given by the new guardian's veterinarian at the proper intervals. De-Worming kills internal parasites that your dog/puppy may have.

Note: No matter how sanitary your conditions, or where you live, your dog will have internal parasites, because it is not a matter of cleanliness.

It is recommended by the Center for Disease Control (CDC) that puppies be dewormed every 2 weeks until they are 3 months old, and then every month after that, in order to control worms.

Many vets recommend worming dogs for tapeworm and roundworms every 6-12 months. Tail docking, also referred to as tail shortening or bobbing to reduce the length of a dog's natural tail length has come to be a hot subject of discussion, with many believing that the method, which was originally executed for efficient health and wellness associated factors, ought to be banned for all breeds.

It is also worth pointing out that while docking is legal in the US, it is banned with the exception of certain cases in the UK. For example, in England and in Wales, docking is only permitted for certain breeds of working dogs, while Scotland is strict, stating that docked tails are only allowable in cases of injuries.

With respect to the Shih Poo crossbreed, some breeders will dock the tails while others will avoid it. There is some talk among breeders that the tail style should follow that of the mother. A Shih Poo with a poodle mother, for example, may have its tail docked as poodles often do have this procedure performed, while a Shih Poo with a Shih Tzu mother should have its tail left full.

Remember when making this decision that there is strong evidence to suggest that docked tails result in lifelong pain for the dog that undergoes it. In addition to that, it can affect the muscles throughout the dog's hindquarters.

Nowadays, docking or shortening the tail has come to be absolutely nothing more than an aesthetic enhancement, especially with regards to a companion breed like the Shih Poo.

There are very few reasons to consider docking your Shih Poo's tail, but if you decide to do so and if you are in an area where it is legal to do so, the best option is to speak to a veterinarian who is skilled in the procedure.

The procedure for reducing or shortening the top section of an older new puppy's or dog's tail needs to be performed by an accredited veterinarian specialist and as this treatment will certainly be a lot more painful for an older puppy or dog, they should be fully anesthetized.

20) Special Care When Pregnant

As pregnancy only last nine weeks, and a Shih Poo female will go into labor within 56 to 66 days after becoming pregnant, a pregnant Shih Poo will require immediate attention when the first signs of pregnancy appear.

Immediately upon noticing signs of pregnancy you will want to take your Shih Poo to the veterinarian to confirm the pregnancy and to receive instructions for the proper feeding and care.

During the first days of pregnancy your Shih Poo may experience morning sickness.

Your veterinarian may recommend increasing food intake or adding an egg or cottage cheese to your Shih Poo's meals and switching to puppy kibble, which is higher in protein, at around the 30 day mark.

As the Shih Poo female becomes heavier with the puppies, she will lose interest in exercising and her other normal activities and will need to sleep more.

When the time for birthing is drawing near, the Shih Poo female will start to display "nesting" characteristics where she will search for a warm and safe place to give birth.

You can help by providing a nesting box and she will likely want to take things into the box to make it more comfortable, such as towels or even a stuffed toy that she will begin to mother.

When the time draws near to whelping, the Shih Poo female may completely lose her appetite and show distress by pacing, panting, and acting uncomfortable.

Her temperature needs to be checked, and should be around 100.2

to 100.8 degrees Fahrenheit (37.89 to 38.22 degrees Centigrade), and when it drops to approximately 98 to 99.4 degrees Fahrenheit (36.67 to 37.44 degrees Centigrade), the puppies will usually be born within 24 hours.

If you are at all worried about the birthing process you will want to take the mother Shih Poo immediately to your veterinarian's office.

If all goes well at home, within 5-6 hours of the last puppy's birth, you will need to take the Shih Poo female and her puppies to your veterinarian for a check up to ensure that the female has not retained any puppies or placentas and that the puppies are all in good health.

21) A Note About Breeding

A lot of people are interested in breeding their Shih Poos, but the truth is unless you have years of experience with one or both of the parent breeds and an established place in the breeding world, this is something that you should generally avoid.

When it comes to breeding, it takes a lot of work, a lot of time and a lot of work on your reputation before you do much more than break even. Remember that the money that you pay for a Shih Poo puppy goes right into it vaccinations and care if you are dealing with a good breeder.

Overall, it is far better for you to simply purchase puppies from a breeder and support the ones who do a good job.

On top of that, if you are a good breeder, you must always guarantee that your puppies will go to a good home. If you cannot sell them then that means that you should be willing to keep them. The shelters are overflowing with all kinds of dogs, and even purebreds are often put down for want of a better home.

Other people state that they want to show their children the miracle of life, but there are documentaries for that. Set your children a far better example by not taking on more than you can handle with a litter of designer puppies.

Across the board, when you are dealing with puppies, it is far better to buy than to breed!

Chapter 16) Poisonous Foods & Plants

When it comes to taking care of your Shih Poo and keeping it from harm, you need to make sure that its environment is safe. This means that you must be are of the fact that dogs curious about anything that they can put in their mouths and that Shih Poos can be susceptible to poisoning. The things that can poison a dog are numerous, so make sure that you know what you need to watch to keep your puppy safe!

1) Poisonous Foods

While some dogs are smart enough not to want to eat foods that can harm or kill them, other canine companions will eat absolutely anything they can get their teeth on.

As conscientious guardians for our fur friends, it will always be our responsibility to make certain that when we share our homes with a dog, we never leave foods that could be toxic or lethal to them easily within their reach.

While there are many foods that can be toxic to a Shih Poo, the following alphabetized list contains some of the more common foods that can seriously harm or even kill our dogs including:

Bread Dough: If your dog eats bread dough, their body heat will cause the dough to rise inside the stomach. As the dough expands during the rising process, alcohol is produced.

Dogs that have eaten bread dough may experience stomach bloating, abdominal pain, vomiting, disorientation and depression. Because bread dough can rise to many times its size, eating only a small amount will cause a problem for any dog.

Broccoli: The toxic ingredient in broccoli is isothiocynate. While it may cause stomach upset, it probably won't be very harmful unless the amount eaten is more than 10% of the dog's total daily diet.

Chocolate: Contains theobromine, a chemical that is toxic to dogs in large enough quantities. Chocolate also contains caffeine, which is found in coffee, tea, and certain soft drinks. Different types of chocolate contain different amounts of theobromine and caffeine.

For example, dark chocolate and baking chocolate or cocoa powder contain more of these compounds than milk chocolate does, therefore, a dog would need to eat more milk chocolate in order to become ill.

However, even a few ounces of chocolate can be enough to cause illness or death in a small dog like the Shih Poo, therefore, no amount or type of chocolate should be considered safe for a dog to eat.

Chocolate toxicity can cause vomiting, diarrhea, rapid or irregular heart rate, restlessness, muscle tremors, and seizures. Death can occur within 24 hours of eating.

During many holidays such as Christmas, New Year's, Valentine's, Easter and Halloween, chocolate is often more easily accessible to curious dogs, especially from children who are not so careful with where they keep their Halloween stash and who are an easy mark for a hungry dog.

In some cases, people unwittingly poison their dogs by offering them chocolate as a treat or leaving a luscious chocolate frosted cake easily within licking distance when nobody is looking.

Caffeine: Beverages containing caffeine (like soda, tea, coffee and chocolate) act as a stimulant and can accelerate your dog's heartbeat to a dangerous level. Dogs eating caffeine have been known to have seizures, some of which are fatal.

Cooked Bones: These can be extremely hazardous for a dog because the bones become brittle when cooked which causes them to splinter when the dog chews on them.

The splinters have sharp edges that have been known to become stuck in the teeth, and cause choking when caught in the throat or cause a rupture or puncture of the stomach lining or intestinal tract.

Especially dangerous are cooked turkey and chicken legs, ham, pork chop and veal bones. Symptoms of choking include:

- Pale or blue gums
- Gasping, open-mouthed breathing
- Pawing at the face
- Slow, shallow breathing
- Unconscious, with dilated pupils

Grapes and Raisins: These foods can cause acute (sudden) kidney failure in dogs. While it is unknown what the toxic agent is in this fruit, clinical signs can occur within 24 hours of eating and include vomiting, diarrhea, and lethargy (tiredness).

Other signs of illness caused from eating grapes or raisins relate to the eventual shutdown of kidney functioning.

Garlic and Onions: These contain chemicals that damage red blood cells by rupturing them so that they lose their ability to carry oxygen effectively, which leaves the dog short of oxygen, causing what is called *"hemolytic anemia"*.

Poisoning can occur with a single ingestion of large quantities of garlic or onions or with repeated meals containing small amounts.

Cooking does not reduce the potential toxicity of onions and garlic.

NOTE: Fresh, cooked, and/or powdered garlic or onions are commonly found in baby food, which is sometimes given to dogs when they are sick, therefore, be certain to carefully read food labels before feeding to your Shih Poo.

Macadamia Nuts: These are commonly found in candies and chocolates. Although the mechanism of macadamia nut toxicity is not well understood, the clinical signs in dogs having eaten these nuts include depression, weakness, vomiting, tremors, joint pain, and pale gums.

Signs can occur within 12 hours after eating. In some cases, symptoms can resolve themselves without treatment within 24 to 48 hours, however, keeping a close eye on your Shih Poo will be strongly recommended.

Mushrooms: Mushroom poisoning can be fatal if certain species of mushrooms are eaten.

The most commonly reported severely toxic species of mushroom in the US is Amanita phalloides (Death Cap mushroom) which is also quite a common species found in most parts of Britain. Other Amanita species are also toxic.

This deadly mushroom is often found growing in grassy or wooded area near various deciduous and coniferous trees, which means that if you're out walking with your Shih Poo in the woods, they could easily find these mushrooms.

Eating them can cause severe liver disease and neurological disorders. If you suspect your dog has eaten these mushrooms, immediately take them to your veterinarian, as the recommended treatment is to induce vomiting and to give activated charcoal. Further treatment for liver disease may also be necessary.

Pits and Seeds: Many seeds and pits found in a variety of fruits, including apples, apricots, cherries, pears and plums, contain cyanogenic glycosides that can cause cyanide poisoning in your Shih Poo.

The symptoms of cyanide poisoning usually occur within 15-20 minutes to a few hours after eating and symptoms can include initial excitement, followed by rapid respiration rate, salivation, voiding of urine and feces, vomiting, muscle spasm, staggering, and coma before death.

Dogs suffering from cyanide poisoning that live more than 2 hours after onset of symptoms will usually recover.

Raw Salmon or Trout: Salmon Poisoning Disease (SPD) can be a problem for anyone who feeds their dog a raw meat diet that includes raw salmon or trout. The cause is infection by a rickettsia organism called Neorickettsia helminthoeca.

Nanophyteus salmincola are found to infect some species of freshwater snails. The infected snail is eaten by the fish as part of the food chain. The dog is exposed only when it eats an infected fish.

A sudden onset of symptoms occurs 5-7 days after eating the infected fish. In the acute stages, gastrointestinal symptoms are quite similar to canine parvovirus.

SPD has a mortality rate of up to 90%, can be diagnosed with a fecal sample and is treatable if caught in time.

Prevention is simple, cook all fish before feeding it to your Shih Poo and immediately see your veterinarian if you suspect that your dog has eaten raw salmon or trout.

Tobacco: All forms of tobacco, including patches, nicotine gum and chewing tobacco can be fatal to dogs if eaten.

Signs of poisoning can appear within an hour and include hyperactivity, salivation, panting, vomiting and diarrhea. Advanced signs include muscle weakness, twitching, collapse, coma, increased heart rate and eventually cardiac arrest.

Never leave tobacco products within reach of your Shih Poo, and if you suspect your dog has eaten any of these, seek immediate veterinary help.

Tomatoes: Tomatoes contain atropine which can cause dilated pupils, tremors and irregular heartbeat. The highest concentration of atropine is found in the leaves and stems of tomato plants, next is the unripe (green) tomatoes, followed by the ripe tomato.

Xylitol: This is an artificial sweetener found in products such as gum, candy, mints, toothpaste, and mouthwash that is recognized by the National Animal Poison Control Center to be a risk to dogs.

Xylitol is harmful to dogs because it causes a sudden release of insulin in the body that leads to hypoglycemia (low blood sugar). Xylitol can also cause liver damage in dogs.

Within 30 minutes after eating a product containing xylitol, the dog may vomit, be lethargic (tired), and/or be uncoordinated. However, some signs of toxicity can also be delayed for hours or even for a few days. Xylitol toxicity in dogs can be fatal if left untreated.

Please be aware that the above list is just some of the more common foods that can be toxic or fatal to our fur friends and that there are other foods we should never feed our dogs.

If you have one of those dogs who will happily eat anything that looks or smells even slightly like food, be certain to keep these foods far away from your beloved Shih Poo and you'll help them to live a long and healthy life.

2) Poisonous Household Plants

Many common house plants are actually poisonous to our canine companions, and although many dogs simply will ignore house plants, some will attempt to eat anything, especially puppies who want to taste everything in their new world.

More than 700 plant species contain toxins that may harm or be fatal to puppies or dogs depending on the size of the puppy or dog and how much they may eat. It will be especially important to be aware of the more common household plants when you are sharing your home with a new puppy.

The following is a short list of the more common household plants, what they look like, the different names they are known by, and what symptoms would be apparent if your puppy or dog decides to eat them.

Aloe Plant: (medicine plant or Barbados aloe), is a very common succulent that is toxic to dogs. The toxic agent in this plant is Aloin.

The bitter yellow substance is found in most aloe species and may cause vomiting and/or reddish urine.

←

Asparagus Fern: (emerald feather, emerald fern, sprengeri fern, plumosa fern, lace fern) The toxic agent in this plant is sapogenin — a steroid found in a variety of plants. Berries of this plant cause vomiting, diarrhea and/or abdominal pain or (skin inflammation) from repeated exposure.

Corn Plant: (cornstalk plant, dracaena, dragon tree, ribbon plant) is toxic to dogs. Saponin is the offensive chemical compound found in this plant. If the plant is eaten, vomiting (with or without blood), loss of appetite, depression and/or increased salivation can occur.

Cyclamen: (Sowbread) is a pretty, flowering plant that, if eaten, can cause increased salivation, vomiting and diarrhea. If a dog eats a large amount of the plant's tubers, which are usually found below the soil at the root — heart rhythm abnormalities, seizures and even death can occur.

Dieffenbachia: (dumb cane, tropic snow, exotica) contains a chemical that is a poisonous deterrent to animals. If the plant is eaten, oral irritation can occur, especially on the tongue and lips. This irritation can lead to increased salivation, difficulty swallowing and vomiting.

170

Elephant Ear: (caladium, taro, pai, ape, cape, via, via sori, malanga) contains a chemical similar to that found in dieffenbachia, therefore, a dog's toxic reaction to elephant ear is similar: oral irritation, increased salivation, difficulty swallowing and vomiting.

Heartleaf Philodendron: (horsehead philodendron, cordatum, fiddle leaf, panda plant, split-leaf philodendron, fruit salad plant, red emerald, red princess, saddle leaf) is a common, easy-to-grow houseplant that contains a chemical irritating to the mouth, tongue and lips of dogs. An affected dog may also experience increased salivation, vomiting and difficulty while swallowing.

171

Jade Plant: (baby jade, dwarf rubber plant, jade tree, Chinese rubber plant, Japanese rubber plant, friendship tree) While the toxic property in this plant is unknown, eating it can cause depression, loss of coordination and, although more rare, slow heart rate.

Lilies: Some plants of the lily family are toxic to dogs. The peace lily (also known as Mauna Loa) is toxic to dogs. Eating the peace lily or calla lily can cause irritation of the tongue and lips, increased salivation, difficulty swallowing and vomiting.

Satin Pothos: (silk pothos) If eaten by a dog, the plant may cause irritation to the mouth, lips and tongue, while the dog may also experience increased salivation, vomiting and/or difficulty swallowing.

The plants noted above are only a few of the more common household plants, and every conscientious Shih Poo guardian will want to educate themselves before bringing plants into the home that could be toxic to their canine companions.

3) Poison Proof Your Home

You can learn about many potentially toxic and poisonous sources both inside and outside your home by visiting the ASPCA Animal Poison Control Center website.

Always keep your veterinarian's emergency number in a place where you can quickly access it, as well as the Emergency Poison Control telephone number in case you suspect that your dog may have been poisoned.

Knowing what to do if you suspect your dog may have been poisoned and being able to quickly contact the right people could save your Shih Poo's life.

If you keep toxic cleaning substances (including fertilizers and vehicle products) in your home or garage, always keep them behind closed doors. As well, keep any medications where your Shih Poo can never get to them, and seriously consider eliminating the use of any and all toxic products, for the health of both yourself and your best friend.

4) Garden Plants

Please note that there are also many outdoor plants that can be toxic or poisonous to your Shih Poo, therefore, always check what plants are growing in your garden and if any may be harmful, remove them or make certain that your Shih Poo puppy or adult dog cannot eat them.

Cornell University, Department of Animal Science lists many different categories of poisonous plants affecting dogs , including house plants, flower garden plants, vegetable garden plants, plants found in swamps or moist areas, plants found in fields, trees and shrubs, plants found in wooded areas, and ornamental plants.

5) Grass

Also, be aware that many puppies and adult dogs will eat grass, just because they are bored, or need a little fiber in their diet. Remember that canines are natural scavengers always on the lookout for something they can eat, and so long as the grass is healthy and has not been sprayed with toxic chemicals, this should not be a concern.

6) Antifreeze

Antifreeze is a substance that is found in many garages as it is intended to help you keep your car running smoothly. It is clearly labeled with warnings about its poisonous nature, but of course you cannot expect your Shih Poo to read!

The problem with antifreeze is that it is extremely sweet in flavor. This means that if a small amount of it is spilled, there is a better than average chance that your dog will make a beeline for it!

Make sure that your antifreeze is stored upright and with the cap screwed on tightly after every use. Ideally, you should keep your dog from ever accessing the area where the antifreeze is kept.

If left untreated, antifreeze poisoning is something that can prove fatal to a dog. This poisoning causes severe damage to the dog's liver, and if it is left unchecked for between 8 to 12 hours, there is a good chance that the dog will have to be put down.

If you suspect that your dog has ingested antifreeze, it is time to take an immediate visit to the veterinarian or to the emergency veterinarian. There are only a few specific things that can be done to treat this kind of poisoning and across the board, the sooner they are done, the better your dog's chances of survival are.

If there is the least chance that your dog has ingested this substance, it is better to jump the gun than to realize too late that your Shih Poo might have to be put down. As small as this dog is, even a very small amount of antifreeze can turn into a fatal issue.

7) Signs of Poisoning

When it comes to making sure that your Shih Poo stays safe, make sure that you are aware of the signs that it has been poisoned.

First, look for behavior changes that might indicate that a low level of poison has been ingested. Dogs that have ingested something toxic will often try to drink too much water at once, or they may be anorexic, avoiding food that they usually love.

The dog might also be staggering on its feet, or it might be uncoordinated. A dog that is otherwise sweet might snap without provocation, and a dog that is usually quite graceful might walk into the wall.

Some serious signs of poisoning include seizures where the dog shakes violently, losing control of their bowels or bladder, or a difficulty with breathing. If you check the dog's gums, it might look white or blue due to a lack of oxygen.

If you notice any of these signs in your dog, make sure that you take them to the veterinarian immediately, or that you call one of the emergency lines listed below.

8) Animal Poison Control Centre

The ASPCA Animal Poison Control Center is staffed 24 hours a day, 365 days a year and is a valuable resource for learning about what plants are toxic and possibly poisonous to your dog.

Poison Emergency USA

Call: 1 (888) 426-4435
When calling the Poison Emergency number, a $65 US (£39.42) consultation fee may be applied to your credit card.

Poison Emergency UK

- Call Pet Poison Helpline 800-213-6680 (payable service)

- Call RSPCA 0300 1234 999

www.aspca.org = ASPCA Poison Control. Animal Poison Control.

Chapter 17) Your Aging Shih Poo

Shih Poos have a long life compared to some breeds, but a Shih Poo is considered well into middle age by the time it is seven or eight. A dog that is older is one that requires more care and more attention, and if you catch some of the signs of aging early, you will find that you can keep your canine companion a lot more comfortable and safe.

As a result of advances in veterinarian care, improvements in diet and nutrition and general knowledge concerning proper care of our canine companions, our dogs are able to enjoy longer, healthier lives, and as such, when caring for them we need to be aware of behavioral and physical changes that will affect our dogs as they approach old age.

1) Physiological Changes

As our beloved canine companions become senior dogs, they will be suffering from very similar, physical aging problems that affect people, such as pain, stiffness and arthritis, diminished or complete loss of hearing and sight and inability to control their bowels and bladder. Any of these problems will reduce a dog's willingness to want to exercise.

2) Behavioral Changes

Further, a senior Shih Poo may experience behavioral changes resulting from loss of hearing and sight, such as disorientation, fear or startle reactions and overall grumpiness from any number of physical problems that could be causing them pain whenever they move.

Just as research and science has improved our human quality of life in our senior years, the same is becoming true for our canine counterparts who are able to benefit from dietary supplements and pharmaceutical products to help them be as comfortable as possible in their advancing years.

Although there will be some inconveniences associated with keeping a dog with advancing years around the home, your Shih Poo deserves no less than to spend their final days in your loving care after they have unconditionally given you their entire lives.

3) Geriatric Dogs

Being aware of the changes that are likely occurring in a senior dog will help you to better care for them during their geriatric years.

For instance, most dogs will experience hearing loss and visual impairment. If a dog's hearing is compromised, then using more hand signals will be helpful.

Deaf dogs will still be able to hear louder noises and feel vibrations, therefore hand clapping, using a loud clicker or stomping your foot on the floor may be a way to get their attention.

If a senior dog loses their eyesight, most dogs will still be able to easily navigate their familiar surroundings, and you will only need to be extra watchful on their behalf when taking them to unfamiliar territory. If they still have their hearing, you will be able to assist your dog with verbal cues and commands.

Dogs that have lost both their hearing and their sight will need to be close to you so that they can relax and not feel nervous, and so that you can communicate by touching parts of their body.

Generally speaking, even when a dog becomes blind and/or deaf, their powerful sense of smell is still functioning, which means that they will be able to tell where you are and navigate their environment by using their nose.

Bathroom breaks may need to become more frequent in older dogs that may lose their ability to hold it for longer periods of time, so be prepared to be more watchful and to offer them opportunities to go outside more frequently during the day.

You may also want to place a pee pad near the door, in case they just can't hold it long enough, or if you have not already taught them to bathroom on an indoor potty patch, or pee pad. Now may be the time for this alternative bathroom arrangement.

A dog who has been house trained for years will feel the shame and upset of not being able to hold it long enough to get to their regular bathroom location, so be kind and do whatever you need to do to help them not to have to feel bad about failing bowel or bladder control.

Our beloved canine companions may also begin to show signs of cognitive decline and changes in the way their brain functions, similar to what happens to humans suffering from Alzheimer's, where they start to wander about aimlessly, sometimes during the middle of the night. Make sure that if this is happening with your Shih Poo at nighttime, that they cannot accidentally harm themselves.

Being aware that an aging Shih Poo will be experiencing many symptoms that are similar to an aging human, will help you to understand how best to keep them safe and as comfortable as possible during this golden age in their lives.

4) Regular Checkups

During this time in your Shih Poo's life, when their immune systems become weakened and they may be experiencing pain, you will want to get into the habit of taking your senior Shih Poo for regular veterinarian checkups. Take them for a veterinarian checkup every six months so that early detection of any problems can quickly be attended to and solutions for helping to keep your aging Shih Poo comfortable can be provided.

5) No Rough Play

An older Shih Poo will not have the same energy or willingness to play that they did when they were younger, therefore, do not allow younger children to rough house with an older dog. Explain to them that the dog is getting older and that as a result they must learn to be gentle and to leave the dog alone when it may want to rest or sleep.

6) Mild Exercise

Dogs still love going for walks, even when they are getting older and slowing down. Although an older Shih Poo will generally have less energy, they still need to exercise and keep moving, and taking them out regularly for shorter walks will keep them healthier and happier long into old age.

7) Best Quality Food

Everyone has heard the saying, "you are what you eat" and for a senior dog, what they eat is even more important as their digestive system may no longer be functioning at peak performance. Therefore, feeding a high quality, protein-based food will be important for their continued health.

As well, if your older Shih Poo is overweight, you will want to help them shed excess pounds so that they will not be placing undue stress on their joints or heart, and the best way to do this is by feeding smaller quantities of a higher quality food.

Clean and Parasite Free

The last thing an aging Shih Poo should have to deal with is the misery of itching and scratching, so make sure that you continue to give them regular baths with the appropriate shampoos and conditioners to keep their coat and skin comfortable and free from parasites.

8) Plenty of Water

Proper hydration is essential for helping to keep an older Shih Poo comfortable. Water is life-giving for every creature, so make certain that your aging dog has easy access to plenty of clean, fresh water which will help to improve their energy and digestion and also prevent dehydration which can add to joint stiffness.

9) Keeping Warm

Just as older humans feel the cold more, so do older dogs. Keeping your senior Shih Poo warm will help to alleviate some of the pain of their joint stiffness or arthritis. Make sure their bed or kennel is not kept in a drafty location. You might consider a heated bed for them.

Be aware that your aging Shih Poo will be more sensitive to extremes in temperature, and it will be up to you to make sure that they are comfortable at all times, which means not too hot and not too cold.

10) Indoor Clothing

People tend to wear warmer clothing as we get older, simply because we have more difficulty maintaining a comfortable body temperature and the same will be true of our senior Shih Poo companions.

Therefore, while you most likely already have a selection of outdoor clothing appropriate to the climate in which you live, you may not have considered keeping your Shih Poo warm while inside the home. Now would be the time to consider doggy t-shirts or sweater clothing options to help keep your aging companion comfortably warm both inside and out.

11) Stairs and Ramps

If your Shih Poo is allowed to sleep on the couch or chair, but they are having difficulties getting up there as their joints are becoming stiff and painful, consider buying them a set of foam stairs so that they do not have to make the jump to their favorite sleeping place.

Some Shih Poos who were valiant jumpers in their youth will end up getting a lot more frustrated when they can no longer get up on the places that they were used to. Steps are one way to solve this issue, but another option for you to consider is the creation of a ramp.

Ramps should be pitched at a fairly low slope so that your Shih Poo can handle it without a problem. For example, many people who build their own ramps for their dogs end up using the standards set by the American with Disabilities Act. To be suitable for wheelchair use, a ramp must only have a rise of 1 inch per 1 foot, or 2.5 centimeters per 30 centimeters. A low slope makes it much easier for your Shih Poo to get where it is going.

To make sure that your Shih Poo does not slip on the ramp, considering making sure that it is wrapped with carpeting. Because some dogs with arthritis end up dragging the affected paw, the last thing that you want to worry about is your Shih Poo scraping its paw raw on the ramp you built!

12) Comfortable Bed

While most dogs seem to be happy with sleeping on the floor, providing them with a padded, soft bed will greatly help to relieve sore spots and joint pain in older dogs.

If there is a draft in the home, generally it will be at floor level, therefore a bed that is raised up off of the floor will be warmer for your senior Shih Poo who will be much more comfortable sleeping in a cozy dog bed.

One way to make sure that your Shih Poo's bed stays nice and warm is to consider wrapping a towel around a heating pad and setting it on low. This is best for Shih Poos that do not gnaw, and of course you should check it on a regular basis to make sure that it does not overheat.

Remember that when it comes to warmth, many dogs end up loving the chance to sleep or nap with you. For an older dog, spending some time in your day cuddling with it is a great way to make sure that it stays warm, healthy and happy.

13) More Love and Attention

Last, but not least, make sure that you give your senior Shih Poo lots of love and attention and never leave them alone for long periods of time.

When they are not feeling their best, they will want to be with you all that much more because you are their guardian whom they trust and love beyond life itself.

The more time you can spend with an aging dog, the happier it will be. You may not be able to play anymore, and you may find that your interactions are mostly limited to snuggling on the couch instead of playing fetch, but this is something that will both comfort your dog and allow you to adjust to your pet's new stage of life.

Remember that your Shih Poos life is short, comparatively, so celebrate all parts of it!

Chapter 18) Traveling With a Shih Poo

Thanks to the fact that your Shih Poo is quite a small dog, you will discover that for the most part, it can go nearly anywhere you can go. However, because of its small size, it needs to be kept safe!

As we have mentioned before, your Shih Poo is fragile, and the more time you spend ensuring that your dog is safe and comfortable, the happier it and you will be. When you are ready to take your Shih Poo traveling, make sure that you have the right tools handy!

1) Beware of Faulty Restraints

Many dog lovers may be laboring under the misconception that they are doing the right thing by buckling their canine companions into a safety harness because they are unaware that many of these dog harnesses that are supposed to keep furry passengers safe have a 100% failure rate.

Statistics collected by the Center for Pet Safety (CPS) have shown that every popular restraint tested with dog dummies, traveling at a sedate 30 mph (48.28 km/h), not only failed, but also indicated that serious injuries or deaths were highly likely.

Most restraints that were tested in the CPS study allowed dogs to easily become flying projectiles during vehicle accidents because the harnesses were simply not strong enough to keep them in their seats, and in many cases the restraints could actually choke the dog during a crash.

When the MGA Research Corporation carried out a pilot study for The Center for Pet Safety (CPS), in which they tested 12 major brands of pet harnesses, the results indicated a 100% failure rate.

According to the American Kennel Club, these safety harness tests were carried out using the average weights of the ten most popular breeds of dogs, including the Labrador Retriever, the German Shepherd, the Golden Retriever, the Beagle, the Bulldog, the Yorkshire Terrier, the Boxer, the Poodle, the Rottweiler and the Dachshund.

The founder and chairman of CPS, believes that, "Saying that these products prevent your pet from becoming a projectile in an accident is a potentially misleading statement."

Law enforcement agencies, safety advocates, insurance companies, and concerned dog owners need to keep pressing for the development of a standard for dog safety equipment, to insist that all such equipment pass a government regulated crash test before being sold as safe for travel.

The safest travel arrangement for any dog is to secure them inside a travel bag or kennel, followed by finding a safety restraint that is crash and strength tested and certified to be safe for your dog.

2) Kennels

If you opt to contain your best friend inside a kennel, crate or travel bag, you absolutely must make sure that the kennel or bag is very securely attached with the vehicle's seatbelt or even better, with special tie downs that are bolted to the floor of the vehicle.

A small dog kennel or crate will easily fit on the back seat of most vehicles and can be secured with the vehicle's restraint system. A Shih Poo riding inside a kennel, crate or travel bag inside your vehicle will have the best protection in the case of a rollover accident.

There is at least one manufacturer of a travel bag restraint system, called 'Sleepypod™', designed for pets up to 15 pounds (6.8 kg) that goes the extra mile for safety and actually puts its own products through the child safety seat test. All four models of the Sleepypod™ have passed the 30 mph (48.28 km/h) crash test.

3) Harness Restraints

The Kurgo Tru-Fit Smart harness has been crash and strength tested and with its steel nesting buckles has a tensile strength tested to withstand a force of 2250 pounds (1,581,906 ksm). The crash test videos of this product depict a 35 pound (15.9 kg) dummy dog traveling at 30 miles per hour (48.28 km/h), recorded at an accredited University test facility.

The Ruff Rider Roadie® harness successfully passed the preliminary test criteria for both dynamic and static load limits.

Ruff Rider's only product is the Roadie® travel restraint which was invented by dog owner, Carl Goldberg, after his pet was ejected through the front windshield in a minor collision.

The design of the Roadie® is so unique it was awarded three (3) patents. Over the past 20 years Roadie® has helped protect many dogs during vehicle accidents.

Sleepypod™ manufactures a safety harness called "Clickit Utility" that is the first dog safety harness to incorporate three-points of attachment to absorb force in a frontal collision by dissipating energy and keeping the dog in the car seat during an impact (patents pending). Clickit Utility can also be used in the cargo area and includes a d-ring on the back of the vest so it can be used as a walking harness.

Keep your Shih Poo safe when traveling in your vehicle. Do your research and either transport your dog inside a kennel, or find a safety harness that is strength tested and certified to be able to keep your Shih Poo safe in the event of an accident.

4) Sherpa for Small Dogs

The Sherpa is a name that refers to a soft-sided dog carrier with zippered pockets for carrying important papers, treats, baggies, etc. It has mesh sides for superior ventilation.

While there is an actual "Sherpa" brand name, this name has become synonymous with any type of soft sided carrier bag.

The bag has handles as well as a shoulder strap and some even have wheels, so your Shih Poo puppy or dog will be able to safely travel anywhere in style and comfort.

A Shih Poo puppy will remain small when fully grown; therefore they are the perfect candidate for learning to travel about inside a Sherpa or soft-sided travel bag, such as the Sleepypod™.

When they are young puppies, get them used to Sherpa travel by putting them inside their bag every time they need to go outside, and before you bring them back inside. When you do this, a Shih Poo puppy will very quickly learn to love scooting into their bag because they associate it with the fun activity of going outside with you.

Once your Shih Poo puppy becomes used to Sherpa travel, it will be very easy for them to travel with you wherever you go, including public transportation (buses), boats, planes and vehicles, and the best way to start them getting used to this idea is as soon as you bring your new puppy home.

"Sleepypod™" manufactures various styles of high end travel bags for small dogs, such as the Shih Poo, and puts their bags through rigorous crash testing to ensure they are totally safe.

Although these bags are considerably more costly than many other canine travel bags or Sherpas, you will have peace of mind knowing that your little Shih Poo will always be safe when riding inside one.

5) Air Travel

A small dog, like the Shih Poo, can be "carry-on baggage" if the carrier fits the airline regulations, which state that a pet carrier must be able to fit under the seat in front of you. Most soft carriers are airline approved and under seat dimensions are generally as follows:

Window Seat: 19" L x 14" W x 8.25" H

[48.26 cm L x 35.56 cm W x 20.955 cm H]

Middle Seat: 19" L x 19" W x 8.25" H

[48.26 cm L x 48.26 cm W x 20.955 cm H]

Aisle Seat: 19" L x 14" W x 8.25" H

[48.26 cm L x 35.56 cm W x 20.955 cm H]

For in-cabin travel by plane, your pet must be able to stand up and turn around comfortably in the bag. Airlines also require an absorbent liner in the bag, which could be a pee pad, an old towel, a favorite blanket, or a cozy, faux lambskin liner.

Many styles of canine carrier bags are officially approved for airline travel, and when you make your flight reservations, don't forget to reserve for your Shih Poo as well because there is generally a small charge for in-cabin travel.

Chapter 19) Euthanasia and the Death of a Pet

There comes a point in the lives of many dogs when their owners have to make a very difficult decision. Shih Poos may grow old and ill, or they may stumble into an accident that leaves them unable to continue.

The decision to euthanize your animal, or more euphemistically, to put it to sleep, is one that every dog owner dreads, but it is one that you must be willing to confront if you want to take care of Shih Poo.

Veterinarians will usually ask you to consider quality of life versus life-prolonging therapies, and they will always be willing to give you the facts. However, the decision will always be up to you, and even though this decision is hard, it is something that you need to understand.

1) The Process of Euthanizing

Every veterinarian will have received special training to help provide all incurably ill, injured or aged pets that have come to the end of their natural lives with a humane and gentle death, through a process called "euthanasia".

When the time comes, euthanasia, or putting a dog "to sleep", will usually be a two-step process.

First, the veterinarian will inject the dog with a sedative to make them sleepy, calm and comfortable.

Second, the veterinarian will inject a special drug that will peacefully stop their heart. These drugs work in such a way that the dog will not experience any awareness whatsoever that their life is ending. What they will experience is very much like what we experience when going under anesthesia during a surgical procedure.

Once the second-stage drug has been injected, the entire process takes about 10 to 20 seconds, at which time the veterinarian will then check to make certain that the dog's heart has stopped.

There is no suffering with this process, which is a very gentle and humane way to end a dog's suffering and allow them to peacefully pass on.

2) When to Help a Dog Transition

The impending loss of a beloved dog is one of the most painfully difficult and emotionally devastating coping experiences a canine guardian will ever have to face.

For the sake of our faithful companions, because we do not want to prolong their suffering, we will have to do our best to look at our dog's situation practically, rather than emotionally, so that we can make the best decision for them.

They may be suffering from extreme old age and the inability to even walk outside to relieve themselves, and thus suffering the indignity of regularly soiling their sleeping area, or they may have been diagnosed with an incurable illness that is causing them much pain, or they may have been seriously injured.

Whatever the reason for a canine companion's suffering, it will be up to their human guardian to calmly guide the end-of-life experience so that any further discomfort and distress can be minimized.

3) When There is Uncertainty

In circumstances where it is not entirely clear how much a dog is suffering, it will be helpful to pay close attention to your Shih Poo's behavior and keep a daily log or record so that you can know for certain how much of their day is difficult and painful for them, and how much is not.

When you keep a daily log, it will be easier to decide if the dog's quality of life has become so poor that it makes better sense to offer them the gift of peacefully going to sleep.

During this time of uncertainty, it will also be very important to discuss with a veterinarian what signs of suffering may be associated with the dog's particular disease or condition, so that you know what to look for.

Often a dog may still continue to eat or drink despite being distraught, having difficulty breathing, excessively panting, being disoriented or in much pain, and as their caring guardians, we will have to weigh their love of eating against how much they are really suffering in all other aspects of their life.

Obviously, if a canine guardian can clearly see that their beloved companion is suffering throughout their days and nights, it will make sense to help humanely end their suffering by planning a euthanasia procedure.

We humans are often tempted to delay the inevitable moment of euthanasia, because we love our dogs so much and cannot bear the anticipation of the intense grief we know will overwhelm us when we must say our final goodbyes to our beloved fur friend.

Unfortunately, we may regret that we allowed our dog to suffer too long, and find ourselves wishing that if only we had the same option, to peacefully let go, when we reach such a stage in our own lives.

4) Grieving a Lost Pet

Often we do not fully recognize the terrible grief involved in losing a beloved canine friend. There will be many who do not understand the close bond we can have with our dogs, which is often unlike any we have with our human counterparts.

Your friends may give you pitying looks and try to cheer you up, but if they have never experienced such a loss themselves, they may also secretly think you are making too much fuss over "just a dog".

For some of us, the loss of a beloved dog is so painful that we decide never to share their lives with another, because we cannot bear the thought of going through the pain of loss again.

Expect to feel terribly sad, tearful and yes, depressed because those who are close to their canine companions will feel their loss no less acutely than the loss of a human friend or life partner. The grieving process can take some time to recover from, and some of us never totally recover.

After the loss of a family dog, first you need to take care of yourself by making certain that you keep eating and getting regular sleep, even though you will feel an almost eerie sense of loneliness.

Losing a beloved dog is a shock to the system which can also affect your concentration and your ability to find joy or want to participate in other activities that may be part of the rest of your life.

During this early grieving time you will need to take extra care while driving or performing tasks that require your concentration as you may find yourself distracted.

If there are other dogs or pets in the home, they will also be grieving the loss of a companion, and may display this by acting depressed, being off their food or showing little interest in play or games. Therefore, you need to help guide your other pets through this grieving process by keeping them busy and interested, taking them for extra walks and spending more time with them.

Many people do not wait long enough before attempting to replace a lost pet and will immediately go to the local shelter and rescue a deserving dog. While this may help to distract you from your grieving process, this is not really fair to the new fur member of your family.

Bringing a new pet into a home that is depressed and grieving the loss of a long time canine member may create behavioral problems for the new dog that will be faced with learning all about their new home while also dealing with the unstable energy of the grieving family.

A better scenario would be to allow yourself the time to properly grieve by waiting a minimum of one month to allow yourself and your family time to feel happier and more stable before deciding upon sharing your home with another dog.

The grieving process will be different for everyone and you will know when the time is right to consider sharing your home with another canine companion.

5) The Rainbow Bridge Poem

"Just this side of heaven

is a place called Rainbow Bridge.

When an animal dies that has been

especially close to someone here,

that pet goes to Rainbow Bridge.

There are meadows and hills for all of our special friends

so they can run and play together.

There is plenty of food, water and sunshine,

and our friends are warm and comfortable.

All the animals that had been ill and old

are restored to health and vigor;

those who were hurt or maimed

are made whole and strong again,

just as we remember them in our dreams

of days and times gone by.

The animals are happy and content,

except for one small thing;

they each miss someone very special to them,

who had to be left behind.

They all run and play together,

but the day comes when one suddenly stops

and looks into the distance.

His bright eyes are intent; His eager body quivers. Suddenly he

begins to run from the group,

flying over the green grass,

his legs carrying him faster and faster.

You have been spotted,

and when you and your special friend finally meet,

you cling together in joyous reunion,

never to be parted again.

The happy kisses rain upon your face;

your hands again caress the beloved head,

and you look once more into the trusting eyes

of your pet, so long gone from your life

but never absent from your heart.

Then you cross Rainbow Bridge together...."

-Author Unknown

6) Memorials

There are as many unique ways to honor the passing of a beloved
pet as each of our fur friends is unique and special to us.

For instance, you may wish to have your fur friend cremated and preserve their ashes in a special urn or sprinkle their ashes along their favorite walk.

Perhaps you will want to have a special marker, photo bereavement, photo engraved Rainbow Bridge Poem, or wooden plaque created in honor of your lost friend.

You may wish to keep their memory close to you at all times by having a DNA remembrance pendant or bracelet designed.

As well, there are support groups, such as Rainbow Bridge, which is a grief support community, to help you and your family through this painful period of loss and grief.

Chapter 20) Rescue Organizations

When you are considering rescuing a specific breed or cross breed of dog or puppy, the first place to start your search will be with your local shelter and rescue groups.

1) Shelters

Here you can expect to pay an adoption fee to cover the cost of spaying or neutering, but this will be only a small percentage of what you would pay a breeder, and you will be saving a life at the same time, without supporting puppy mills.

2) Online Resources

Sites such as Petango, Adopt A Pet and Pet Finder can be good places to begin your search.

Each of these online resources is a central gathering site for hundreds and hundreds of local shelters, humane societies and rescue groups.

3) Canine Clubs

Another place to search will be Poodle and Shih Tzu Clubs in your local area. These groups may often have rescue dogs available, including a Shih Poo crossbreed.

Chapter 21) Resources & References

The following resources and references are listed alphabetically within their specific category

1) Poison Control

ASPCA Poison Control

www.aspca.org

2) Breeders, Registries & Rescues

Adopt A Pet

www.adoptapet.com

American Canine Hybrid Club

www.achclub.com

Canine Registry

www.designercanineregistry.com

Designer Dogs - The Kennel Club

www.thekennelclub.org.uk

International Designer Canine Registry®

www.designercanineregistry.com

Little Rascals

www.littlerascaluk.com

Mini Pups Breeder

www.minipups.ca

National Hybrid Registry

www.nationalhybridregistry.com

Petango

www.petango.com

Poodle Club of America

http://www.poodleclubofamerica.org/

American Shih Tzu Club

http://www.americanshihtzuclub.org/

Miniature Poodle Club

http://miniaturepoodleclub.weebly.com/

Shih Tzu Club

http://www.theshihtzuclub.co.uk/

Pet Finder

www.petfinder.com

Poisonous Plants Affecting Dogs - Cornell University, Department of Animal Science

www.ansci.cornell.edu/plants/dogs

3) Equipment and Supplies

Andis Dog Clippers

www.andis.com

Dog Bowl for Your Dog

www.dogbowlforyourdog.com

Modern Puppies

www.modernpuppies.com

Oster Dog Clippers

www.osterpro.com

Remove Urine Odors

www.removeurineodors.com

Sleepy Pod

www.sleepypod.com

Wahl Dog Clippers

www.wahl.com

4) Memorials

Rainbow Bridge

www.rainbowbridge.com

Index

Published by IMB Publishing 2014

CPSIA information can be obtained
at www.ICGtesting.com
Printed in the USA
BVHW042049100222
628633BV00008B/833

A BASIS FOR SENSORIMOTOR DEVELOPMENT— NORMAL AND ABNORMAL

The Influence of Primitive, Postural Reflexes on the Development and Distribution of Tone

By

MARY R. FIORENTINO, Mus.B., O.T.R., F.A.O.T.A.

Consultant and Lecturer
Wethersfield, Connecticut

With a Foreword by

Josephine C. Moore, Ph.D., O.T.R.

Professor
University of South Dakota
School of Medicine
Department of Anatomy
Vermillion, South Dakota

CHARLES C THOMAS • PUBLISHER
Springfield • Illinois • U.S.A.

Published and Distributed Throughout the World by
CHARLES C THOMAS • PUBLISHER
Bannerstone House
301-327 East Lawrence Avenue, Springfield, Illinois, U.S.A.

© *1981, by* **CHARLES C THOMAS • PUBLISHER**
ISBN 0-398-04179-2
Library of Congress Catalog Card Number: 80-24600

*With THOMAS BOOKS careful attention is given to all details of
manufacturing and design. It is the Publisher's desire to present books that are
satisfactory as to their physical qualities and artistic possibilities and appropriate for their particular use. THOMAS BOOKS will be true to those laws of
quality that assure a good name and good will.*

Library of Congress Cataloging in Publication Data

Fiorentino, Mary R
    A basis for sensorimotor development-normal and abnormal.

    Bibliography: p.
    Includes index.
    1. Motor ability in children. 2. Child development. 3. Reflexes. 4. Movement
disorders in children. I. Title. [DNLM: 1. Central nervous system diseases—Diagnosis. 2. Motor skills. 3. Reflex. 4. Reflex, Abnormal. WL 141 F518b]
RJ133.F54   618.92'7   80-24600
ISBN 0-398-04179-2

Printed in the United States of America
PS-OK-1

To "Jo"
With Deep Appreciation
For Her Many Years
Of Friendship
And For Her
Professional Support

FOREWORD

Retirement is a gift of time that may be spent in the pursuit of leisure, long neglected hobbies, or perhaps in travel. For some it may constitute a new era when one is free from the demands of work, research, and publications. Not so for Mary. Once again Mary has used her precious time and talents for writing and sharing her depth and breadth of knowledge with her professional colleagues.

Mary's gift to all of us has been her ability to analyze the various stages of normal and abnormal development in relation to reflex/responses and movement and to put this complex subject into an integrated and meaningful sequence of events. Each and every critical stage of sensorimotor development, behavioral pattern, and/or changes in posture and muscle tone resulting from underlying reflex/responses is well documented with photographs. Explanations accompanying each photograph are succinct. Important points, critical for understanding each overlapping yet fundamental stage of development, are clearly presented.

Mary's writing technique utilizes two vital and conjugate avenues for learning: pictorial analysis accompanied by precise explanatory sentences. This enables the beginner, as well as the experienced clinician, to use this text as an invaluable teacher, especially while observing infants and children in a home environment or in a clinical setting.

This book also teaches one how to observe, what to observe, and to understand that which is being observed. By the time the last chapter is read, the necessity of memorizing this volume of material is negated. Instead, one realizes that through the active process of personally synthesizing this information, i.e. comparing this richly endowed text with actual behavioral patterns of normal and neurologically involved infants and children, one has gained an in-depth understanding of this important subject. Learning, per se, has become a *fait accompli*.

Josephine C. Moore, Ph.D., O.T.R.

PREFACE

Our total postural behavior is the result of the interaction of reflexes and the relative strength of each one of them. Postural reflexes involve changes in tone and distribution which primarily affects posture and movement.

Early reflexes and postures are basic developmental patterns that are processed within the CNS. They are integrated, modified, and incorporated into more complex patterns in order to form the background for normal, voluntary movement and skills.

ACKNOWLEDGMENTS

Grateful appreciation is extended to the children and parents who allowed their pictures to be used in this book; to Josephine Moore and Margot van Homm for their review of the text; to Donald Gale and Raymond Martin of the photography department; to Jean Long, medical librarian, all of the Newington Children's Hospital; to Kathleen Bagioni for preparation of the index; and to Dorothe Gustafson, former secretary, and friend, for all of their assistance.

M.R.F.

CONTENTS

A BASIS FOR SENSORIMOTOR
DEVELOPMENT—
NORMAL AND ABNORMAL

INTRODUCTION

Movement is an essential characteristic of living organisms. The simplest, like the fish, make spontaneous and rhythmical movements. Man, with his complex movements, shows more complicated patterns of motor activities. The basic elements of these activities include tone, control, and strength. These underlie specific functions such as movement, postural stability, balance, and coordination, and the integration of these functions leads to the development of skill.

This monograph is not intended to be a highly theoretical, neurophysiological treatise on the components underlying CNS function and influences. It is an attempt to place the reflexes in their proper perspective to tone and its distribution, and how they relate to the development of movement.

To understand and interpret the normal processes of sensorimotor development as this relates to the development of normal postural behavior and total patterns of motor coordination, it will be necessary to:

1. Identify and sequence normal, developmental, postural reflexes.
2. Relate postural reflex sequences to sensorimotor development.
3. Place postural reflexes in their proper perspective to movement, tone, and intervention.

PURPOSE

The purpose of this book is to orient occupational, physical, and speech students and therapists, physical educators, movement therapists, physicians, and any other professional involved with sensorimotor development as to the importance of knowing the processes involved in creating change, and consequently development, in the motor system. An explanation of the influence of reflexes on tone and movement and the relative control or dominance each one has that is basic to sensorimotor development, normal and abnormal, will be given.

5

PROCEDURE

The following pages will present certain basic neonatal and postural reflexes that contribute to the enhancement of tone to develop the balance between flexor and extensor muscles. In this way, the basis for movement at higher levels is provided and coordinated skills will result.

Photographs, with accompanying interpretations, will illustrate this development, modification, and integration in normal and abnormal sensorimotor development.

DEFINITIONS

arm: upper arm from shoulder to elbow

ASTN: asymmetrical tonic neck reflex

asymmetry of movement: dissociation of movement from one part or side to the other part or side

body: total anatomical structure including head, neck, trunk, and extremities

CNS: central nervous system

crawling: moving along the floor on the abdomen (marine crawl)

creeping: mobility in the 4-foot quadruped position, on hands and knees

digits: total hand, four fingers and thumb

dissociation: movement of one part(s) separate from another part(s), as limb movements separate from the trunk

forearm: lower part of the limb, from elbow to wrist

leg: foreleg of the lower limb from knee to ankle

long sit: sitting position with hips flexed and knees extended

lower limb: includes thigh, leg, and foot

quadruped: 4-foot position, on hands and knees

raking movement: an early developmental stage in which the baby uses a swiping movement of the hand on attempting to pick up an object

scratching movements: palmomandibular reflex; flexion-extension movements of the fingers as the baby is feeding at the breast or the bottle, or on clothing

STN: symmetrical tonic neck reflex

symmetry of movement: the infant moves the extremities, two lower limbs and/or two upper limbs, in the same direction at the same time, such as both in flexion or both in extension

thigh: upper part of the limb from the hip to the knee

upper limb: includes arm, forearm, and hand

windswept position: both lower extremities turned in the same direction, resulting in one limb in external rotation and the other limb in internal rotation

Chapter I

BASIC CONCEPTS IN THE MATURATION OF NORMAL SENSORIMOTOR DEVELOPMENT

POSTURAL BEHAVIOR

Figure 1

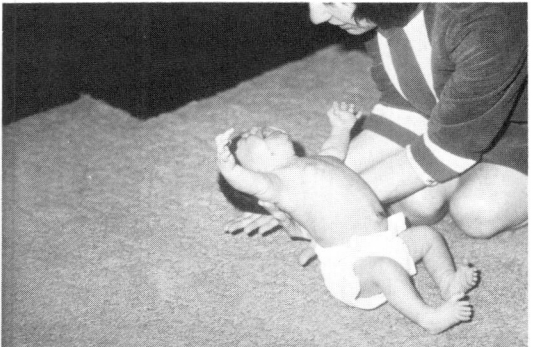

Figure 2

The total postural behavior of an individual (Fig. 1) is the result of the interaction of all reflexes and the relative strength of each one of them. Postural reflexes and their interaction and integration form the background of normal, voluntary movement and skills. Man with an intact CNS can, and does, perform in a coordinated, smooth, highly complex manner. The continuing upward spiral moves in an integrated manner (Fig. 2) from mass excitation to controlled (Fig. 3), voluntary, cortical movements in a cephalo-caudal, proximal-distal, and gross-fine sequence. With maturation and integration of the lower centers contributing to the development of higher centers, with more inhibitory control from the higher centers, the mass movements are integrated and goal-directed movements, which depend on the higher control within the CNS, are developed.

Figure 3

At birth, the body is under the un-opposed control of the lower centers of the CNS (Fig. 4), which basically generate involuntary reflex movements and postures. The baby is influenced by neonatal reflexes, which are stereotyped and are predictable responses. The body responds mechanically and automatically to a number of influences, such as head or body position. This affects changes in muscle tone, which then affects posture and/or movement in a number of consistent patterns termed "primitive reflexes." The term "reflex" is used to designate a specific, automatic, patterned response that is elicited by a particular stimulus and does not involve any conscious control.

During the first year there is a great deal of maturation that takes place in the CNS. As stated previously, the baby at birth is motorically at a primitive, crude level, a reflex level (Fig. 5). His movements are automatic with no component of voluntary control or meaningful direction.

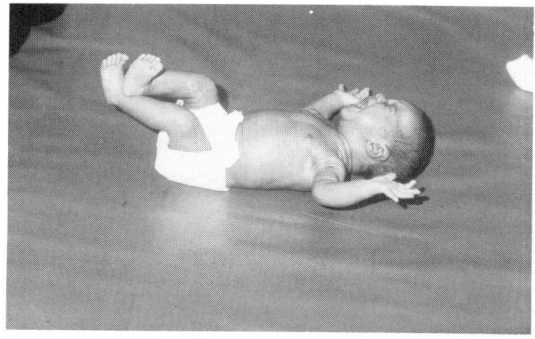

Figure 4

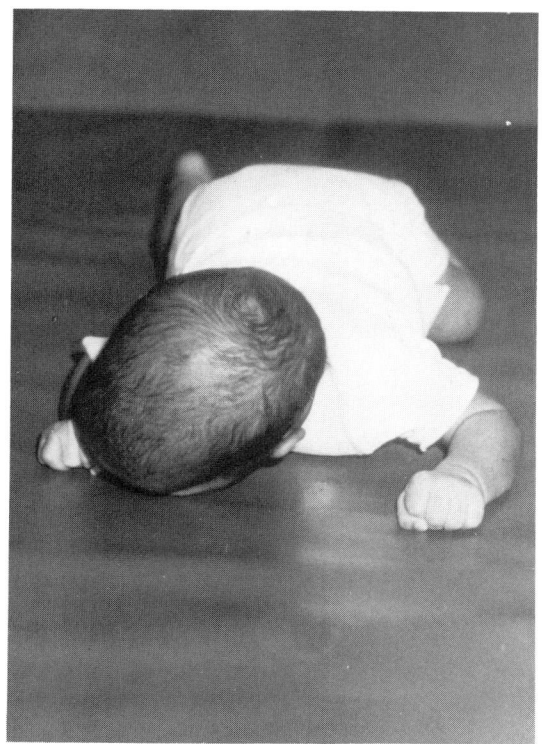

Figure 5

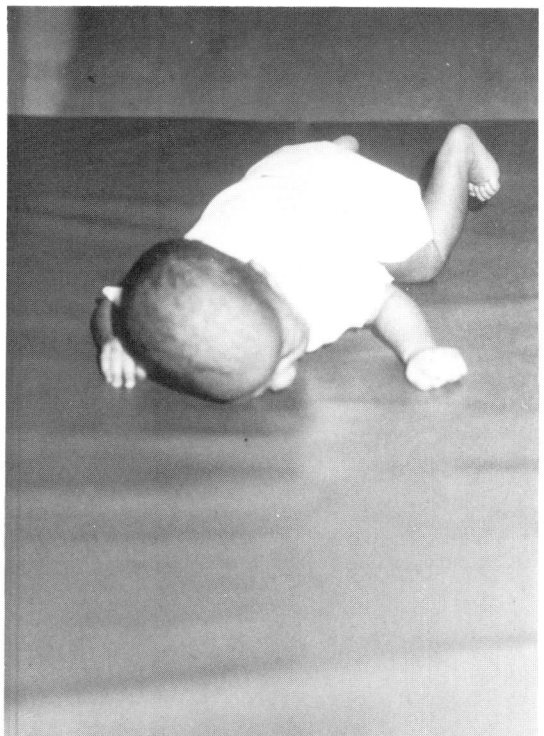

Figure 6

The primitive, postural reflexes primarily involve changes in tone and distribution, which affects posture and movement (Fig. 6). These the body responds to automatically and mechanically. As the higher CNS centers mature, they gradually suppress the influences of the primitive reflexes, which then integrates the involuntary reflex patterns in order to develop a wider range of voluntary movements (Fig. 7). The more primitive motor patterns are modified. Subsequent patterns develop sequentially, building from one pattern to the next in a gross to fine sequence.

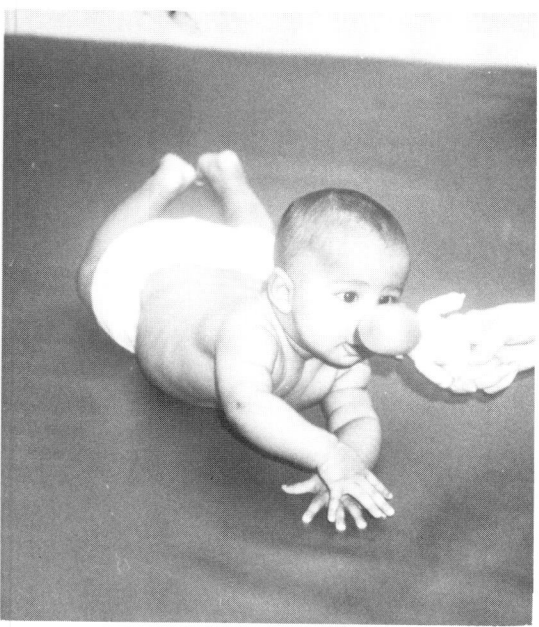

Figure 7

Therefore, at about fifteen months of age the motor system matures and progresses to a level of proficiency in the basic motor functions (Fig. 8) so that the child is able to accomplish a number of motor skills. The development of these early functions and skills is the foundation and basis for all future sensorimotor development.

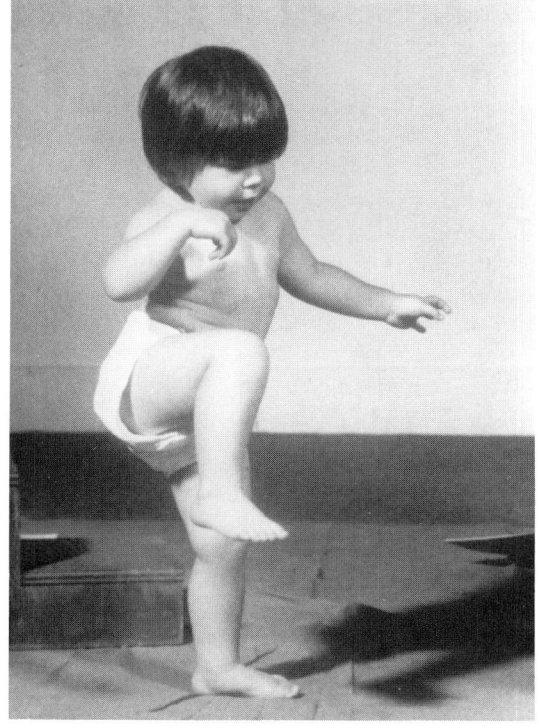

Figure 8

There are four basic components in these patterns of movement that are necessary for the acquisition of motor skills. It is necessary to have gross developmental patterns of movement directed toward the stabile position, especially against gravity.
1. The first major component is head control, which is influential in the development of tonal distribution and much of motor movement.
2. It is necessary to have increased extensor tone (the baby is born with a reflexive flexor tone predominating) in order to establish the maintenance of positions against gravity.
3. The third component, and one of major consequence, is the ability to rotate within the body axis, thus developing the rotary components for the development of righting reactions and higher levels of sensorimotor development.
4. Finally, equilibrium reactions develop, making possible the maintenance of balance in sitting, standing, and walking. As a result, the upper limbs are released from their early function of support so that they may become the tools for skilled, manipulative activities. The development of these functions is the foundation and basis for all future sensorimotor development.

HIGHER LEVEL MOVEMENTS

In the developmental continuum the postural reflexes supply the basic balance of tone. They develop the component parts to form the balance for coordinated movement. For the first five-to-six months, movements are in patterns of total flexion and extension against gravity, e.g. flexor and extensor musculature must develop until tone is balanced. (Other muscle groups will develop sequentially. During this initial phase of development these groups are not as functional as the flexor and extensor groups. As rotation is developing, complete balance of all muscles will be acquired.) Righting reactions also influence sensorimotor development. When these elements all blend and interact, they create smooth, coordinated patterns of movement that are efficiently executed to perform highly skilled activities.

Righting reactions are a chain of actions that sequentially interact with each other to create a smooth transition from one developmental stage to the next and to maintain a proper relationship to the environment of nose vertical and eyes and mouth horizontal. The attainment and maintenance of upright postures against gravity are essential requirements for the successful sensorimotor development of the infant. The labyrinths are the most important organs at this stage of life that are concerned with the development of antigravity postures and balance. Movement of the head in any dimension stimulates some part of the labyrinths and, after the early weeks postnatally, produces appropriate responses.

For example, labyrinthine head righting along with optical righting is not present at birth (Fig. 9) but develops in the early months. When this is developed (Fig. 10), the head will always attempt to right itself to nose vertical and eyes and mouth horizontal no matter in what position the child's body is placed. As this response is gained, a series of chain reactions come about as various reflexes interact and influence the body position and attitudes and movements of the limbs. For example, in the prone position (Fig. 11), the labyrinthine and optical righting of the head interact with the symmetrical tonic neck reflex to develop the tone for acquiring the quadruped position.

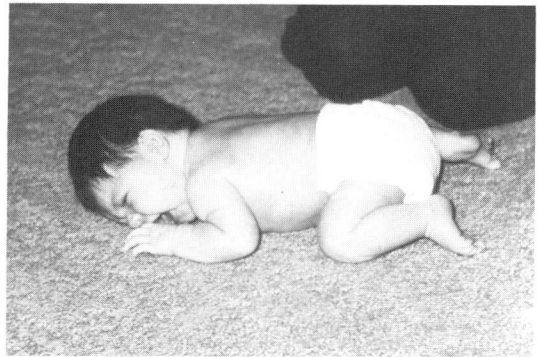

Figure 9

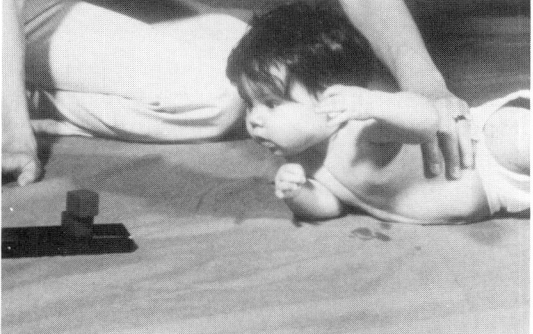

Figure 10

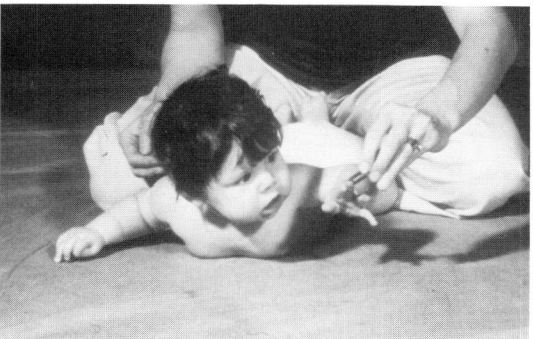

Figure 11

Figure 12

As the head rights, extensor tone develops in the upper limbs so that the child sequentially assumes the prone-on-elbows (Fig. 12), to extended elbows (Fig. 13), to quadruped position (Fig. 14) and, finally, reciprocal creeping (Fig. 15). Flexor tone is reinforced in the hips. Both extensor and flexor tone are developed to create the balance between progravity and antigravity positioning and movement.

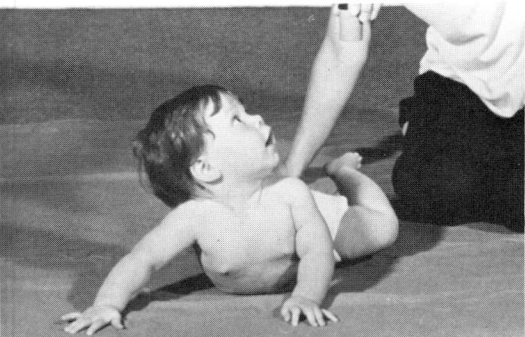

Figure 13

Figure 14

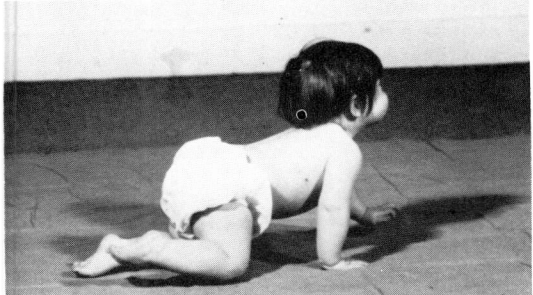

Figure 15

Correlating with this development of tone, as the head rights into extension, extensor tone starts to develop down the neck and trunk (Fig. 16), influencing the initiation of the Landau reaction. Figures 15 and 16 demonstrate how tone is developed and distributed by a given stimulus to develop higher sensorimotor movements and development.

The baby is born with a minimal neck righting reflex (Fig. 17), which acts as a protective reaction to prevent suffocation when placed in the prone position. Once the head has been turned in response to the labyrinths and body-on-head righting reflexes (Fig. 18), the neck muscle proprioceptors become stimulated and the body follows as a unit in the direction of the head rotation.

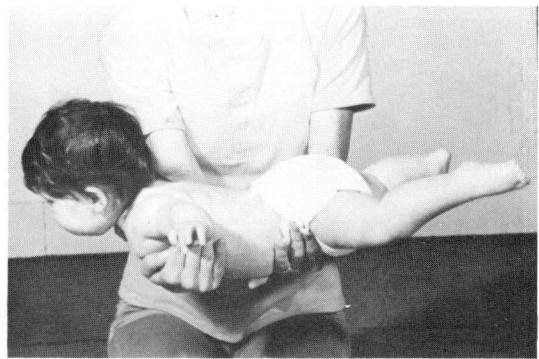

Figure 16

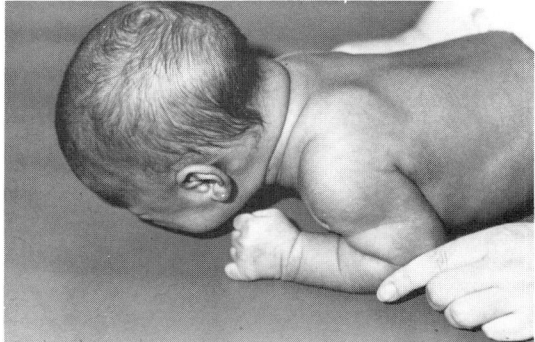

Figure 17

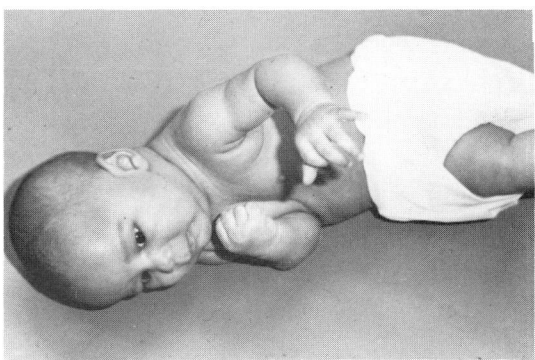

Figure 18

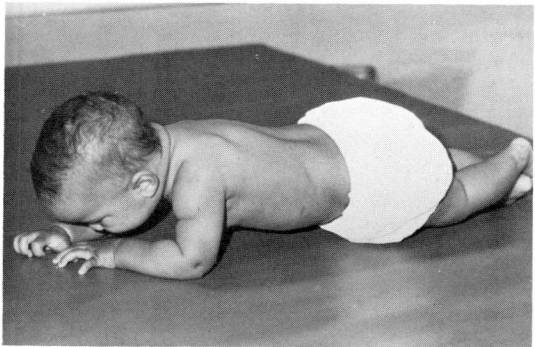

Figure 19

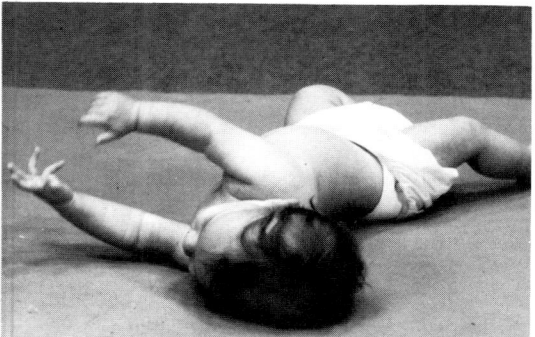

Figure 20

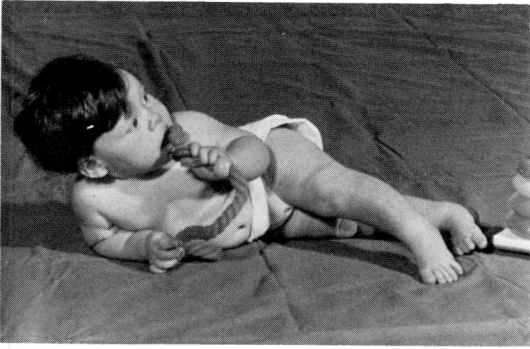

Figure 21

As the asymmetrical tonic neck reflex integrates (Fig. 19), neck righting becomes more mobile so that by four to five months of age the baby is turning from sidelying to prone.

The next higher level of turning is body-righting-on-the-body (Fig. 20). This is necessary for the development of the rotatory components of movement and for developing higher skills for assuming the sitting and quadruped positions.

Body righting acting on the head is stimulated by the contact of the body surface with a hard surface (Fig. 21) as a result of the asymmetrical stimulation of the exteroceptive sense organs of the body surface. When the body is in the lateral position, the head will right itself to nose vertical and eyes and mouth horizontal.

Integrating with the development of the righting reactions is the method used by the baby to get to higher levels of sensorimotor development from prone to standing. When using neck righting and body righting (Fig. 22), complete rotation of the body is used to turn to prone or supine. By eighteen to twenty-four months of age (approximate), the righting reactions and postural reflexes are well integrated and the child uses a partial rotation (Fig. 23) to get to sitting, then turns to the quadruped position and up to standing.

By four and a half to five years of age, (approximate), the adult method of symmetrical sitting is used to assume the sitting and standing positions (Fig. 24).

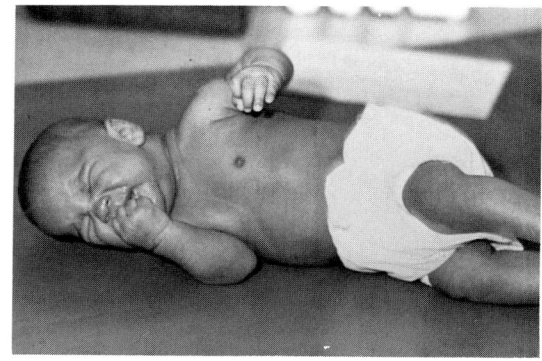

Figure 22

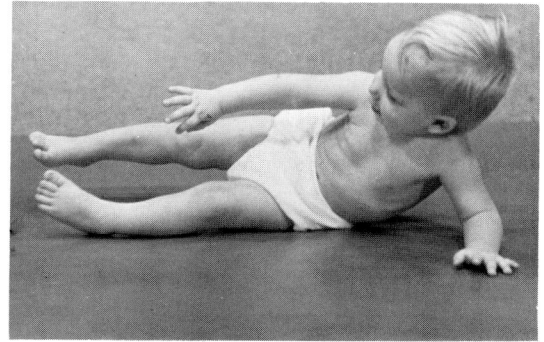

Figure 23

Figure 24

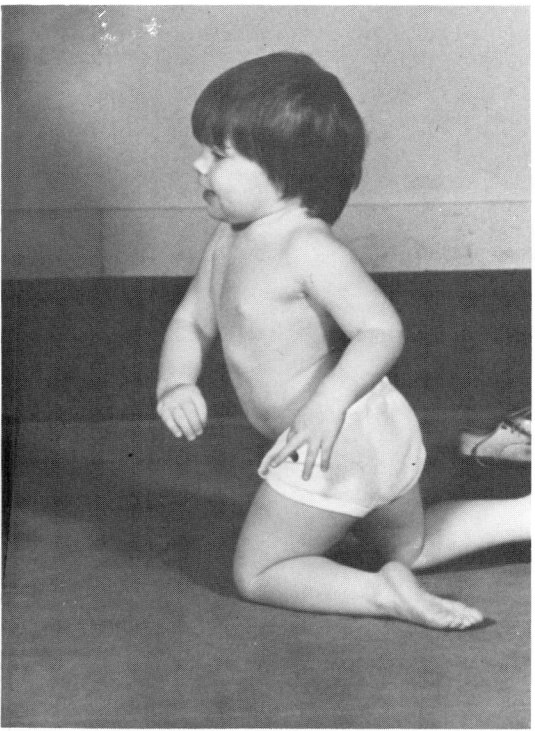

Figure 25

Weiscz has stated that "the development of the equilibrium reactions overlaps with that of the righting reactions and are responsible for the modification and transformation of the righting reactions."

Equilibrium reactions develop (Fig. 25) as the child progresses developmentally to create the stability in balance needed for independent function no matter what position the body is in. If postural reflexes and tone are dominant (Fig. 26), righting and equilibrium reactions cannot be elicited or may be compromised. This further delays and/or prevents normal sensorimotor development.

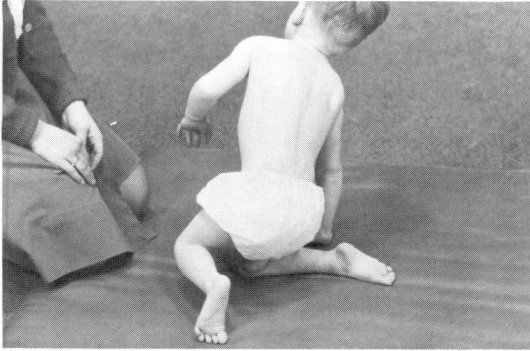

Figure 26

Maintenance of equilibrium is much more complicated than previously considered. Briefly and cursorily, the vestibular apparatus, the maculae of the utricle and saccule, the ampullae of the semicircular canals and ducts and their respective receptive organs, the vestibular nerve and nucleus, and the cerebellum are all involved in the maintenance of equilibrium.

The semicircular canals/ducts detect the rate of change or rotation of the head in any plane. This is called angular acceleration and deceleration. They predict that the person is turning and will fall off balance unless a correction is made. The utricles are also important for maintaining equilibrium. The maculae of the utricle and saccule with their varying orientation and also that of their hair cells detect the position of the head in space. The cerebellum integrates information received from the vestibular system and all other systems of the body and responds with an appropriate discharge of signals that will set up appropriate responses concerned with muscle tone, coordination, and synergy of movement patterns. The vestibular apparatus is the sensory organ primarily used by the infant for detecting sensations concerned with equilibrium.

At a later time, the CNS relies more upon a multitude of exteroceptive and proprioceptive signals of the entire body, plus visual input and integrative cerebellar functions for orientation in space. Therefore, appropriate information must be detected by the nervous system for orientation of the head with respect to the body as well as the orientation of the different parts of the body with respect to each other. Exteroceptive sensations are also important in the maintenance of equilibrium. If there is malfunctioning of the vestibular apparatus and some of the proprioceptive information from the body, visual feedback is of major importance in the maintenance of equilibrium. Equilibrium reactions are not present at birth. However, they develop progressively as the need arises to maintain balance for independent function, especially in standing and walking.

Chapter II
THE DEVELOPMENT AND DISTRIBUTION
OF BASIC TONE

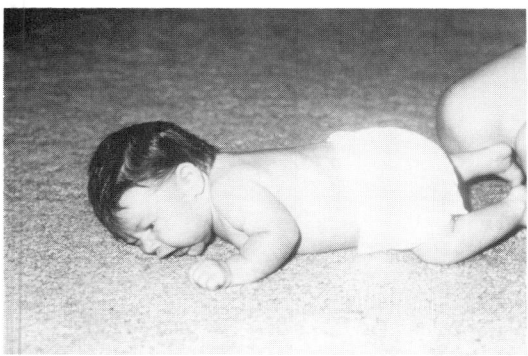

Figure 27

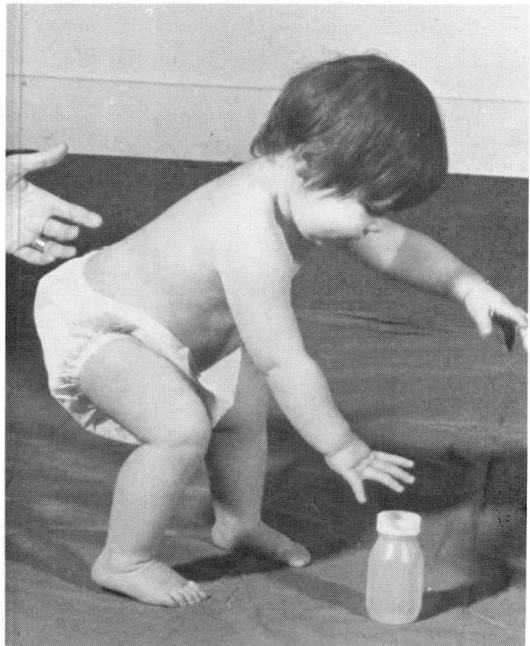

Figure 28

Figure 29

At birth a normal full-term baby is dominated by flexor tone (Fig. 27). Over a period of ten to twelve months, extensor tone has developed (Fig. 28), flexor tone has strengthened, and a balance has been created to allow for coordinated patterns of movement from gross to skill. Also, as this balance occurs, rotation within the body axis is initiated and once this develops, the rotatory components of movement for higher development occur. With the combined maturity, all necessary movements are possible and are available to protect, balance, and support the child for mobility and skill.

What mechanisms are involved in the development of muscle tone, in the distribution of this muscle tone for balanced, coordinated movement? Primitive and postural reflexes (Fig. 29) are basic developmental patterns that must be processed through the CNS to contribute to the stability and mobility required for the ultimate development of skill. Reflexes play a dominant role in the regulation of the degree, strength, balance, and distribution of muscle tone. They regulate muscle tone for the maintenance of posture and for the performance of movements. The state of muscle tone and the coordination of posture and movement are closely related, and postural reflexes determine the strength and distribution of muscle tone and regulate it during movement.

Automatic and voluntary movements are difficult if tonic reflex activity is in a state of exaggerated, static (Fig. 30), postural activity, i.e. hypertonus. This, of course, depends upon the degree and type of hypertonus, whether it is etiological and/or reinforced by the reflexes. Each reflex produces specific postural patterns. However, the total postural behavior of a child is the result of the interaction of all the reflexes and the relative control or dominance each one has. Normal muscle tone (Fig. 31) is the result of the total integration of postural reflex activity at all levels in the CNS.

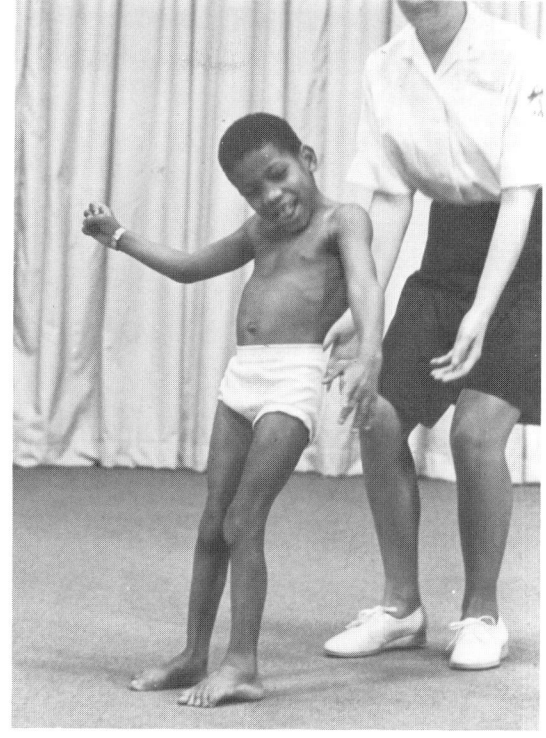

Figure 30

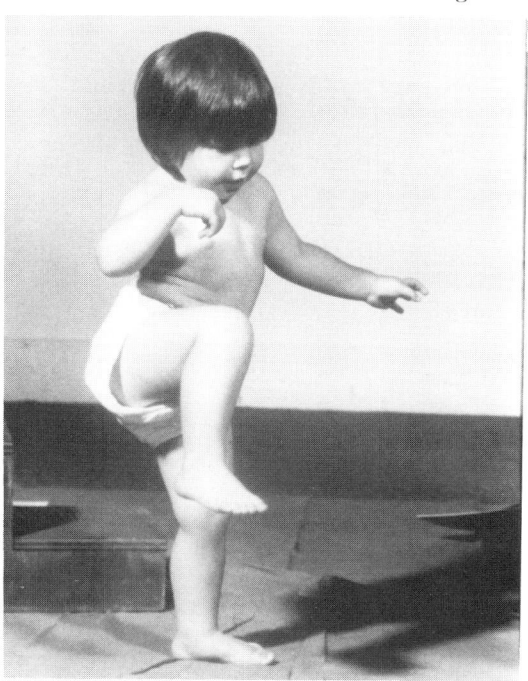

Figure 31

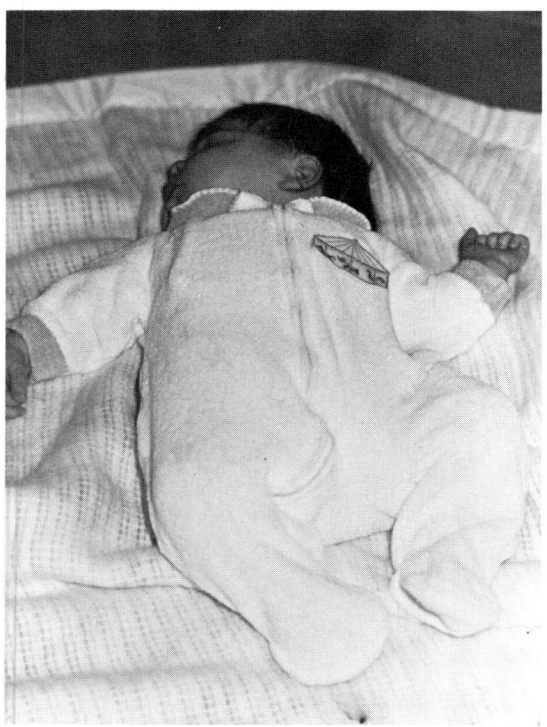

A reflex action consists of a prompt, stereotyped response to a specific stimulus. The neonatal, primitive, and postural reflexes (Fig. 32) interact and integrate to form the background of normal, voluntary movements and skills (Fig. 33), supplemented by the blending of righting and equilibrium reactions for higher skills. Each reflex produces specific postural patterns. Without their full development and integration, normal tone, distribution, and normal activities might not be realized or might be delayed or compromised.

Figure 32

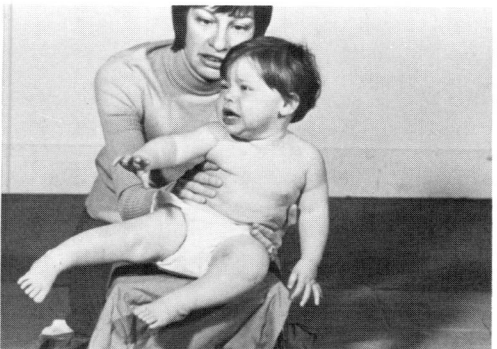

Figure 33

As the nervous system develops, many of the early reflexes are inhibited and others are modified and incorporated into more complex actions. (These reflexes remain subliminal unless the individual is under stress or there has been trauma to the CNS.) Developmental changes are necessary because the continued activity of the early reflexes interferes with the development of other actions. When reflex tone interferes to any extent with the normal asynchronous discharge of agonist and antagonist during a movement or postural pattern, it would be considered abnormal, as seen in the cerebral palsied child (Fig. 34).

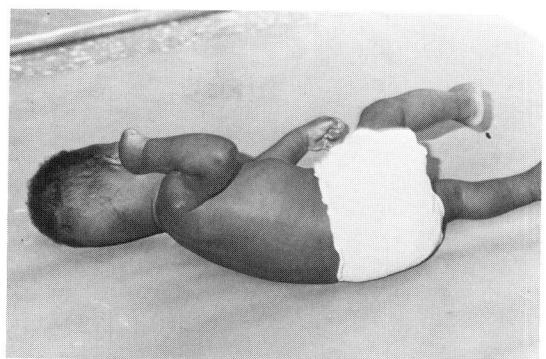

Figure 34

Cerebral palsy is a nonprogressive, static neurological disability resulting from a brain lesion that occurs prenatally, natally, or postnatally. Damage to the CNS causes a release of postural reflexes, abnormal tone, and movement. These children are dominated, to one degree or another, by reflexive, postural behaviors, combined with abnormal tone. These abnormalities prevent the child from exhibiting all the potential that he may possess relative to higher kinds of sensorimotor activity. Other neurological disabilities, such as the patient with a CVA or head trauma, will demonstrate similar abnormal influences and should be considered from this point of view.

Chapter III
CONTRIBUTION OF REFLEXES

This chapter will present the influence of these early reflexes in their contribution to the development of tone and its distribution, which forms the background of normal, voluntary movements leading to sensorimotor development. Photographs will demonstrate this with normal children. Parallel photographs of cerebral palsied children will demonstrate the abnormal distribution of tone, resulting in the deviation from normal movement, leading to delays in sensorimotor development.

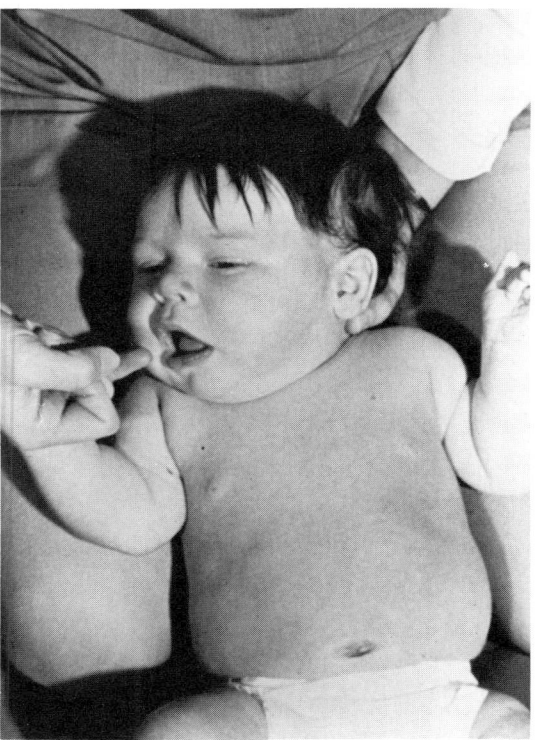

Figure 35

Rooting Reflex

This reflex (Fig. 35) is mediated reflexively through the V and VII cranial nerves and associated pathways. This reflex is sometimes called the "cardinal points" reflex because it is elicited by stimulation of cardinal points in all four quadrants around the mouth.

Of prime importance is its functional role for survival as well as its adaptive role. It is best seen during breast feeding.

Note: stroking the newborn's cheek/or palm, the infant's mouth will root, the arm will flex, and the hand will come up to his open mouth.

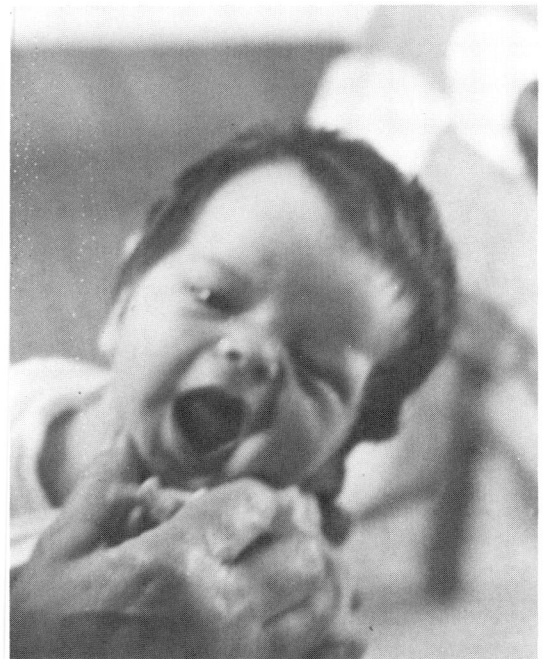

Figure 36

Contributions

Develops opening of the mouth (Fig. 36).

Helps find the breast and the sucking reflex follows (Fig. 37).

Touching inside of the mouth, which is more sensitive than external area, stimulates this reflex the most. A bottle is thus easier to suck than the breast because the bottle touches this area.

Utilization of the reflex during feeding ensures that the infant takes the nipple well into its widely opened mouth and so avoids painful pressure on the end of the mother's nipple.

Develops various positions of the tongue (lateralization).

Reinforces initial head turning (neck righting rotation).

Stimulates neck receptors feeding into the asymmetrical tonic neck reflex.

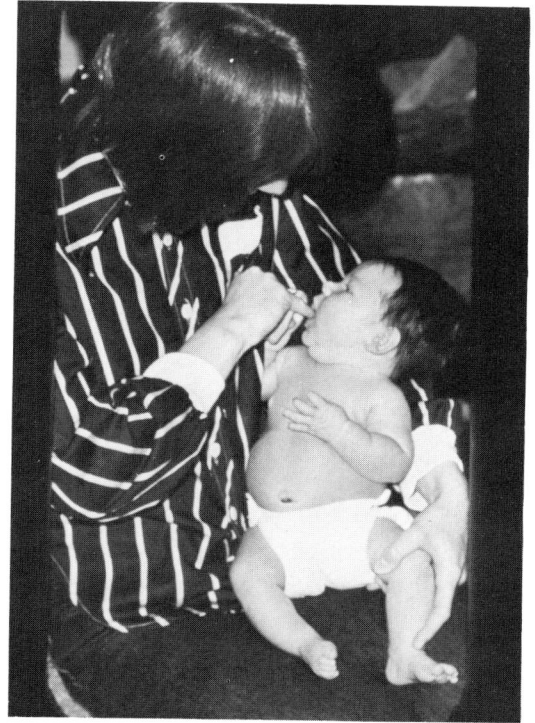

Figure 37

Absence

May compromise head turning. Tongue may retract or movement may be compromised (Fig. 38).

If persists, mouth opening may be too strong (an avoidance reaction) and tongue will retract.

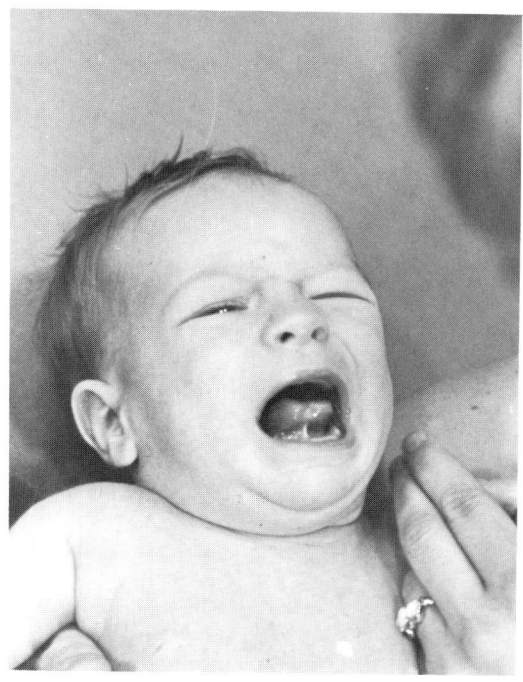

Figure 38

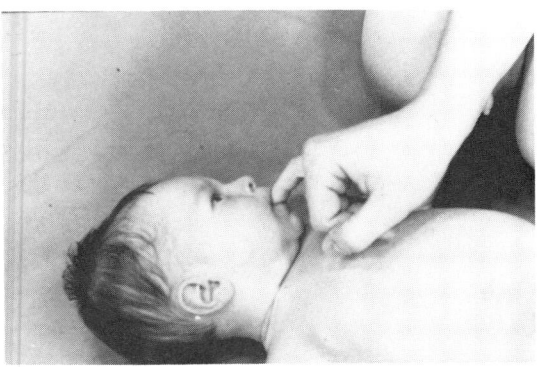

Figure 39

Sucking Reflex

Mediated through the sensory of the trigeminal and motor nuclei of the trigeminal nerve, facial nerves and hypoglossal nerve (Fig. 39).

The pons and medulla contain centers concerned with sucking. Integrative center regarding the sucking reflex may be in the medulla, but this is dependent on both pons and medulla to function.

The swallowing and respiratory centers are found close by.

Care should be taken in treating the premature infant as the muscles of deglutition are not developed.

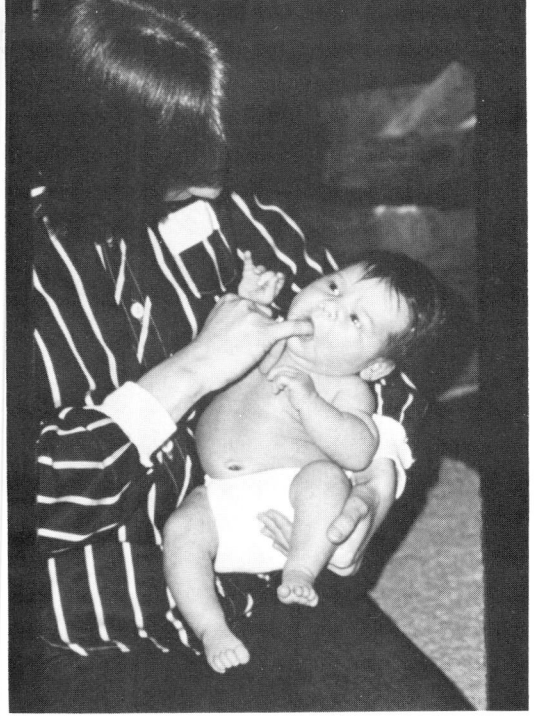

Figure 40

Contribution

Development of oral muscles, tongue placement, swallowing, and gag reflex inhibition (Fig. 40).

Development of sucking pattern for preservation (Fig. 41).

Figure 41

Absence

Ability for feeding and drinking could be compromised (Fig. 42).

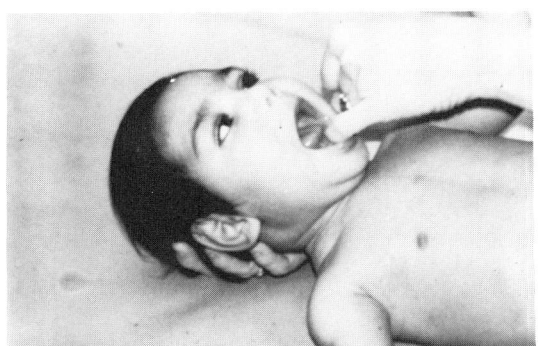

Figure 42

Compromise or none of the contributions (Fig. 43).

Note: a premature newborn struggling to survive can actually clear his air passages by sucking on his fist and swallowing the mucous that is choking him.

Both rooting and sucking are found in the second and third months of gestation and are felt to be two very primitive neurologic functions.

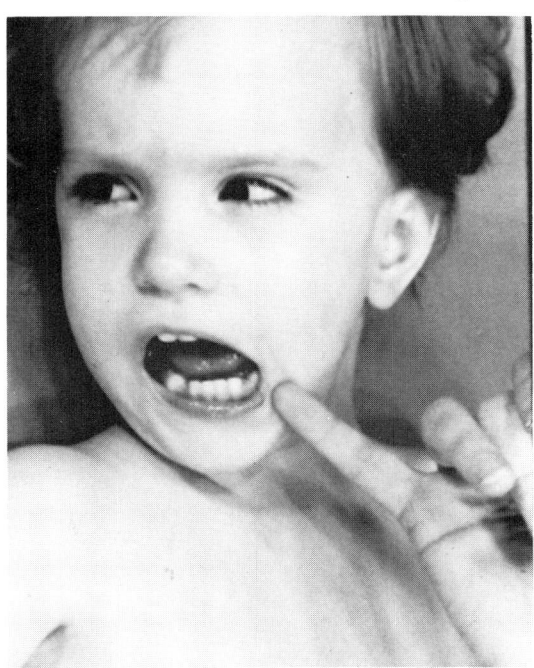

Figure 43

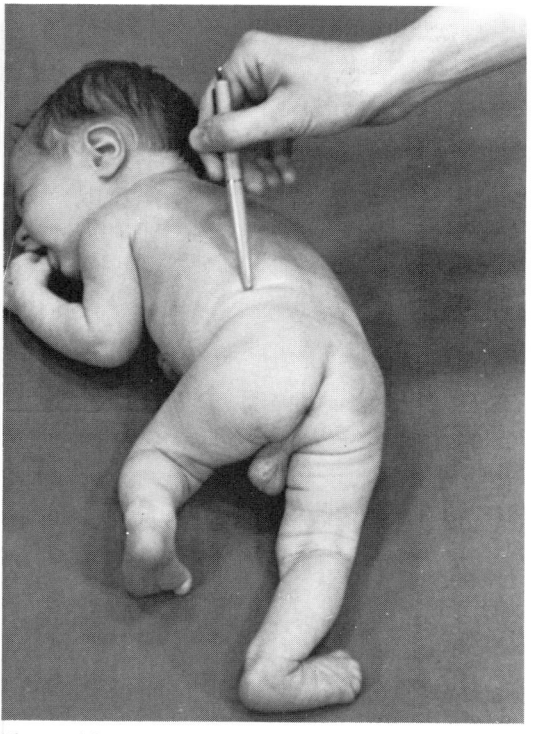

Figure 44

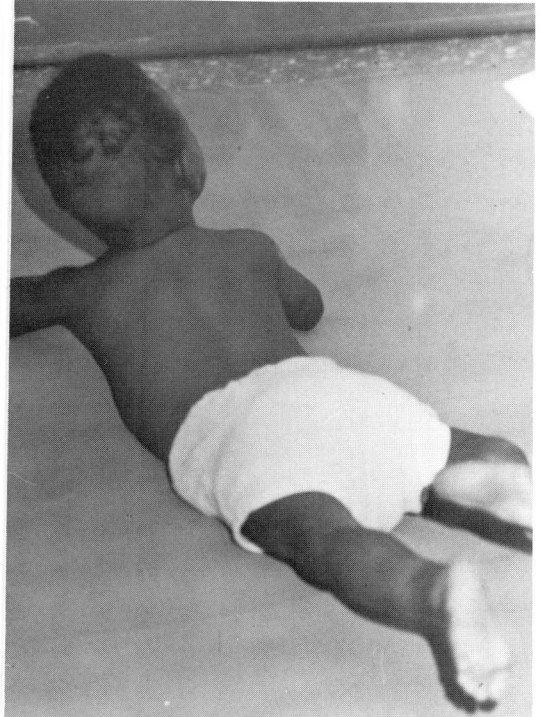

Figure 45

Galant Reflex

Believed to be a spinal reflex (Fig. 44) with the input an exteroceptive one through the sensory components of the thoracic and lumbar nerves.

Almost constantly present whatever the gestational age. Its absence may indicate a spinal cord lesion or general CNS depression.

Contribution

Initiates unilateral trunk muscle mobility (lateral flexors) (Fig. 45).

Initial movement for rotation.

Initiates amphibian movement necessary for crawling, creeping, and walking.

Breaks up the symmetrical patterns of movement of the infant (both limbs moving in the same direction at the same time). Creates asymmetrical pattern.

Can determine segmental spinal nerve lesion through stimulation along the paravertebral borders.

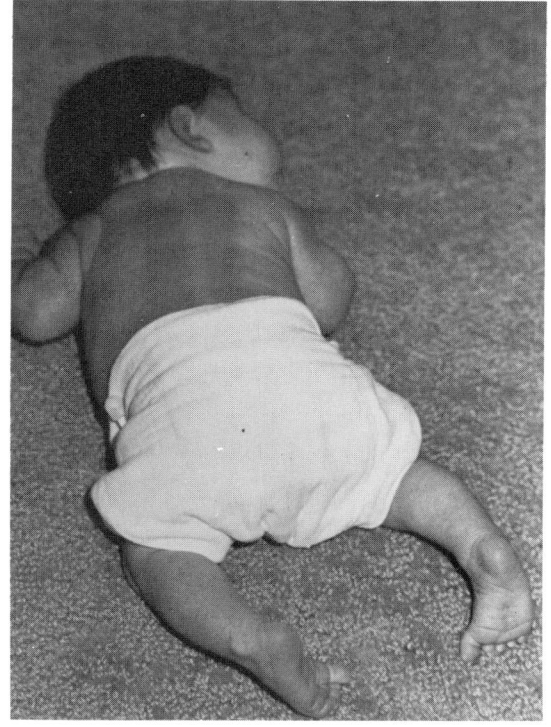

Figure 46

Absence

Eliminates or compromises the contributions (Fig. 47).

May cause delay in the development of symmetrical stabilization of the trunk and of independent movements of the head that are necessary for sitting, standing, and walking.

This instability of the trunk seems to be further aggravated by persistence of the asymmetrical tonic neck reflex.

Note: persistence raises the question whether this could predetermine a future scoliosis, especially if combined with an asymmetrical tonic neck and tonic labyrinthine-supine reflexes.

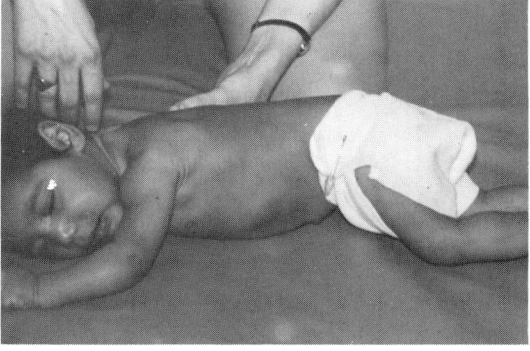

Figure 47

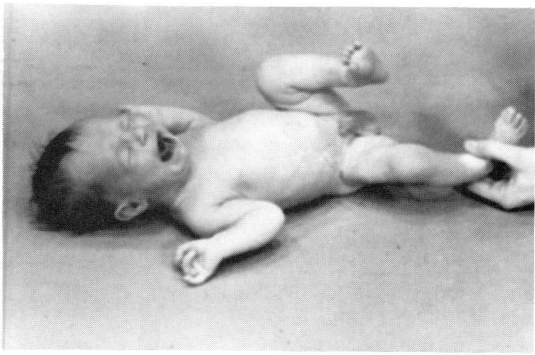

Figure 48

Crossed Extension Reflex

A spinal reflex (Fig. 48) with the reflex arc limited to the lumbosacral sensory and motor segments.

The sensory input may involve both exteroceptive (superficial sensory) and proprioceptive stimuli from the foot and knee.

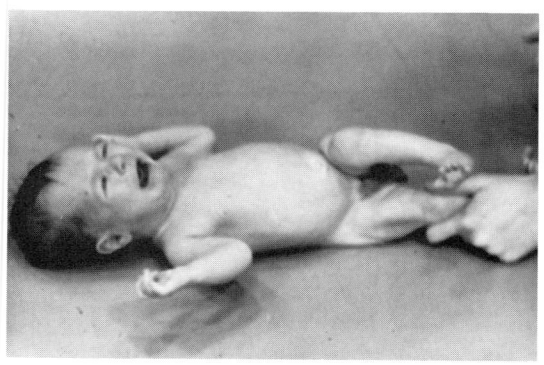

Figure 49

A premature infant does not have a full response to the stimulus. An infant at full term (Fig. 49) demonstrates the complete response of withdrawal, extension, and adduction of the lower limb.

Persistence may be indicative of a pyramidal/extrapyramidal lesion affecting the lower extremities.

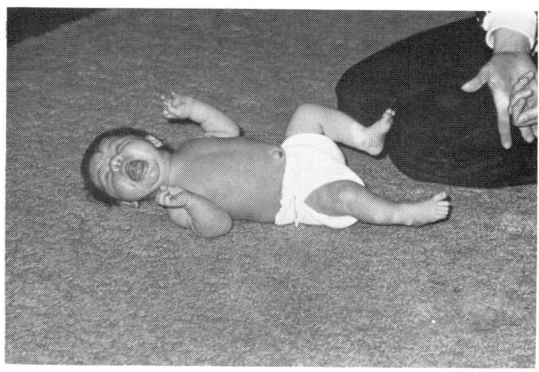

Figure 50

Contribution

Develops alternating extensor tone in the lower extremities (Fig. 50). (Flexors, adductors)

Breaks up symmetrical flexion and extension movements.

Precursor to amphibian movements (Fig. 51) in preparation for crawling, creeping, and walking patterns.

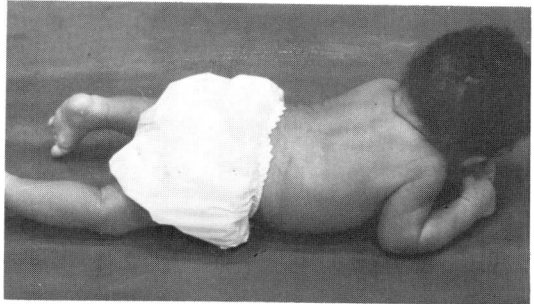

Figure 51

Combines with the positive supporting reflex in the early stages to supply sufficient extensor tone to stand on one lower limb while the opposite limb flexes (Fig. 52).

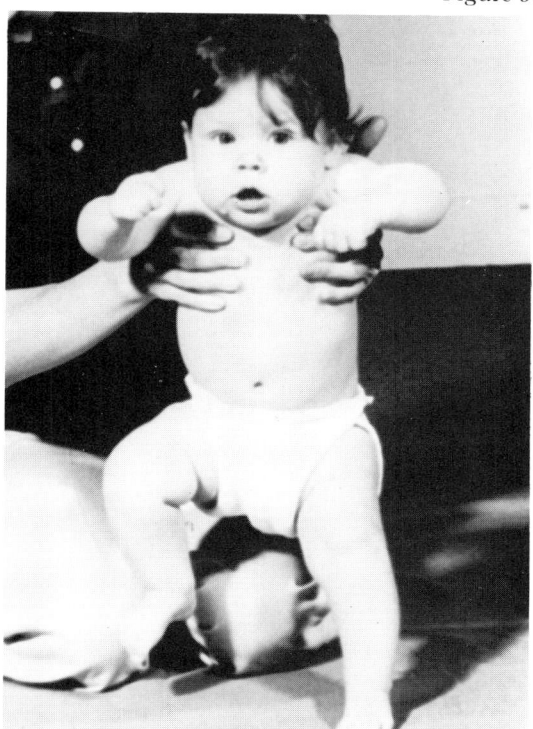

Figure 52

Persistence

Prevents reciprocal movements required for mobility at any level (Fig. 53).

Prevents alternate weight-bearing position required for balance and mobility.

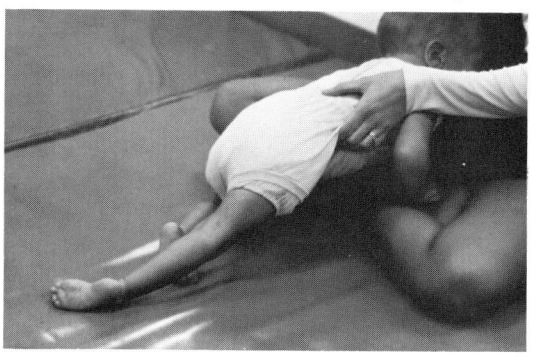

Figure 53

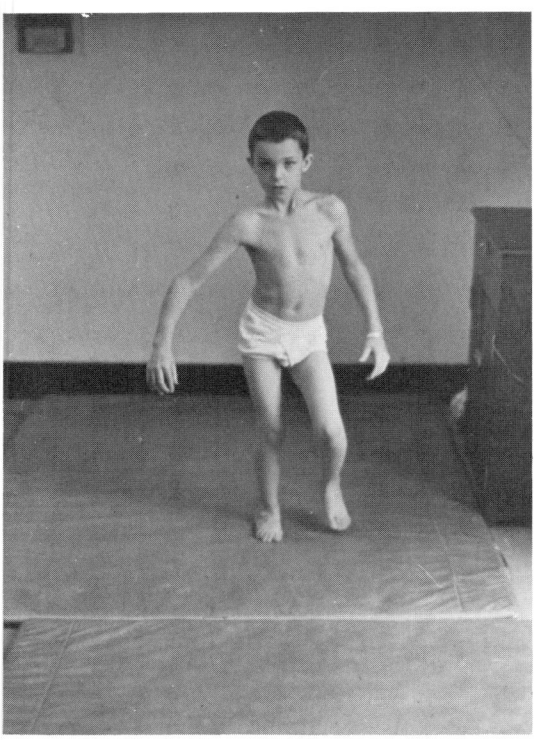

Figure 54

Can create strong extensor spasm combined with the positive supporting to cause loss of balance, clawing of toes, hyperextended knee, and prevents child from falling by flexing at the hips (Fig. 54). Compensation is possible with a lordosis and forward flexion of the head.

The hemiplegic patient can stand on his affected limb with no exaggerated tone, foot dorsiflexed and heel down, body weight over the middle of the foot. This position will be maintained as long as the foot of the sound limb touches the floor. As soon as an attempt is made to lift the sound foot off the floor by flexing the hip and knee, a strong extensor spasm affects the involved limb due to the crossed extension reflex. The patient loses his balance as he pushes against the ground with the ball of his foot (influence of the positive support reflex), claws his toes, hyperextends at the knee, and protects himself from falling forward by flexing the trunk at the hips. In attempting to walk, the sound limb is brought together with the complete sound side in a forward step, leaving the affected limb, hip, and shoulder behind (influence of both positive support and crossed extension reflexes), accounting for the hyperextension of the knee and the affected side lagging slightly behind the other side in walking.

Flexor Withdrawal Reflex

A protective reflex (Fig. 55). Transmitted from pain receptors in the skin and mediated through the afferent nerves of S1 or S2 and possibly from L4 and L5.

The motor response is from several lumbosacral segments and completes what is clearly a spinal cord reflex.

Constantly present whatever the gestational age. It may be weak or absent after a breech presentation as the limbs are extended.

It can be absent with sciatic nerve damage.

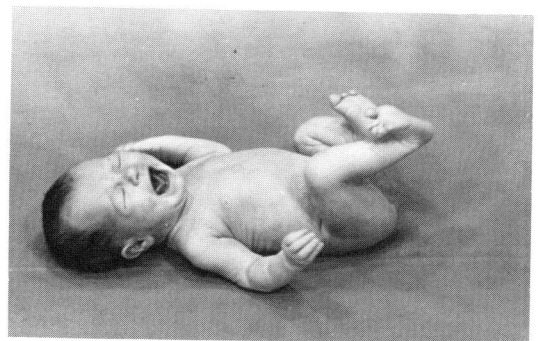

Figure 55

Contribution

A protective reaction (see Fig. 55).

Helps to develop a balance between flexor and extensor tone (Fig. 56).

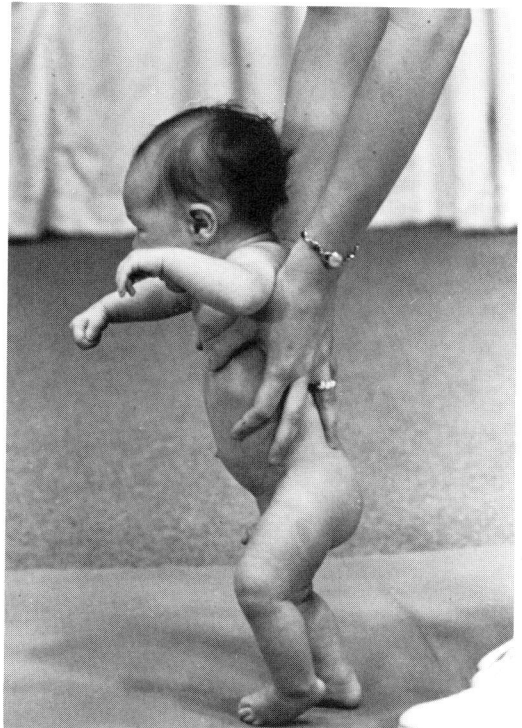

Figure 56

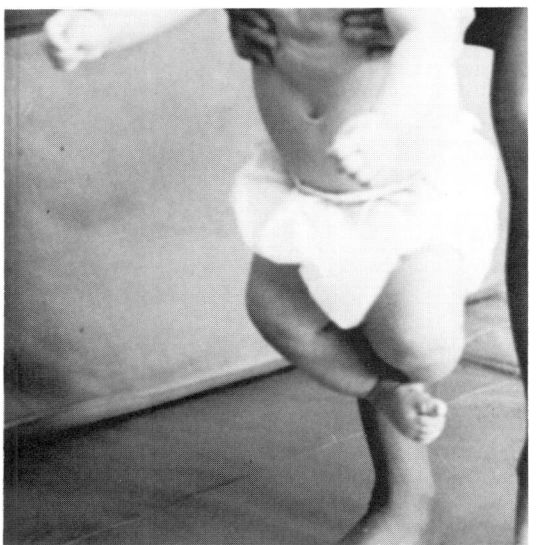

Figure 57

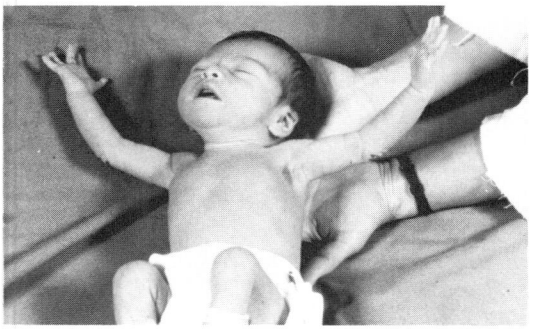

Figure 58

Persistence

Prevents extensor development for weight bearing and the ability to walk (Fig. 57).

Moro Reflex

Any sudden change—exteroceptive, proprioceptive, including vestibular or auditory input—can cause a Moro (Fig. 58).

The afferent impulses are transmitted to the brain stem, which appears to be the upper limit of the reflex arc.

Several methods are projected as the stimulus for this reflex. One method is that retroflexion of the neck stimulates or stretches the muscles and joints around the cervical vertebrae as well as the surrounding skin and the vestibular receptors. With this method, the "head drop" stimulus changes and ultimately disappears much earlier than the other two methods.

The second method is to "lift" the baby about one inch off of a surface and then suddenly lower him. With this method, the extension/abduction components can be observed longer than the flexion/adduction components (upper limbs.)

The third method is to hit the surface on which the baby is lying with the palm of one's flat hand. The flexion/adduction components of the limbs can be observed longer than the extension/abduction components.

The Moro appears at approximately seven months gestation and has been identified in many small prematures. It persists longer postnatally (than the usual four to six months) in these premature infants.

Its absence in the first four months of life usually suggests diffuse CNS depression and is frequently associated with other brain stem signs.

Asymmetry in neonates is a useful sign in recognizing brachial plexus, unilateral fracture of the clavicle or humerus, and hemiplegia.

Contribution

Develops extensor tone bilaterally in the upper limbs and fingers (Fig. 59).

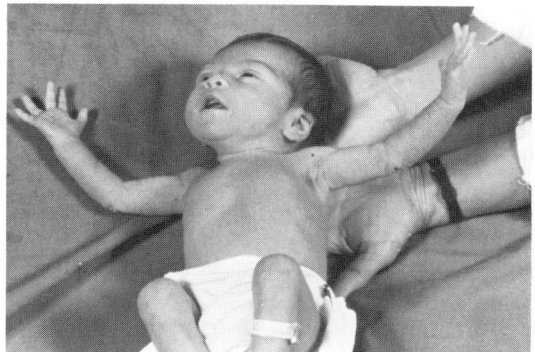

Figure 59

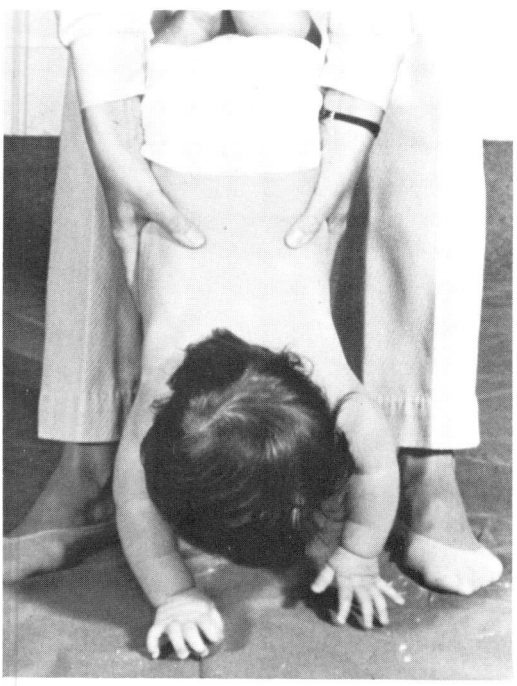

As the Moro reflex matures and integrates, the upper limbs are prepared for the propping and parachute reactions (Fig. 60).

Figure 60

Prepares propping to establish sitting independence (Fig. 61).

Figure 61

Persistence

Excess development of extensor tone to fingertips (Fig. 62).

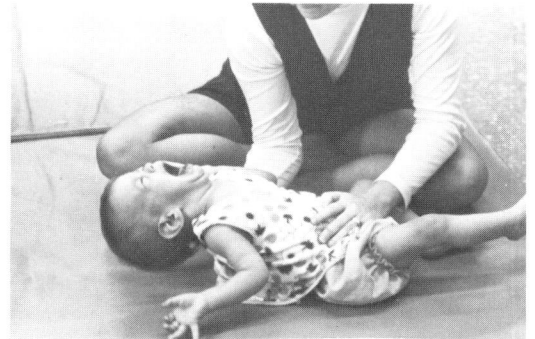

Figure 62

Prevents propping to establish sitting independence, weight bearing, and transfer (Fig. 63).

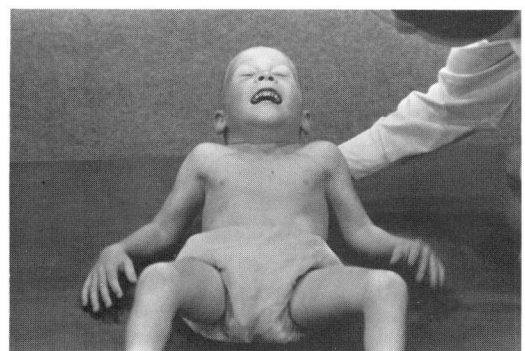

Figure 63

Compromises sitting, standing, and walking due to fear of falling or ability to protect self (Fig. 64).

Absence compromises extensor development.

Figure 64

Figure 65

Parachute Reaction

Probably a vestibular reaction (Fig. 65). The response is independent of visual stimuli since it occurs also when the infant is blindfolded.

As the Moro reflex is integrated, sequential propping and parachute reactions will develop.

An asymmetrical response may be indicative of an orthopedic or neuromuscular disorder.

Contribution

A protective reaction for the remainder of life (Fig. 66).

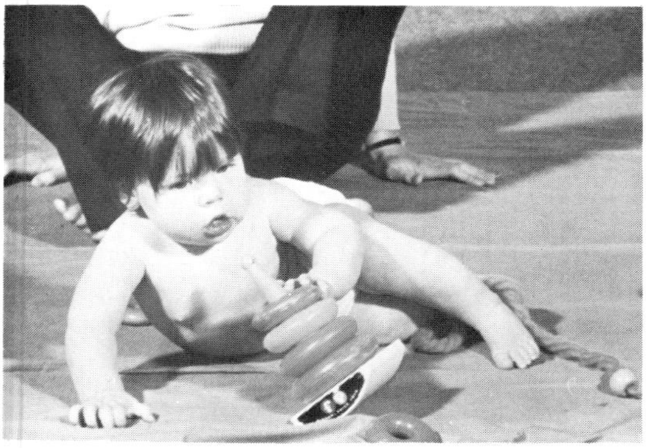

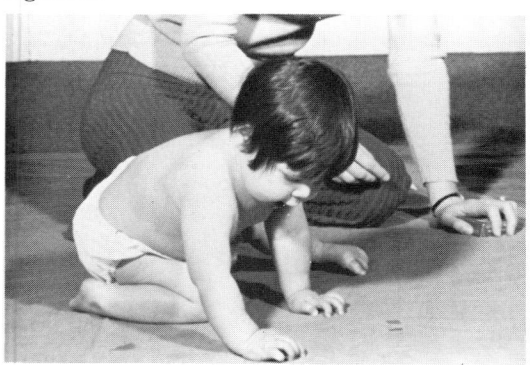

Figure 66

Parachute and propping reactions become functional (Fig. 67).

Figure 67

Propping gives the initial support to sit, and the parachute protects when the body is too far off the center of gravity (Fig. 68).

Contributes to the development of extensor tone.

Figure 68

Absence

Propping and parachute reactions compromised (Fig. 69).

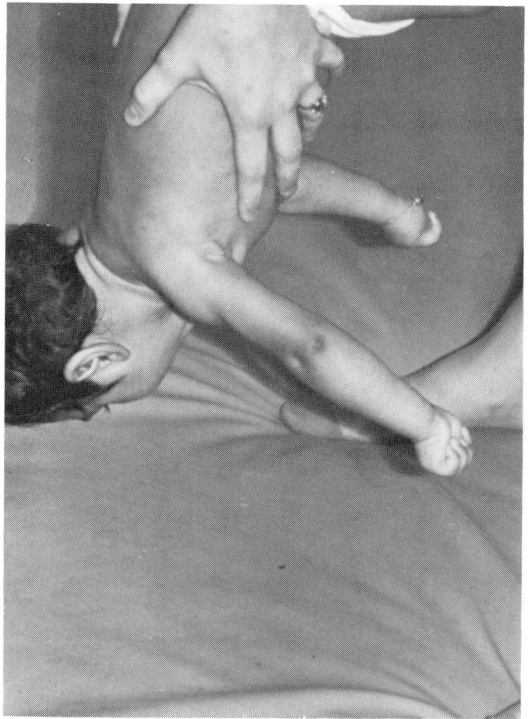

Figure 69

Initial propping support to sit compromised or lacking to prevent independent sitting (Fig. 70).

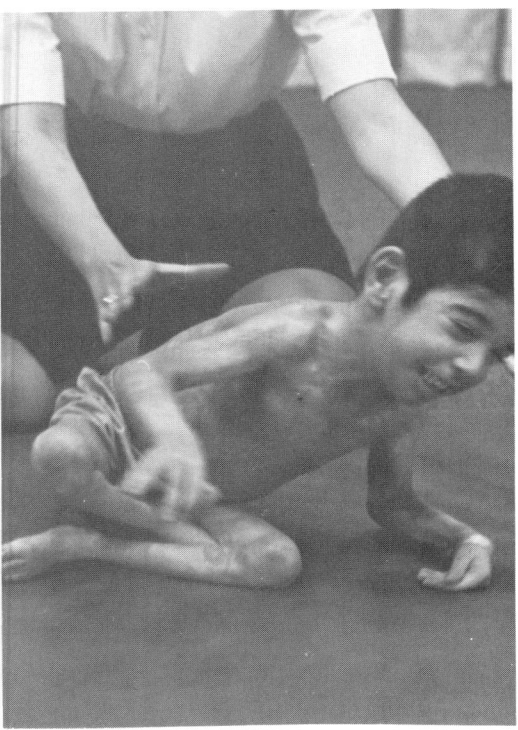

Figure 70

Protective parachute reaction compromised or lacking (Fig. 71).

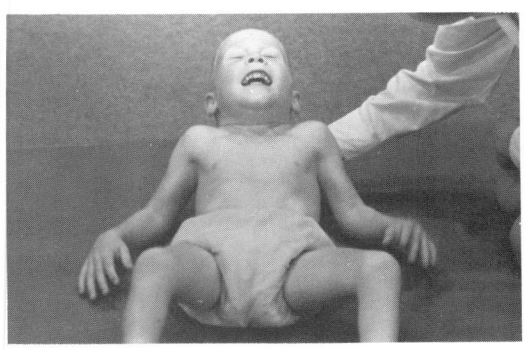

Figure 71

Weight-bearing surface of the upper limbs in the quadruped position may be compromised, especially if full development of the symmetrical tonic neck tone has not occurred (Fig. 72).

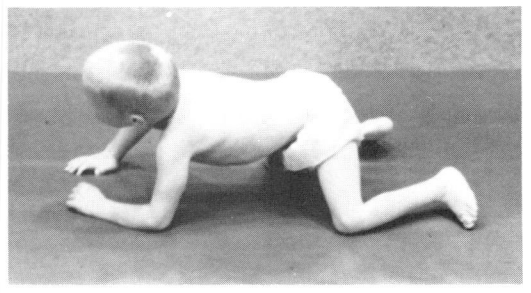

Figure 72

Placing Reaction

Seen in many but not all prematures after thirty-six weeks gestation; seen in all full term babies (Figs. 73, 74, 75, 76).

Some expression of the placing reaction can occur in animals without a cerebral cortex. In man this reaction is probably mediated in the subcortical nuclei (basal ganglia and superior colliculus). It is necessary to have the integrative action of the superior colliculus of the midbrain to be intact and this reaction will function, assuming the rest of the brain stem, spinal cord, and cerebellum are functioning normally.

It is not a visual stimulus as it also occurs in a blindfolded infant.

In testing, do not apply pressure on the forefoot or hand as the pressure brings in a proprioceptive response to the foot or hand.

This response is absent in infants with Werdnig-Hoffman's disease and spinal cord injuries.

Asymmetry could indicate CNS damage, as in hemiplegia.

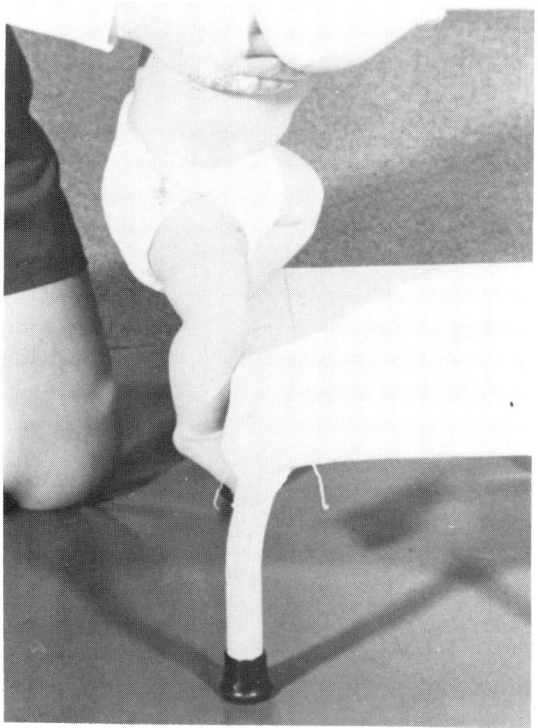

Figure 73

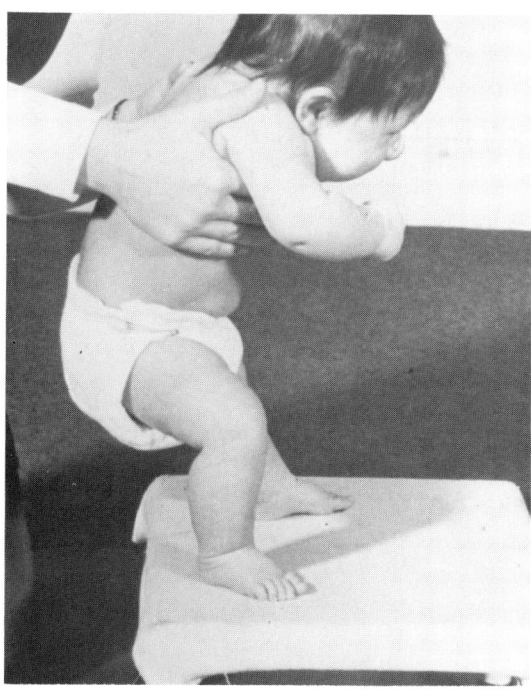

Figure 74

Figure 75

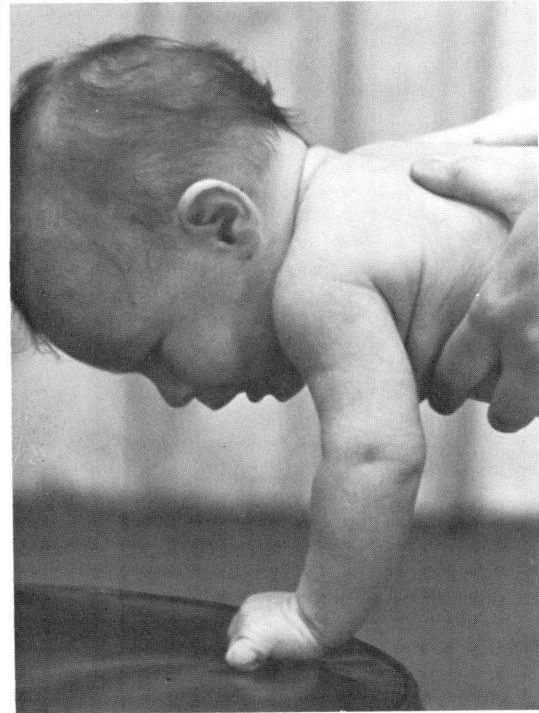

Figure 76

Contribution

Ability to place the foot in the appropriate position for standing and locomotion (Fig. 77).

Initiates the flexion/extension pattern for walking.

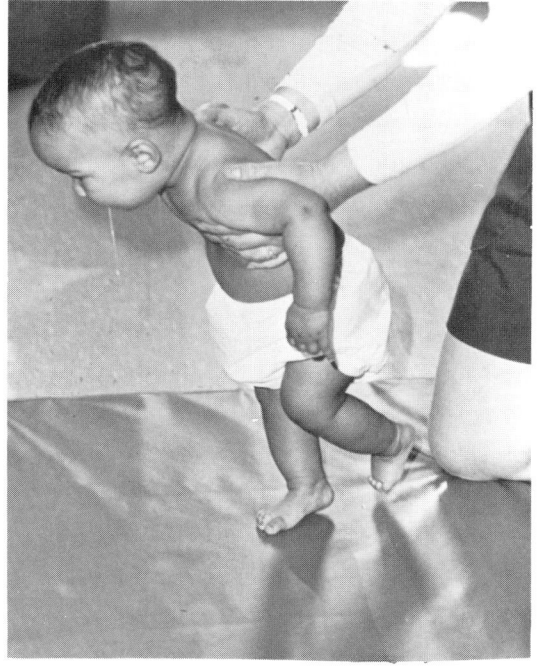

Figure 77

Ability to place the hand and upper limb in a position for support in sitting (Fig. 78) and the quadruped position (Fig. 79).

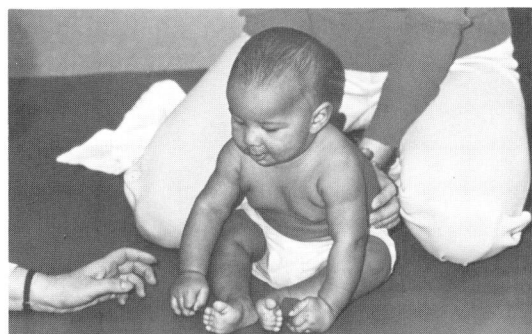

Figure 78

Figure 79

Absence

None or compromising of all of the Contributions (Fig. 80).

Figure 80

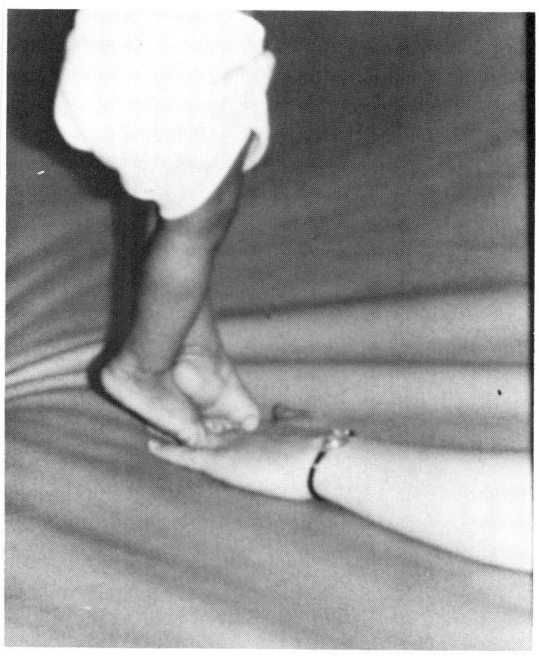

This will alter development for sitting, quadruped, standing, and walking (Fig. 81).

Figure 81

Primary Standing

Present in all newborns; present in prematures but age-specific details lacking (Figs. 82, 83).

Reaction dependent upon spinal responses and may be modified by higher centers for use in standing.

At this time, the support reaction is incomplete. Extensor tone is present to the knees; the hips and knees remain slightly flexed, suggesting that the increased flexor tone of the newborn period cannot be fully overcome.

Magnus likened this initially as the "Magnet" response.

Absence or asymmetry could indicate a spinal cord lesion or higher levels of CNS damage.

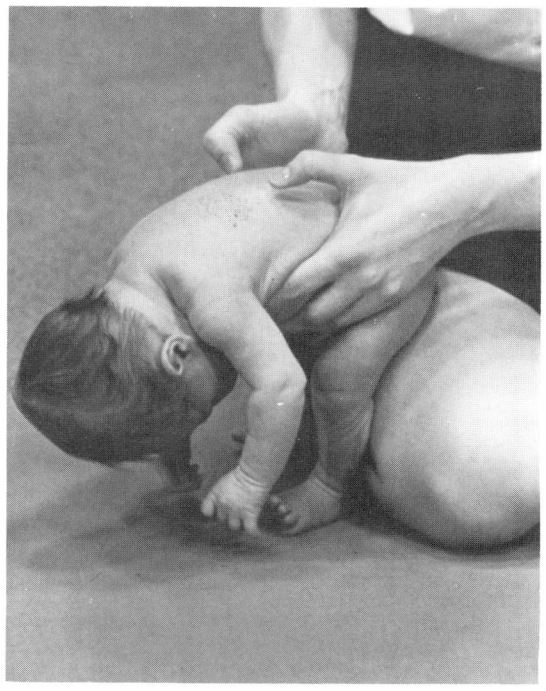

Figure 82

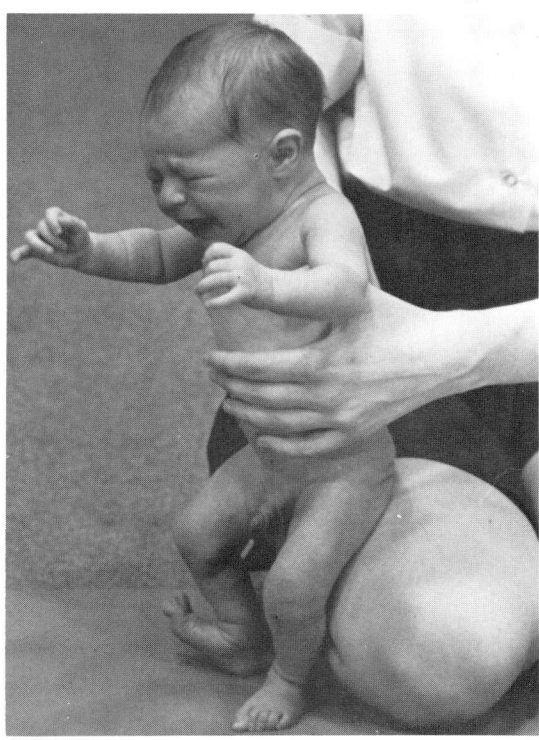

Figure 83

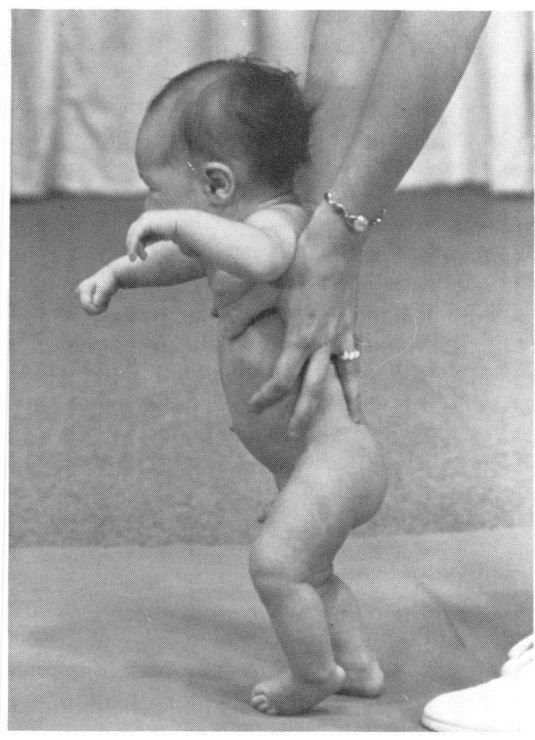

Figure 84

Contribution

Initial ability to assume the standing position (Fig. 84). Develops balance between the flexor and extensor musculature of the trunk.

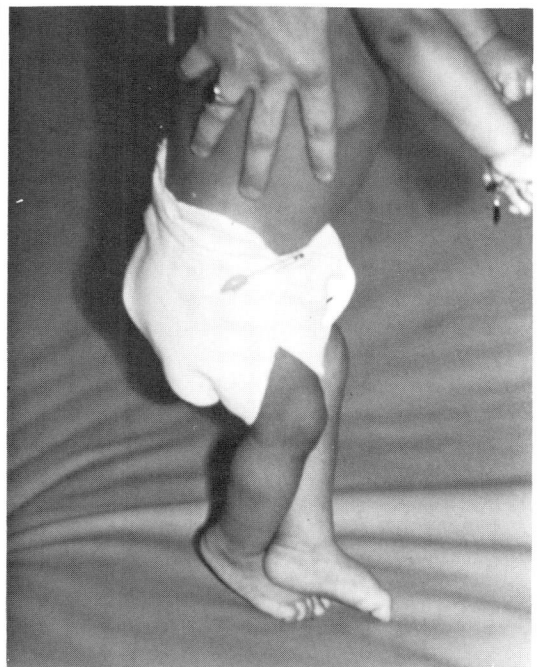

Figure 85

Absence

Compromise or none of the Contributions, which could limit, delay, or alter sensorimotor development to the higher levels (Fig. 85).

Primary Stepping

A reflexive pattern; appears to be localized to spinal segments (Fig. 86). Not a true walking as there is no pelvic stability. Equilibrium reactions of the trunk and cocontraction of the muscles of the trunk and hips for maintaining the upright position are absent and without support the baby will collapse. Extensor tone is present only to the knees.

Occurs infrequently in premature babies of less than thirty-four weeks. It increases in frequency thereafter.

Absent or asymmetrical response could indicate CNS damage.

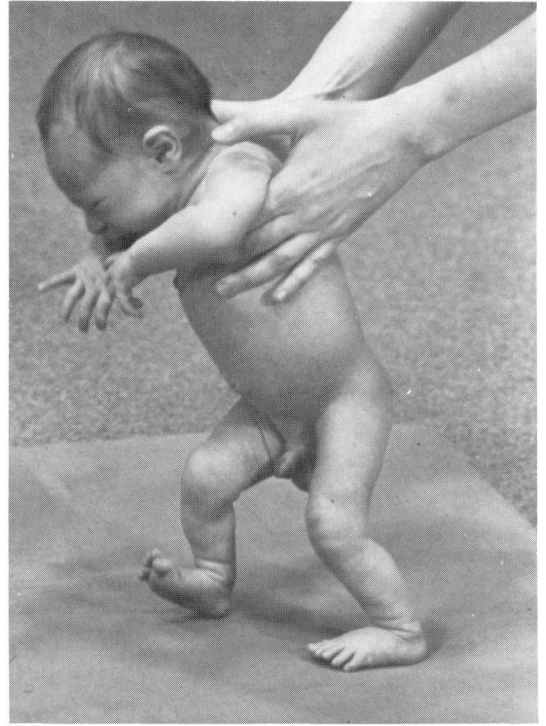

Figure 86

Contribution

Indicates the potential for automatic, reciprocal walking (Fig. 87).

Develops flexor and extensor tone balance for future standing and walking, including dorsiflexion of the foot and extension of the toes.

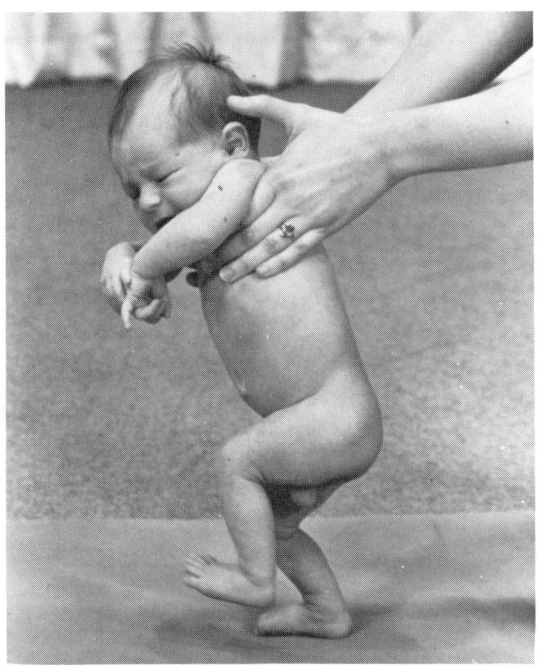

Figure 87

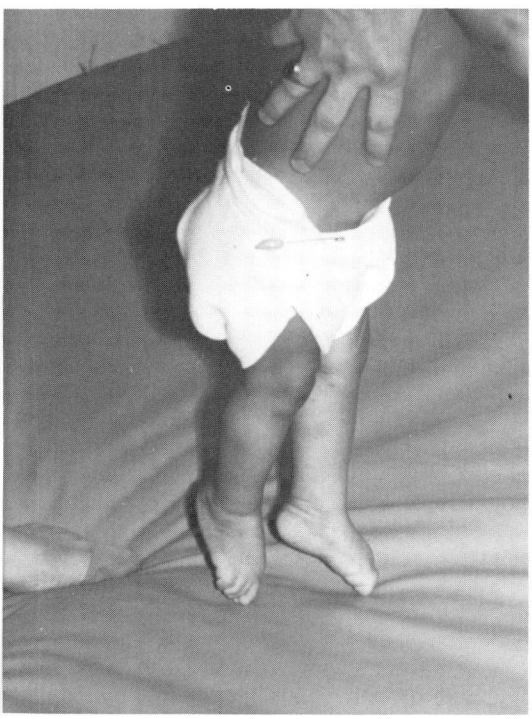

Figure 88

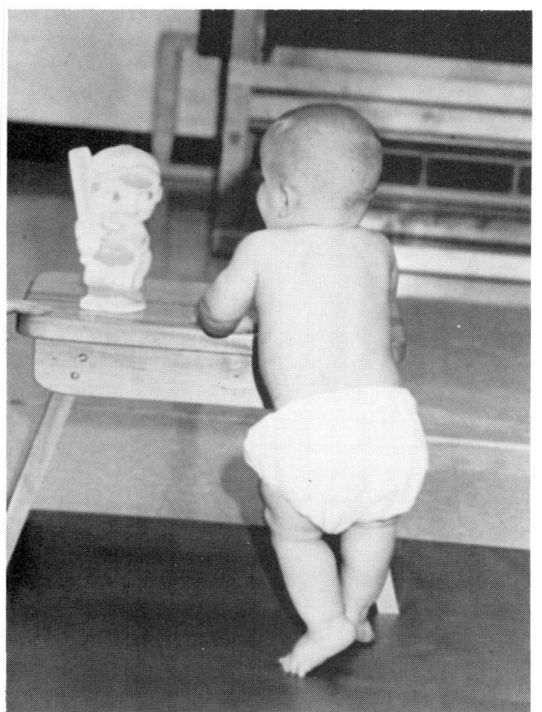

Figure 89

Absence

None of the Contributions. (Fig. 88).

Positive Supporting Reflex

Stimulus is exteroceptive from a touch stimulus to the skin of the toe pads (Fig. 89). This is followed by a proprioceptive stimulus of stretch of the interosseus muscles by separation of the toe pads as well as pressure into the ball of the foot.

If the exteroceptive phase is abolished, the separation of the toe pads promptly initiates the response.

The stretch reflex, which is at the basis of the antigravity response, is not of itself sufficient to fix a given joint. Opposing muscles must contract simultaneously to ensure fixation of the joint.

Joints become fixed and limbs pillar-like through the simultaneous contraction of opposing muscle groups.

Must have relaxation reciprocally when the position of the extremity is changed, even slightly (negative supporting) (Fig. 90).

Failure of this reflex to appear at the appropriate time delays locomotor development.

Persistence and/or excess tone is a sign of neurological abnormality.

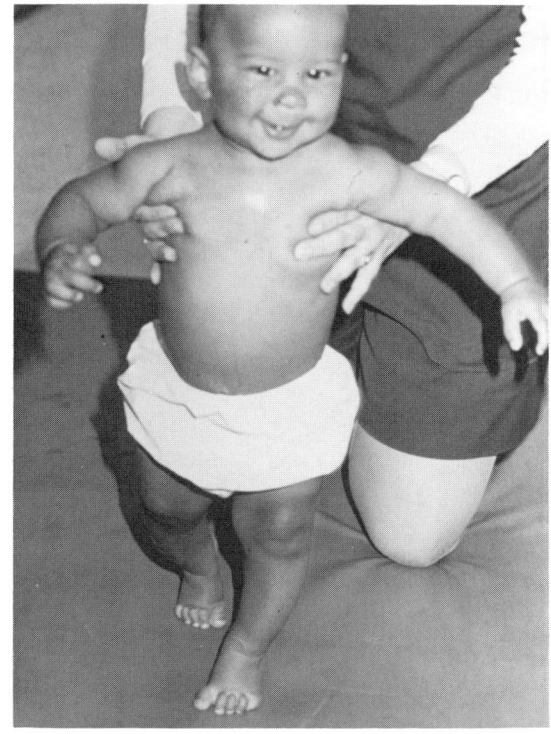

Figure 90

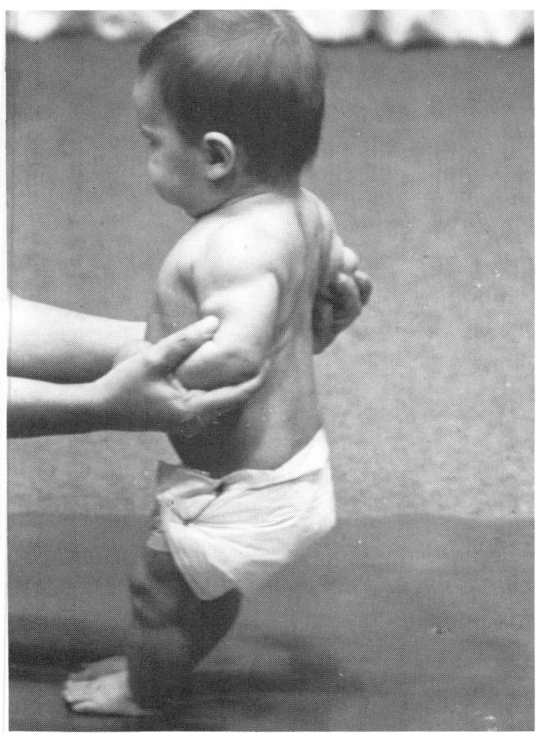

Figure 91

Figure 92

Contribution

Combined with the Landau extension of the trunk, balance between flexors and extensors of the hips and trunk is developed for straight back sitting and standing (Fig. 91).

Precursor to standing and walking through the development of extensor tone in the lower extremities and to a lesser degree in the hips and trunk (Fig. 92).

Flexor and extensor tone stimulated to create the cocontraction necessary for the pillarlike limb of the supporting reaction-tonic phase.

Persistence

Cannot put heel to ground; lower limbs extend, internally rotate, and adduct (Fig. 93).

Creates a narrow base; weight transfer is impossible; cannot stand or walk.

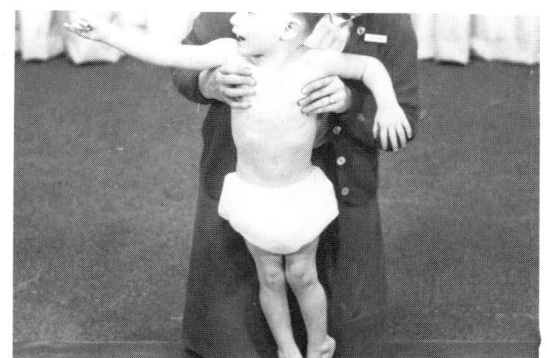

Figure 93

Combined with the crossed extension reflex, the extensor tone may be sufficient to create a backward thrust, thus placing the person off balance (Fig. 94).

Tone may be excessive; prevents good movement or purposeful movement patterns.

Prevents dorsiflexion of the feet and creates clawing of the toes.

Figure 94

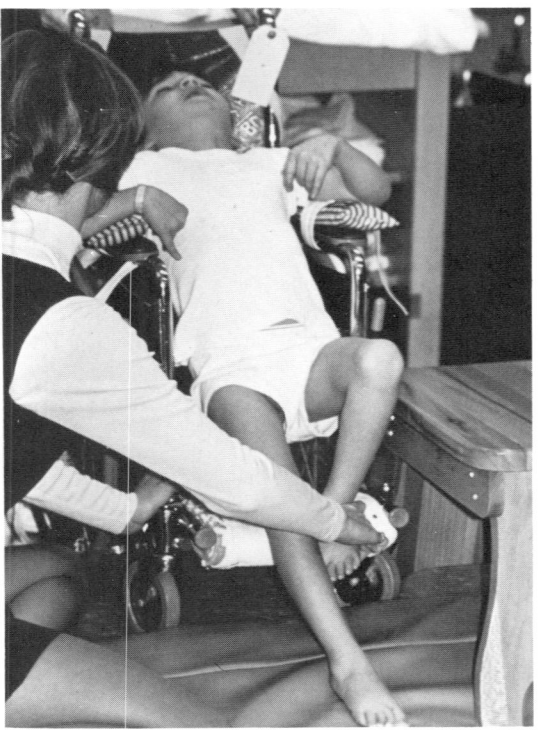

Figure 95

Might have difficulty rising from a chair because the feet may be stimulated as they are placed on the foot rest, thus resulting in an extensor thrust (Fig. 95).

Negative Supporting Reflex

Reflex relaxation of the extensors of the proximal joints of the lower limbs (Fig. 96). The entire limb relaxes sufficiently, especially proximally, and becomes free for movement.

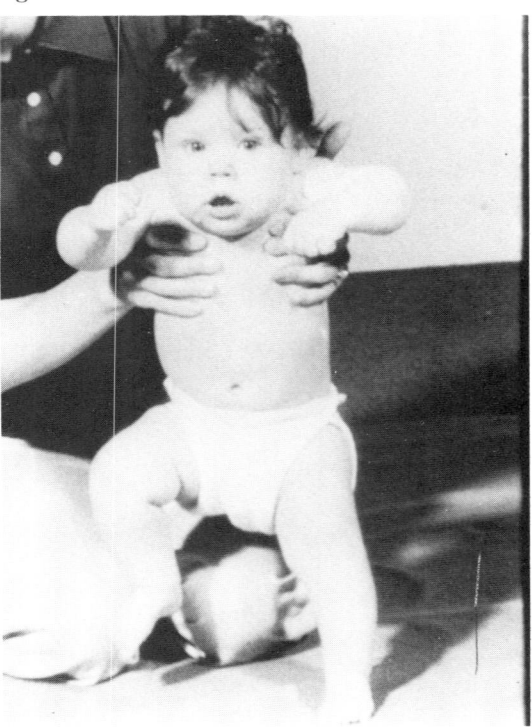

Figure 96

Positive Supporting of the Upper Limbs

A support reflex appears in these extremities similarly to that of the lower limbs (Fig. 97).

Preparation occurs by extension of the upper limbs as the body is tilted forward, sideways, backwards (propping).

Visual and labyrinthine righting reflexes are responsible for the early part of this reflex, but the supporting part follows pressure on the palms of the open hands on a firm surface. This provides the stimulus for tensing of the limb muscles through stimulation of extensor muscles.

Asymmetrical responses may be pathological.

Note: in the development of extensor tone this reflex develops from distal to proximal in the extremities, whereas stimulation of extensor tone from the symmetrical tonic neck reflex develops proximal to distal.

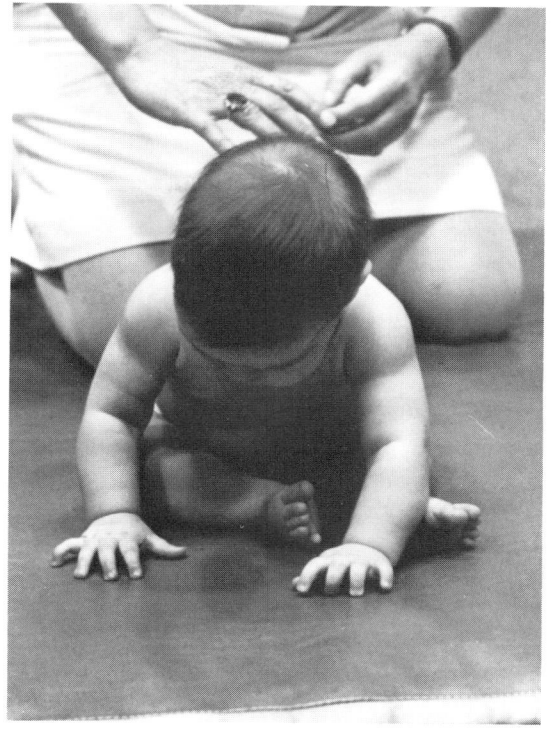

Figure 97

Contribution

Develops extensor tone distal proximal (Fig. 98).

Creates cocontraction for weight bearing positions.

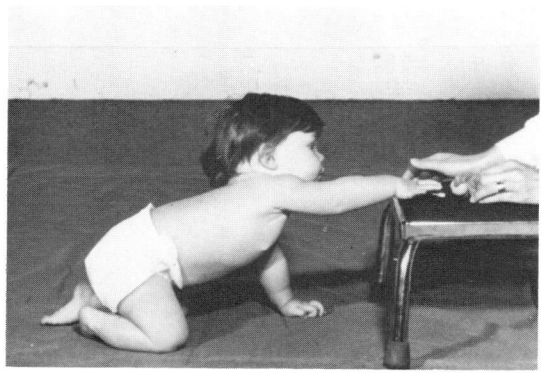

Figure 98

Figure 99

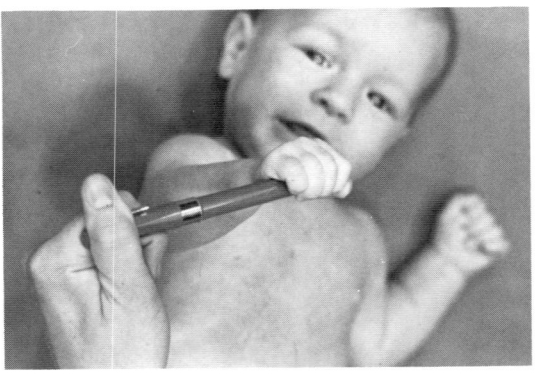

Figure 100

Absence

None of the Contributions (Fig. 99).

Primitive Grasp Reflex

A combination of superficial sensory and proprioceptive stimuli may produce the grasp response (Fig. 100).

The sensory fibers arise from spinal cord levels, C6 through C8. The reflex arc is completed by motor fibers at the same levels.

Weak finger flexion and grasp response can be observed in the human foetus as early as the fourth gestational month; healthy newborns and most premature infants will always have a good palmar grasp.

Light touch of the palm (or sole) produces reflex flexion of the digits (or toes) (Fig. 101).

The most effective way to elicit the reflex is to slide the stimulating object across the palm (or sole) from the ulnar border.

Chain responses follow the initial reflex (seen best in palmar reflex): the first chain response follows initial flexion of the digits and consists of tensing of the flexed muscles to produce a strong grasp. A strong tonic component at this stage of the reflex ensures maintenance of the grasp as long as the stimulus persists.

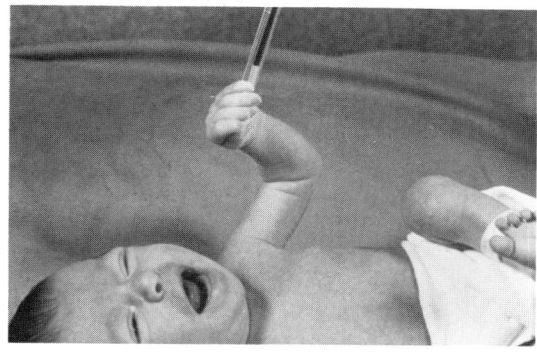

Figure 101

The second stage occurs when traction is exerted by the stimulating digit (Fig. 102). This is followed by progressive contraction of the limb muscles. This response is sufficiently strong so that the baby can be lifted from the bed. Differences occur according to the infant's gestational age.

A neurological organization of the palmar grasp reflex has been described in which finger flexion follows a definite sequence: middle, ring, little, index, thumb. This correlates with the sequence in the development of grasp, which follows the same order: from ulnar to radial grasp to pinch.

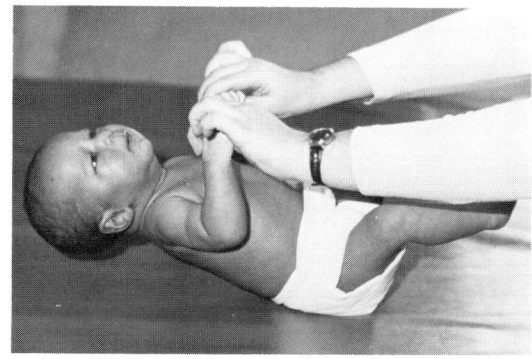

Figure 102

This reflex is reported to be weaker in infants with general CNS depression. It is absent in patients with spinal cord lesions or injuries of the upper limbs, such as traction induced damage to spinal nerve roots as in Erbs and Klumpke-type palsies.

Persistence of automatic grasp is associated with spastic cerebral palsy.

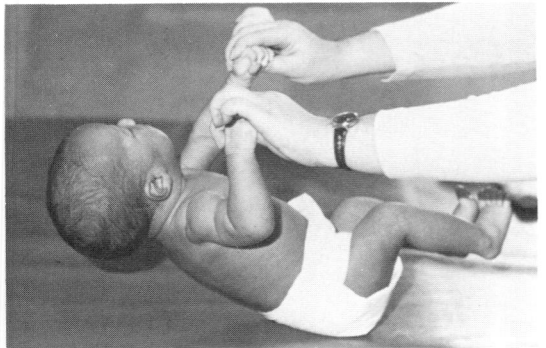

Figure 103

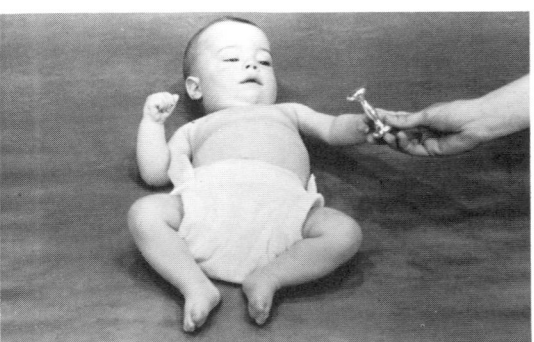

Figure 104

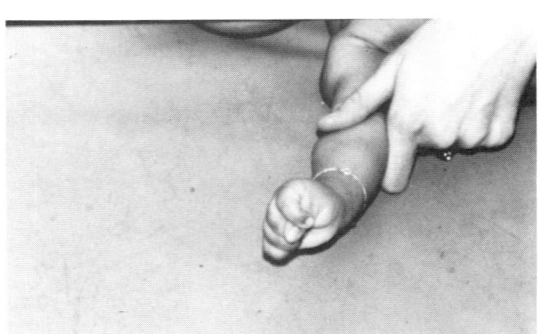

Figure 105

Contribution

Development of the tonic phase of flexor tone in the digits and upper limbs (Fig. 103).

The tactile stimulation in the hand assists in developing coordination between eyes and hand (Fig. 104); coordinates with the response of the asymmetrical tonic neck reflex.

Persistence

Persistence eliminates the Contribution (Fig. 105).

Absence

Creates an inability to hold onto objects that may compromise sensory input tactually; may compromise tonic response of muscles (Fig. 106).

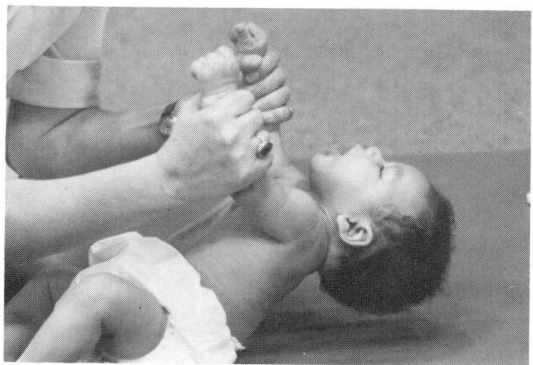

Figure 106

INTERESTING POINTS: the traction/flexion response is a tonic one, but this response can be inhibited by scratching the palmar surface.

Sucking movements appear to facilitate grasping, and the infant's grasp reflex is significantly greater before rather than after feeding.

The palmo-mandibular reflex occurs when the baby is feeding (reflexive flexion/extension movements of the digits).

It is of phylogenetic interest that young animals cling to their mothers with the aid of this reflex. In humans, the reflex can be elicited by stimulation of the hand with hair.

The grasp reflex is superseded, even before it disappears, by achievement of a voluntary grasp response.

Figure 107

Ulnar and Radial Release

Contribution

Ulnar release develops the finger extension and pronation synergy (Fig. 107). Radial release develops the finger flexion and supination synergy.

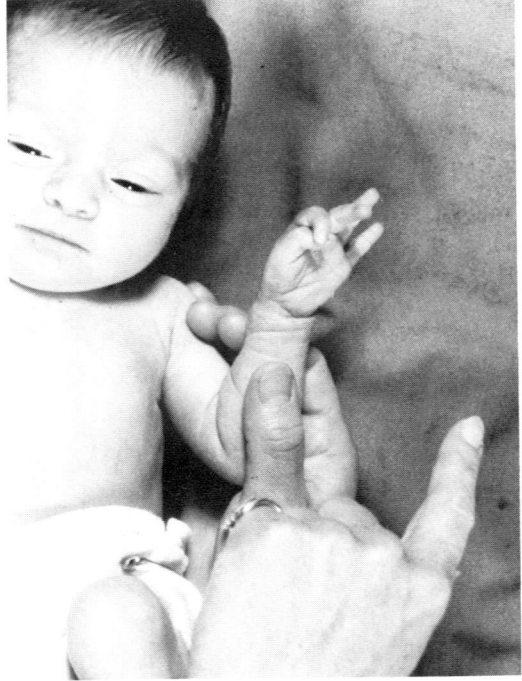

Figure 108

Develops sequencing movements of the fingers (Fig. 108). Develops isolated movements of the fingers. Develops release of the fingers.

Absence

Extension, flexion, supination, pronation, finger sequencing, release, and isolated movements for fine skills may be compromised or lacking (Fig. 109).

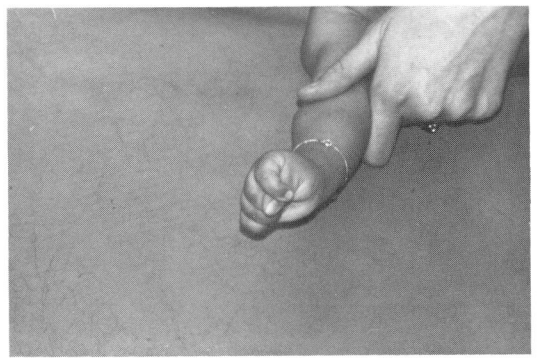

Figure 109

Magnet Response

Demonstrable in the early weeks (Fig. 110). This reflex was designated as occurring prior to the positive supporting reflex.

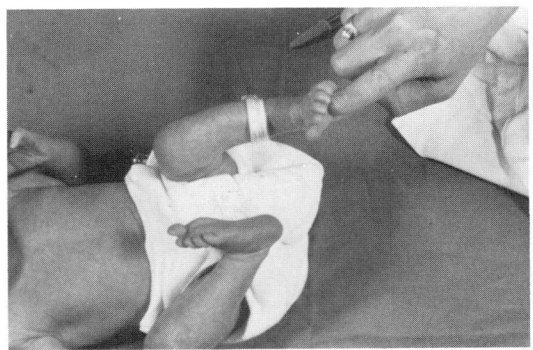

Figure 110

Contribution

Initial development of extensor tone of the muscles controlling the knee and hip joints, bilaterally or unilaterally (Fig. 111).

Development of the foot musculature, invertors, evertors, dorsiflexors, and plantarflexors.

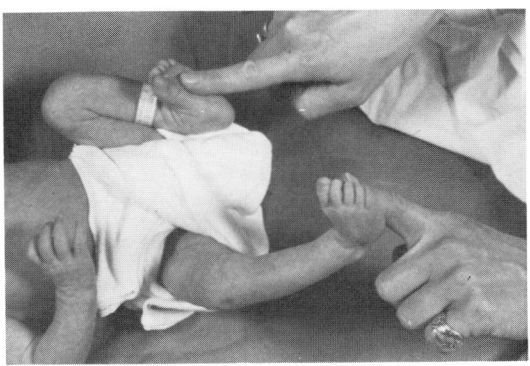

Figure 111

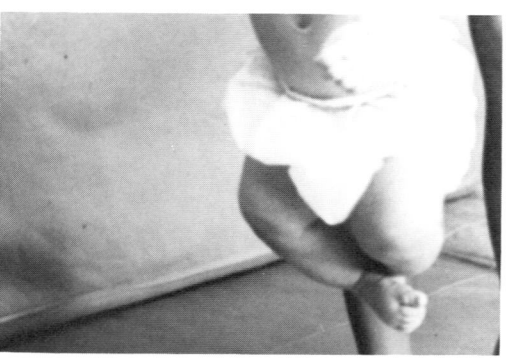

Figure 112

Absence

All the the Contributions may be compromised (Fig. 112).

Babkin Reflex

Possibly mediated by the trigeminal nerve or nucleus, which extends down into the upper cervical cord. In the foetus this is the area of early integration for exteroceptive stimuli from all parts of the body. Hooker states that stimulation of this area in the embryo causes lip and mouth movement as well as head rotation and flexion in the cervical region.

With the baby in the supine position, apply quick pressure simultaneously onto the palms of the hands. The response is rotation of the head to the midline, forward flexion of the head, and mouth opening. (Eyes closing is not regularly seen.) The response disappears with repeated, rapid stimulation, but returns after a short period.

Premature infants response is easier to obtain, possibly due to the immaturity of the CNS, but intensity is greater in the larger infants. Response also depends on the state of the infant.

A primitive reflex demonstrating a hand-to-mouth, neurological sensorimotor link.

Seen from birth to four months.

Contribution

Contributes additional stimulus to neck righting (rotation), to neck flexors to initiate head righting in the supine position, and to mouth opening combined with neck rotation in preparation for the nipple.

Absence

Compromises the Contribution.

Tonic Labyrinthine—
Prone and Supine Reflexes

Stimulation of the labyrinths results in diffuse changes in muscle tone and results in adjustment in posture of a tonic nature.

Changes in the position of the head and body in space affects the labyrinths, which initiates the sensory input for the reflex arc. This reflex is believed to be integrated at brain stem levels.

The labyrinth is believed to have two somewhat distinct mechanisms. One is the maculae, which mediates the static labyrinthine reactions; the other is the ampullae of the semicircular ducts from which angular acceleration reactions occur.

The effects of these receptors and their inability to function normally in both prone and supine are very obvious in the neurologically damaged infant, as in cerebral palsy. Increased tone is seen in these patients, depending on the position of the body and head.

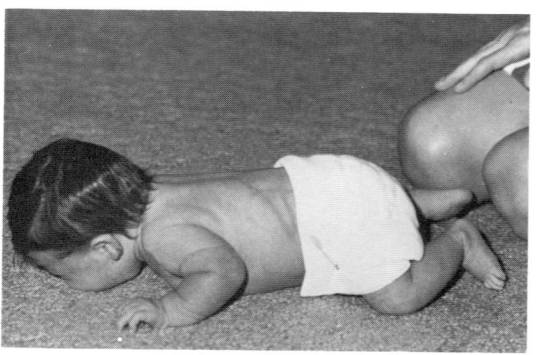

Figure 113

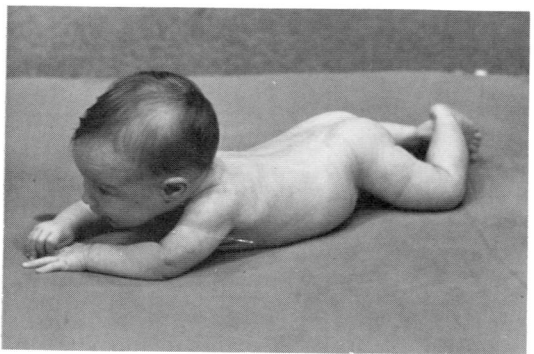

Figure 114

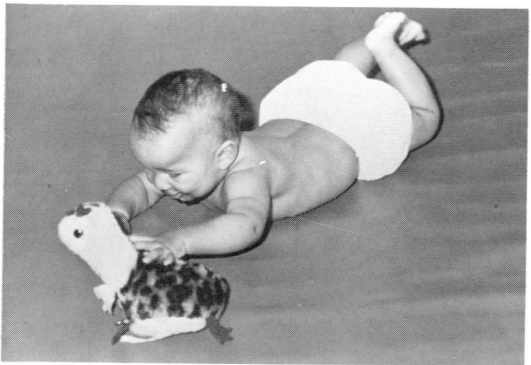

Figure 115

Tonic Labyrinthine—Prone

Contribution

Stimulation to flexor tone of total body (Fig. 113).

Counterbalance to extensor tone developing in supine position.

Balance is maintained (Fig. 114); this gives the stability that is necessary for prone development to proceed to higher levels (Fig. 115).

Persistence

Inability or compromised ability to dorsiflex head for righting reactions and to initiate extensor tone for higher reactions such as the Landau reaction and the symmetrical tonic neck reflex (Fig. 116).

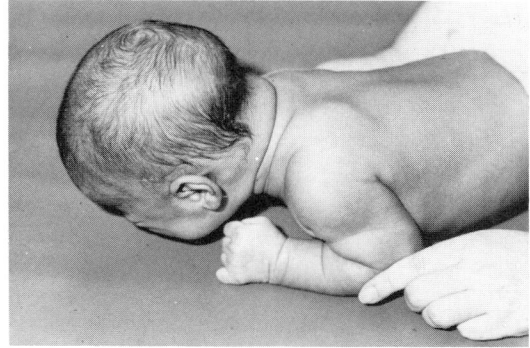

Figure 116

Prevents development of symmetrical tonic neck reflex (Fig. 117), which in turn enables extensor tone to develop for the prone-on-elbows position, to extend elbows, to heel-sitting, and the 4-point quadruped position.

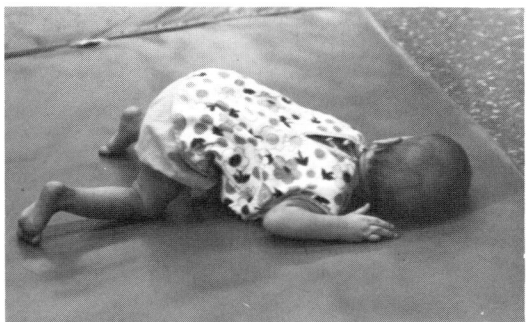

Figure 117

Shoulder protraction and inability to release the arms from under the body compromises function at higher levels (Fig. 118) or weight bearing in the prone position.

Unable to crawl due to inability to use upper limbs and to extend hips.

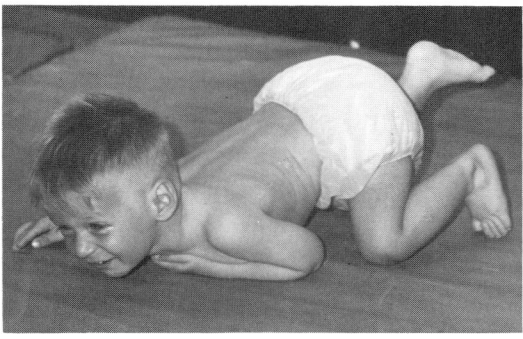

Figure 118

Tonic Neck Reflexes

Sensory input appears to be initiated by stretching of the muscles and joints of the neck. This information is relayed to the CNS via proprioceptive types of neurons.

These reflexes are considered as primary spinal cord reflexes since integration of stimuli and responses probably occurs within the upper segments of the cervical spine.

These reflexes, especially the asymmetrical tonic neck reflex, are normally seen in the premature infant and are more difficult to elicit in the term infant during the neonatal period. Generally, in the term infant, the asymmetrical tonic neck reflex will be seen from two weeks to four months.

The symmetrical tonic neck and the labyrinth system interact with each other to prevent disequilibrium and to detect the orientation and movements of the head. It is essential that the central nervous system receives appropriate information depicting the orientation of the head with respect to the body as well as the orientation of the different parts of the body with respect to each other. This information is transmitted by the proprioceptors of the neck and body.

Asymmetry or an exaggerated response at any time is a clear indication of abnormality in the CNS and is indicative of serious, disruptive sensorimotor development problems.

Symmetrical Tonic Neck Reflex (STN)

Contribution

As the tonic labyrinthine-prone reflex is being integrated, the STN develops.

As the neck is developing dorsiflexion, stimulated by the labyrinthine and optical righting reflexes, extensor tone is developing concurrently in the upper limbs and flexor tone in the lower limbs (Fig. 119).

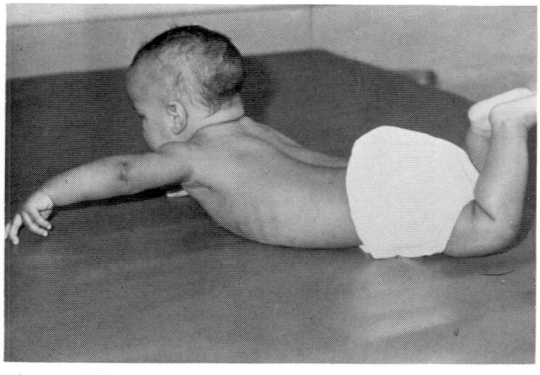

Figure 119

As the neck is ventroflexing, flexor tone in the upper limbs and extensor tone in the lower limbs is elicited (Fig. 120).

This creates a balance between flexors and extensors for stabile positions against gravity.

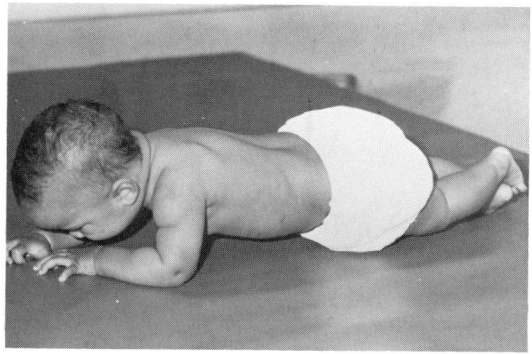

Figure 120

Motorically, the infant gradually develops prone-on-elbows (Fig. 121),

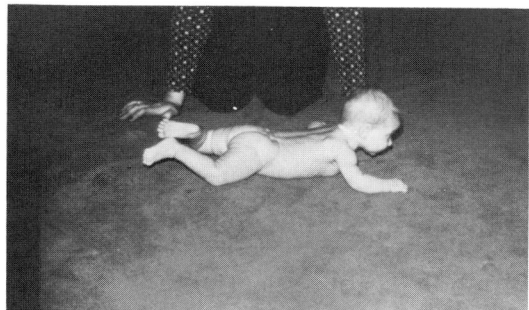

Figure 121

to extended elbows (Fig. 122),

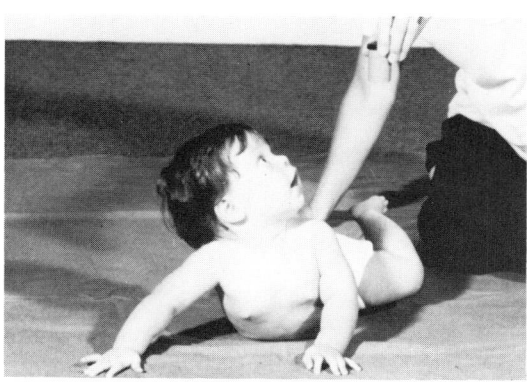

Figure 122

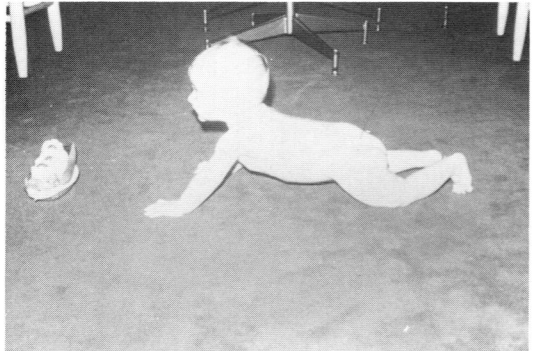

Figure 123

Figure 124

Figure 125

to 4-foot quadruped position (Fig. 123),

to reciprocal creeping (Fig. 124).

Persistence

Differentiating from the tonic labyrinthine-prone reflex, in the quadruped position with the head ventroflexed (Fig. 125), the child will collapse from flexion of the upper limbs and at times extension at the hips.

In this same position with the head dorsiflexed (Fig. 126), it is possible to bear weight on the extended upper limbs and flexed lower limbs and bunny hop, but it is not possible to creep with reciprocal movement.

Figure 126

If there is a delay in this process, either in the development of head righting or insufficient extensor and flexor tone (Fig. 127), this will compromise, delay, or negate higher motor functions.

Figure 127

Tonic Labyrinthine-Supine Reflex

Contribution

Develops extensor tone throughout the body to create balance between flexors and extensors (Fig. 128).

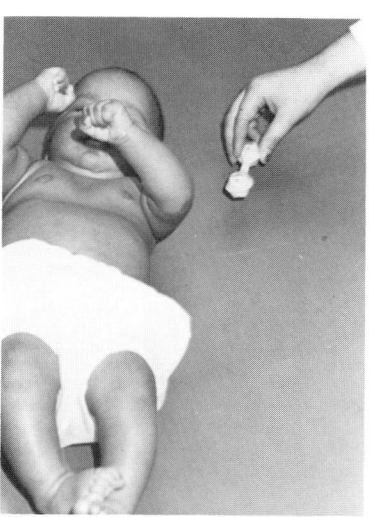

Figure 128

Figure 129

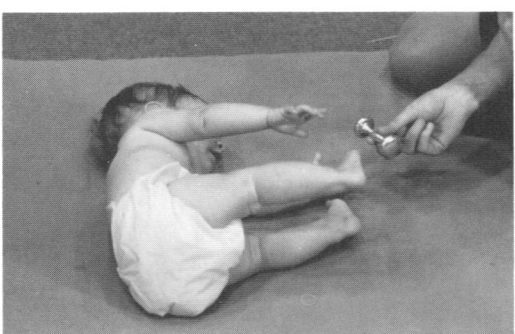

Figure 130

Figure 131

Creates ability to reach, bring limbs to midline, cross midline (**Fig. 129**).

Frees limbs for function away from the body, reach, spatial orientation, and direction (**Fig. 130**).

Enables initial rotation of the body for turning (**Fig. 131**).

Persistence

Persistent extensor tone will retract the shoulders and prevent or compromise head raising, limbs to the midline, rotation, and turning (Fig. 132).

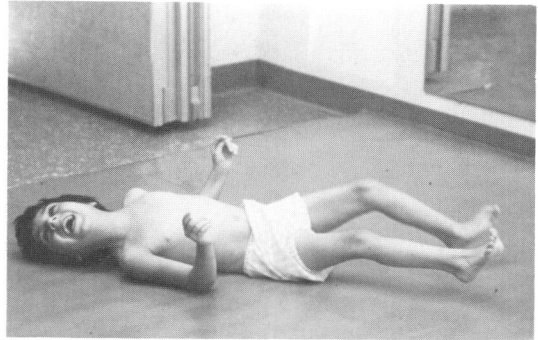

Figure 132

Ability to get to sitting is compromised or prevented (Fig. 133).

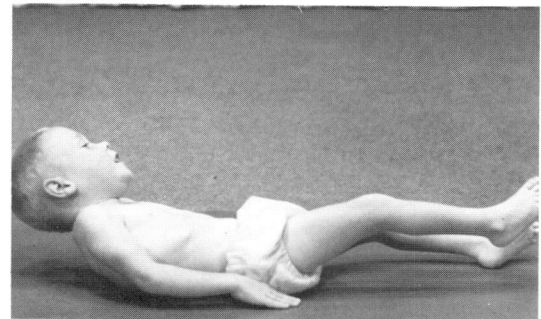

Figure 133

Can be seated with or without support, but the extensor thrust could cause the child to fall backwards (Fig. 134).

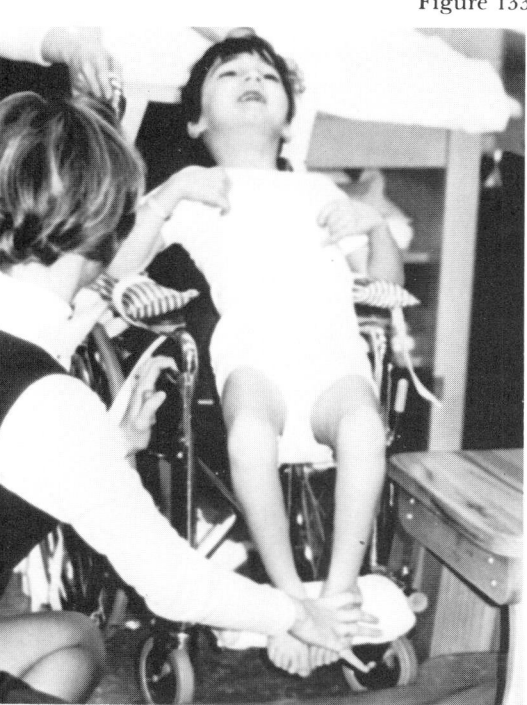

Figure 134

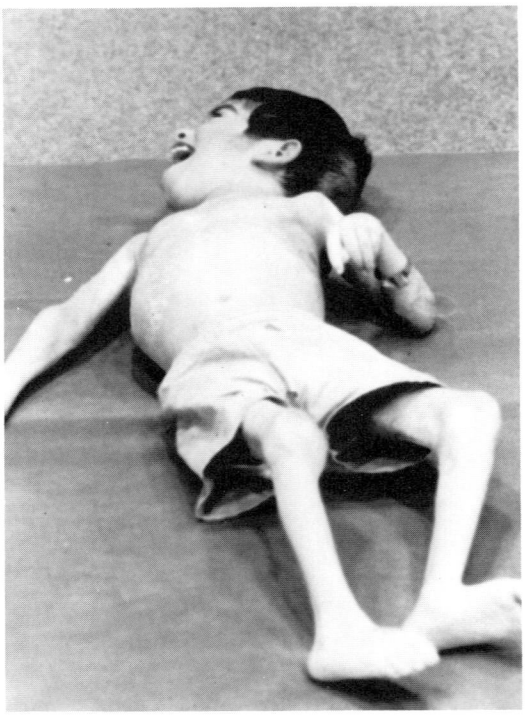

Combined with the asymmetrical tonic neck and the Galant reflexes, if all are persistent, this could initiate or reinforce a scoliosis and/or a subluxed hip and usually creates a windswept position of the lower limbs (both limbs turned in the same direction) (Fig. 135).

Figure 135

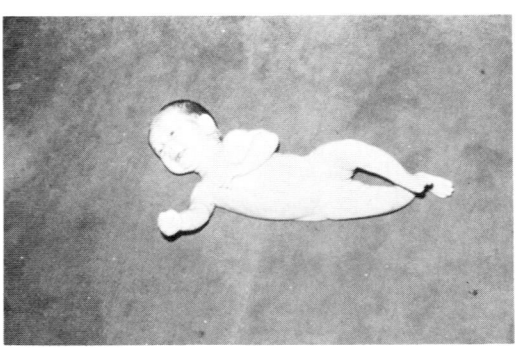

Figure 136

Asymmetrical Tonic Neck Reflex (ASTN)

Contribution

Breaks up the symmetrical flexion and extension patterns of movement (Fig. 136); helps develop alternation of these patterns.

Enables each side of body to be used separately.

Prepares the way for the integration of neck turning, visual fixation, and reaching (Fig. 137).

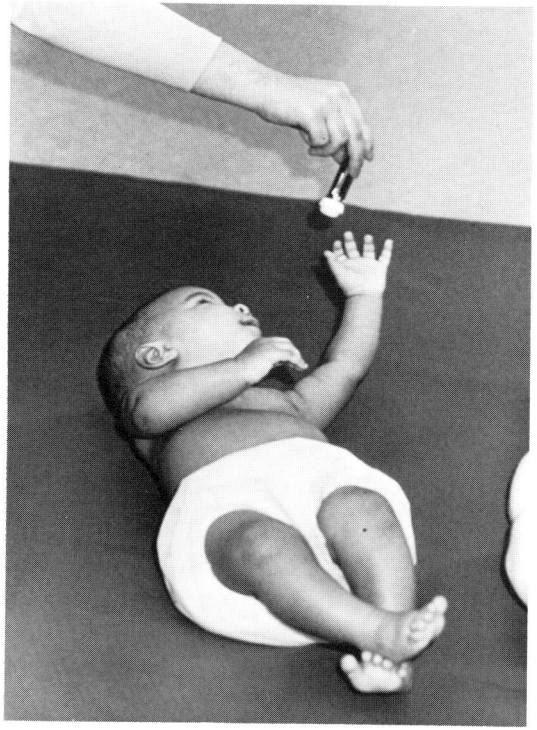

Figure 137

Fundamental to the establishment of visually directed reaching and eye-hand coordination (Fig. 138).

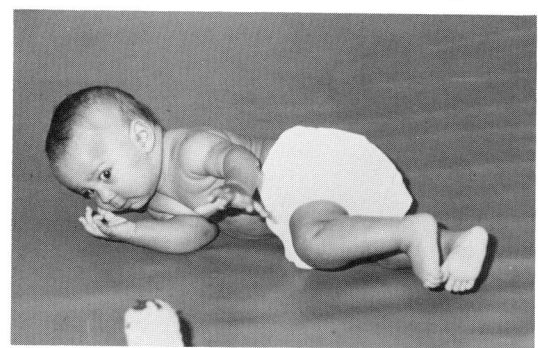

Figure 138

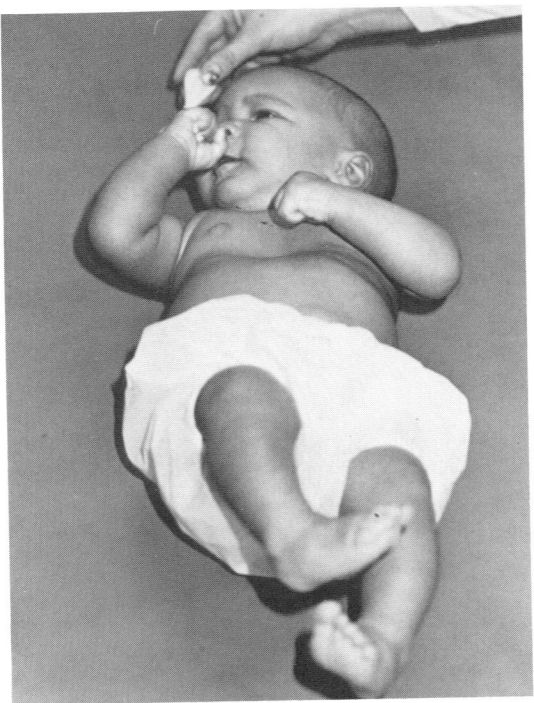

Figure 139

Initiates upper limbs to flex over the body to the midline and eventually to cross the midline (Fig. 139).

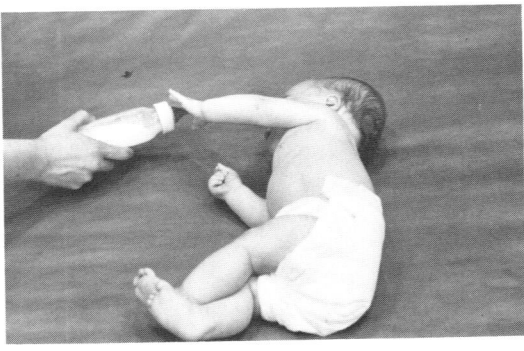

Figure 140

Coordinates with the tonic labyrinthine reflex for turning the body (Fig. 140).

Persistence

May compromise the ability of the flexed arm to reach the midline and/or cross the midline (due to limb retraction) (Fig. 141).

May compromise turning (flexed limb retracted.)

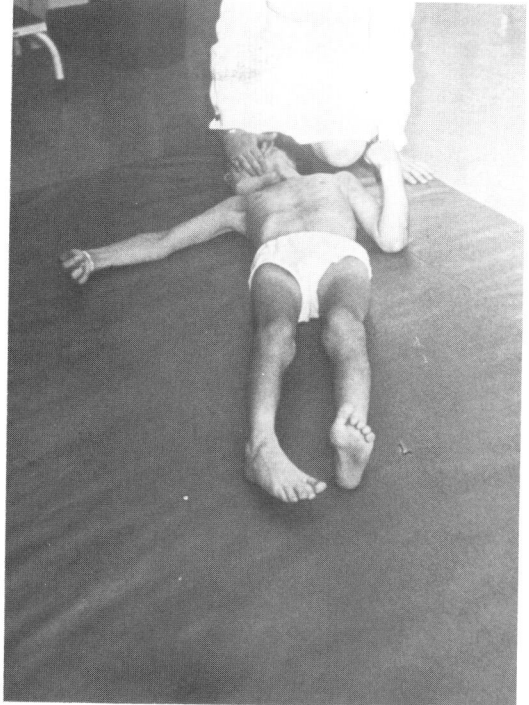

Figure 141

Loses visual fixation, ability to play with an object, or feed self, due to the necessity of turning the head to flex the limb to bring it close to the body (Fig. 142).

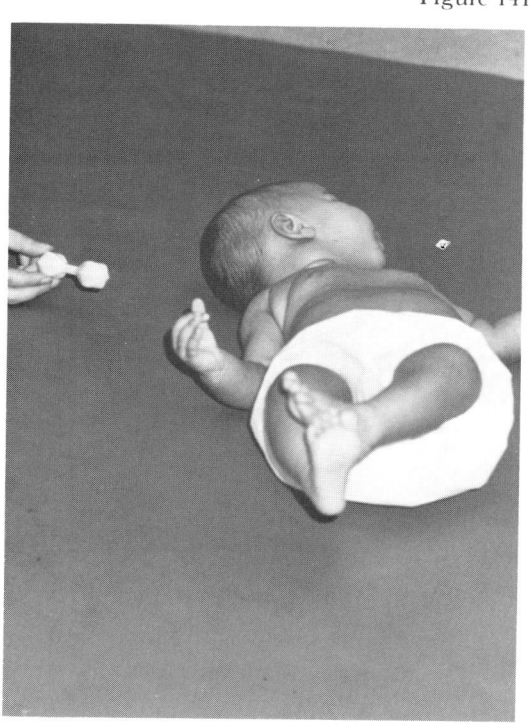

Figure 142

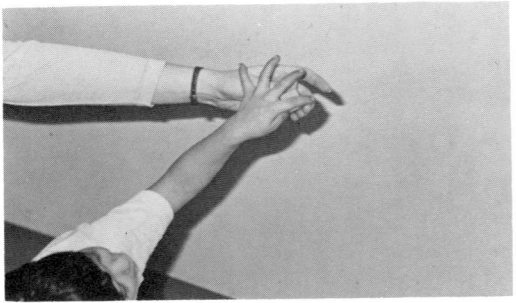

Figure 143

The child may have reach and/or visual fixation through the use of the ASTN, but may have difficulty with grasp (Fig. 143).

Figure 144

Difficulty in the quadruped (Fig. 144) and standing (Fig. 145) positions as loses weight-bearing control, and subsequently balance is lost.

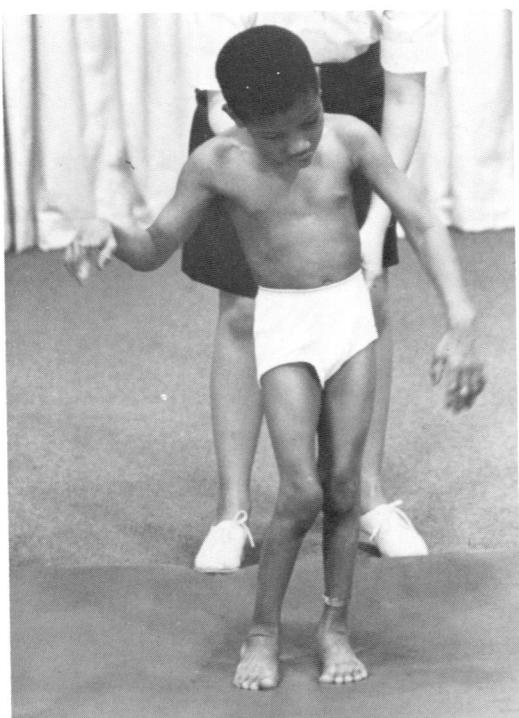

Figure 145

Can create or contribute to a scoliosis and/or a subluxed hip (Fig. 146). (Usually the curve is toward the occiput side. However, if both sides are influenced by the ASTN, the occiput side of the more involved musculature or the most maintained position will be at risk.

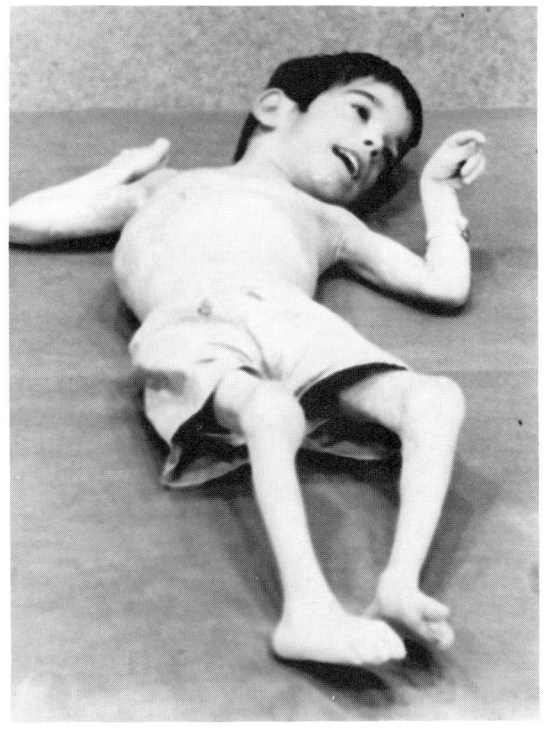

Figure 146

Landau Reaction

Mediation of the interaction of spinal and labyrinthine influences are not fully understood (Fig. 147).

Reaction may be absent with spinal cord abnormalities and with labyrinthine defects.

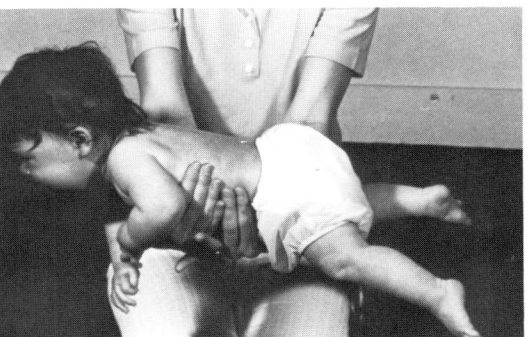

Figure 147

Contribution

The labyrinthine and optical righting reflexes right the head, following which the Landau reaction develops extensor tone in the musculature of the neck, to the trunk, to the hips, knees, ankles, and feet (Fig. 148).

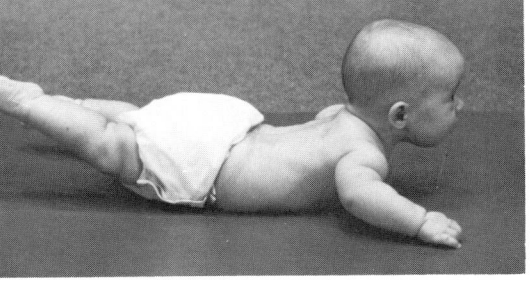

Figure 148

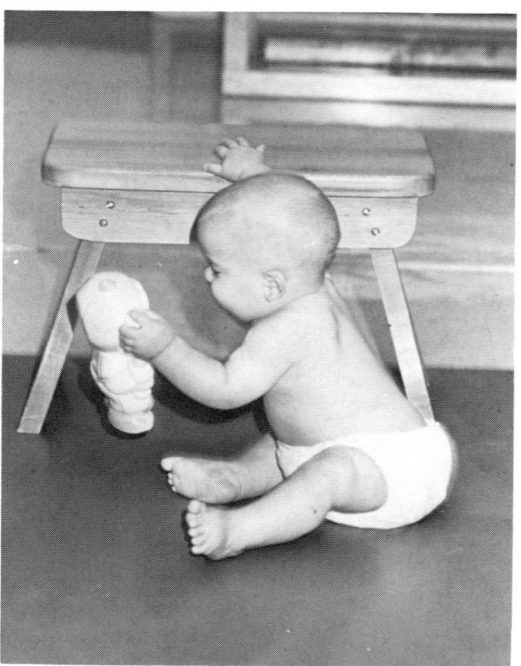

Figure 149

A precursor to good trunk extension for straight sitting (Fig. 149).

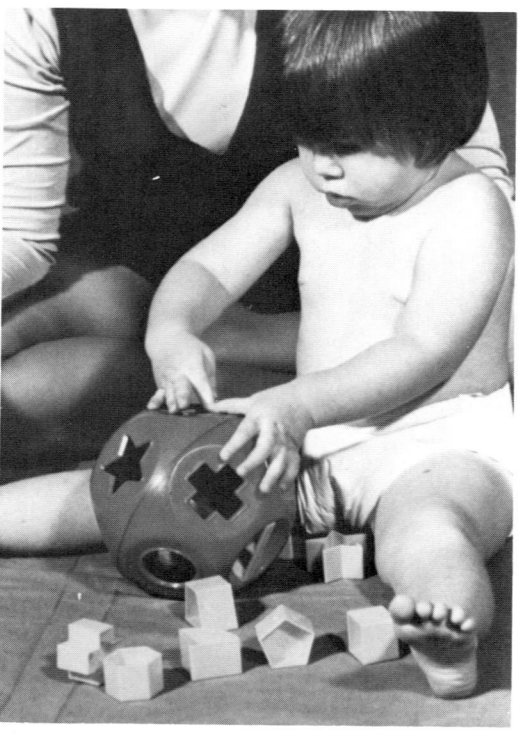

Figure 150

Develops the balance of flexors and extensors for stabile sitting, especially of the hip musculature (Fig. 150).

Absence

Creates a kyphotic position due to the lack of extension in the trunk and the hip musculature (Fig. 151).

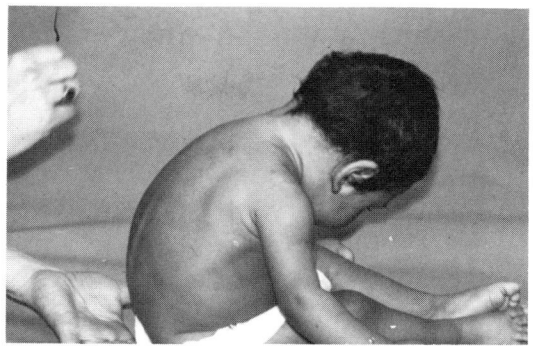

Figure 151

Lack of extensor tone creates unstable sitting (Fig. 152).

INTERESTING POINT: the Landau reaction stimulates extensor tone proximally to distally, and at the same time the positive supporting reflex is stimulating extensor tone distally to proximally. In this way sufficient extensor tone is developed to provide solid weight-bearing antigravity tone.

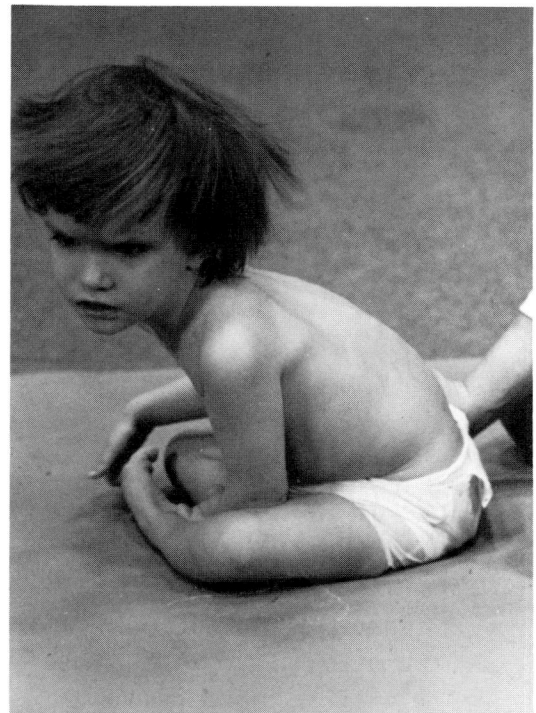

Figure 152

Chart 1 demonstrates the distribution of tone stimulated by the various reflexes. One and/or all of these reflexes affects every part of the trunk and limbs. Distribution of flexor and extensor tone over the entire body assures that every movement will have sufficient tone for balanced motion (within the planes indicated by these reflexes).

DISTRIBUTION OF TONE

REFLEX	MOVEMENT	PART	DISTRIBUTION
TONIC LABYRINTHINE-SUPINE	EXTENSION	BODY	TOTAL
LANDAU	EXTENSION	BODY	TOTAL
POSITIVE SUPPORTING	EXTENSION	LEGS-TRUNK	SYMMETRICAL
POSITIVE SUPPORTING-ARMS	EXTENSION	ARMS-HANDS	SYMMETRICAL
EXTENSOR THRUST	EXTENSION	LEGS	SYMMETRICAL
MAGNET	EXTENSION	LEGS	SYMMETRICAL
PRIMARY STEPPING	EXTENSION	LEGS	SYMMETRICAL
MORO	EXTENSION	ARMS-HANDS	SYMMETRICAL
PARACHUTE	EXTENSION	ARMS-HANDS	SYMMETRICAL
ULNAR RELEASE	EXTENSION-PRONATION	HANDS-FOREARMS	SYMMETRICAL
TONIC LABYRINTHINE-PRONE	FLEXION	BODY	TOTAL
FLEXOR WITHDRAWAL	FLEXION	LEGS	SYMMETRICAL
GALANT	FLEXION-LATERAL	LEG-TRUNK	SYMMETRICAL
PLACING	FLEXION	FEET-HANDS	SYMMETRICAL
GRASP	FLEXION	HANDS-ARMS	SYMMETRICAL
RADIAL RELEASE	FLEXION-SUPINATION	HANDS-FOREARMS	SYMMETRICAL
CROSSED EXTENSION	FLEXION-EXTENSION	LEGS	ASYMMETRICAL
SYMMETRICAL TONIC NECK	FLEXION-EXTENSION	LEGS-ARMS	ASYMMETRICAL
ASYMMETRICAL TONIC NECK	FLEXION-EXTENSION	LEGS-ARMS	ASYMMETRICAL

Chart 2 demonstrates that flexor and extensor tone develop sufficiently in the first four or six months after birth to create the balance necessary for the development of rotatory components of movement.

CNS PROCESSING

REFLEXES	TONE			MONTHS											
				1	2	3	4	5	6	7	8	9	10	11	12
MAGNET	E			X											
GALANT	F	R		X	X										
PRIMARY STEPPING	F	E		X	X										
ROOTING		R		X	X	X									
SUCKING	F			X	X	X									
PRIMITIVE GRASP	F			X	X	X	X								
CROSSED EXTENSION	F	E		X	X	X	X								
FLEXOR WITHDRAWAL	F			X	X	X	X								
ULNAR RELEASE	E			X	X	X	X								
RADIAL RELEASE	F			X	X	X	X								
TONIC LABYRINTHINE-PRONE	F			X	X	X	X								
TONIC LABYRINTHINE-SUPINE	E			X	X	X	X								
SYMMETRICAL TONIC NECK	F	E		X	X	X	X								
ASYMMETRICAL TONIC NECK	F	E		X	X	X	X								
MORO	E			X	X	X	X								
PLACING	F	E		X	X	X	X	X	X						
POSITIVE SUPPORTING	E			X		X	X	X	X	X	X				
POSITIVE SUPPORTING-ARMS	E					X	X	X	X	X	X				
LANDAU	E							X	X	X	X	X	X	X	X
PARACHUTE	E							X	X	X	X	X	X	X	X
NECK RIGHTING	R			X	X	X	X	X	X	X					
BODY RIGHTING ON THE BODY	R							X	X	X	X	X	X	X	X
BODY RIGHTING ON THE HEAD	R								X	X	X	X	X	X	X

Chapter IV

SEQUENTIAL INTERACTION OF REFLEXES

This chapter provides the reader with an example of development and distribution of tone as this relates to the influence of reflexes to sensorimotor development. A group of reflexes that interact and synthesize to provide the components for balanced movement and lead to sequential levels of development is discussed via photographs and an accompanying commentary. All reflexes are not indicated in each exercise, but the reader may incorporate any that may be pertinent to the specific sequence. Exercises 2 through 7 are presented for the reader who may wish to reproduce similar sequential interactions related to sensorimotor development similar to that demonstrated in the first exercise.

Exercise 1: Basic reflexes that need to be integrated for normal prone to sitting positions.

a. Tonic labyrinthine-prone reflex: reflexive flexor tone developing to balance extensor tone.

b. Galant reflex: initial rotation; lateral flexion; amphibian movement enables reciprocal pattern for crawling, creeping, walking; asymmetry of movement.

c. Labyrinthine and optical righting on the head: neck extension; development of extensor tone with subsequent influence from the symmetrical tonic neck reflex and Landau reaction.

d. Symmetrical tonic neck reflex: development of flexor and extensor tone in upper and lower limbs to progress from prone, to prone-on-elbows, to extended elbows, to quadruped positions.

e. Landau reaction: development of extensor tone in muscles of the trunk, hips, and lower limbs as a prerequisite to sitting and standing.

Figures 153, 154, and 155 demonstrate the tonic labyrinthine and Galant reflexes and the Landau reaction in the initial stages of development.

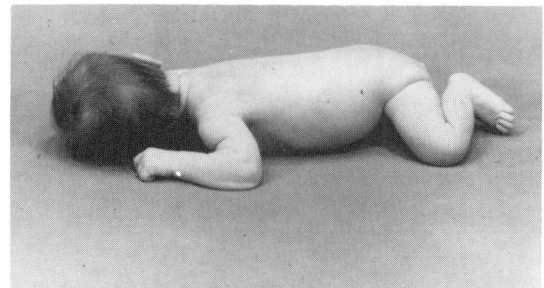

Figure 153

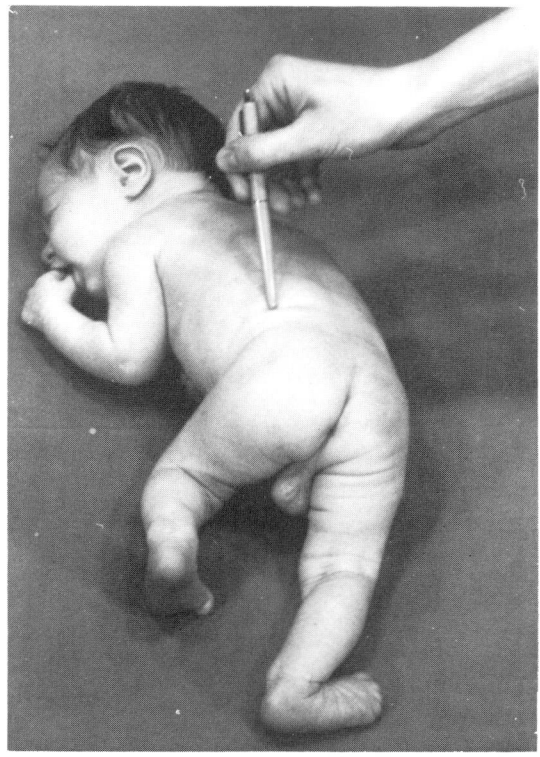

Figure 154

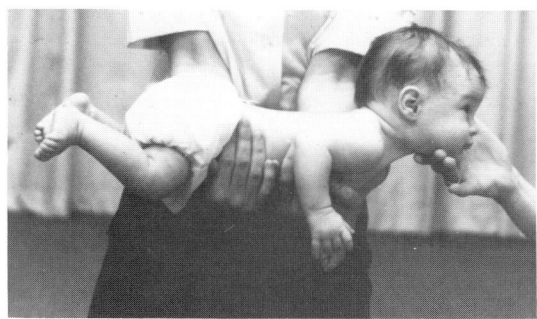

Figure 155

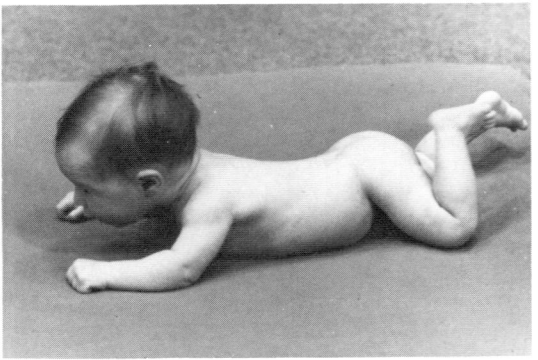

Neck extension to 45°; the STN reflex influences extensor tone to the upper limbs, may assume the prone-on-elbows position; flexor tone increases in hips and in lower limbs, but the position of these limbs is less abducted; weight bearing is beginning; influence of the Galant reflex in this position; weight bearing on the upper part of the body continues; initial scapular stability (Fig. 156).

Figure 156

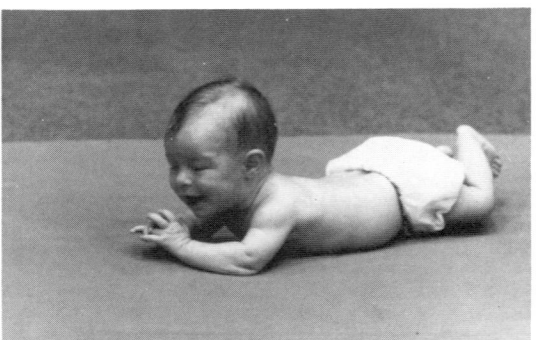

Neck extension to 90°; upper limbs continue prone-on-elbows position, but limbs are closer to the body; hands are coming to the midline; less flexion at the hips (Fig. 157).

Figure 157

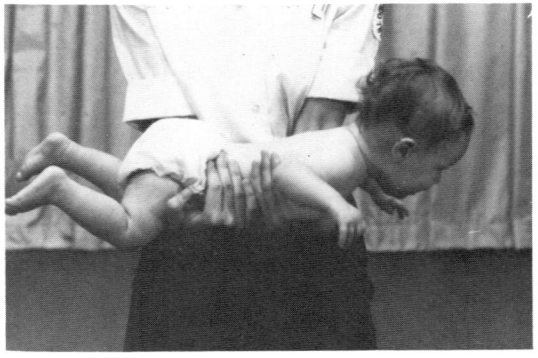

Trunk extension progressing distally due to Landau influence (Fig. 158), which predisposes a less kyphotic curve in the trunk when child is placed in the sitting position.

Figure 158

Increased active head righting influences extensor tone in upper limbs (Fig. 159), i.e. position of extended elbows (influence of positive support—upper limbs for increased extension distal to proximal).

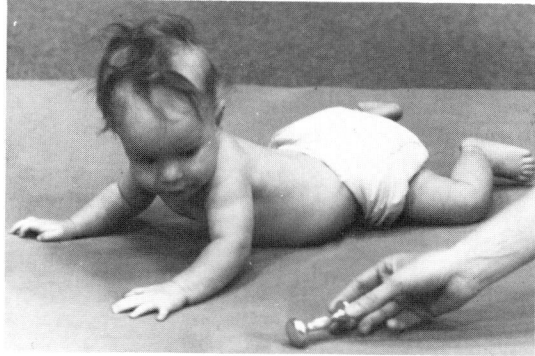

Figure 159

Ability to flex or extend neck (head righting) to initiate turning, with complete neck rotation but minimal initiation of rotation in upper trunk (Fig. 160); weight transfer on lateral side (initiates body righting on the head); use of extensor tone to assist in turning; asymmetry of movement (Fig. 161) (Galant and crossed extension reflexes) and turning is complete, prone to supine.

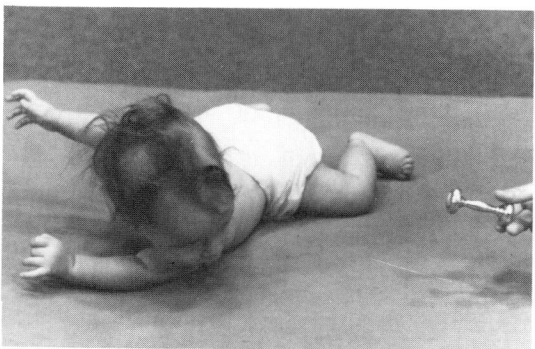

Figure 160

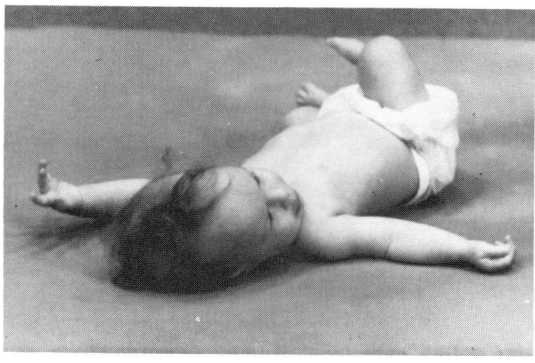

Figure 161

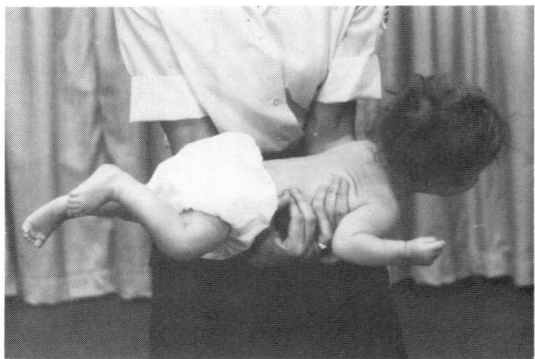

Increased extensor tone at trunk, hips, and knees (Landau reaction) (Fig. 162) that leads to the ability to sit with support (Fig. 163); trunk is less kyphotic; upper limbs have sufficient extensor tone to support body by propping.

Figure 162

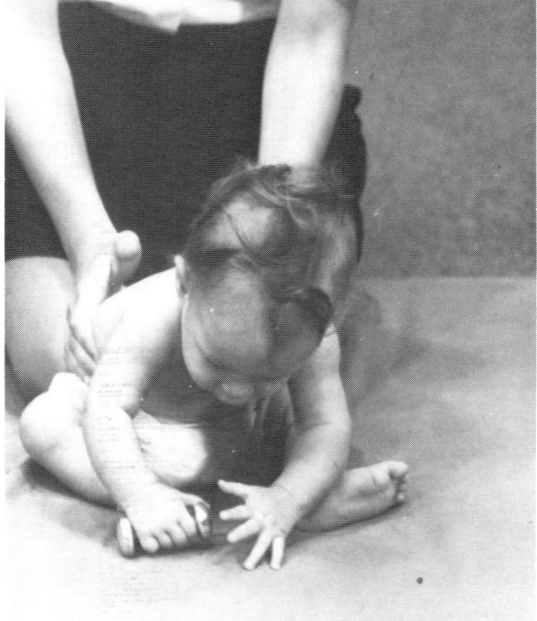

Figure 163

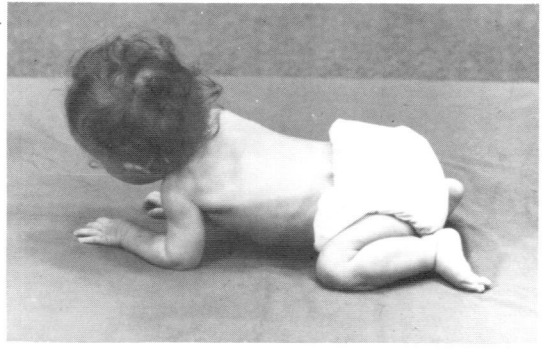

Initial ability to assume the quadruped position indicates the increase in balance between flexor and extensor musculature (Fig. 164); upper limbs are positioned under shoulders, but hips continue to be in abducted position.

Figure 164

STN influence with balanced tone for antigravity quadruped position/trunk rotation, weight transfer and weight bearing on one side to allow function on contralateral side (Fig. 165); dissociated movement of all limbs from the trunk enabled by asymmetry of movement; results in eye-hand coordination (influence of ASTN) and extension of fingers plus pronation (influence of ulnar release reflex). Side propping by upper limb and protective reaction available if needed.

Figure 165

Extensor tone exists at this time, cephalo-caudally, i.e., down the trunk, spreads to hips and knees, especially under stress (Fig. 166).

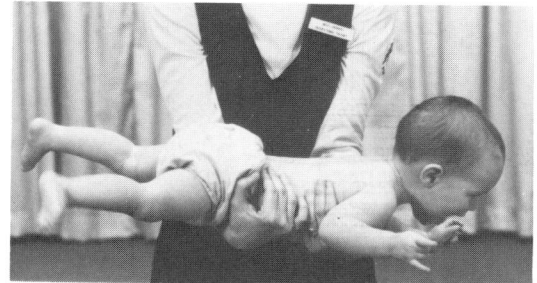

Figure 166

This predisposes straight-back independent sitting (Fig. 167), pelvis functionally dissociated from the trunk; freedom of upper extremities to function in any plane.

Figure 167

The following exercises each indicate the basic reflexes that need to be integrated for normal function.

Exercise 2: supine position to turning to prone position.
a. Crossed extension reflex
b. Tonic labyrinthine-supine reflex
c. Labyrinthine and optical righting on the head

Exercise 3: supine position, to turning, to eye-hand coordination.
a. Rooting reflex
b. Neck righting
c. Asymmetrical tonic neck reflex

Exercise 4: supine position to supported sitting position.
a. Moro reflex
b. Propping reaction
c. Parachute reaction
d. Positive support—upper limbs reflex

Exercise 5: standing position to walking.
a. Primary standing reflex
b. Positive supporting reflex
c. Negative supporting reflex

Exercise 6: hand function—grasp to release.
a. Primitive grasp reflex
b. Ulnar release reflex
c. Radial release reflex

Exercise 7: head orientation in space.
a. Labyrinthine and optical righting on the head
b. Body righting on the head

Chapter V
NORMAL DEVELOPMENT

This chapter presents an overview of a monthly account of development with special reference to the regulation of the degree, strength, balance, and distribution of tone as it relates to sensorimotor development. Average monthly ages are specified. However, this is relative and merely gives a perspective in relation to the approximate time for each developmental stage. It is more important to consider the sequential developmental stages for each child, depending on his/her own rate of change. Specific time should not be of major importance. Refer to Chapter III for correlating development and distribution of tone.

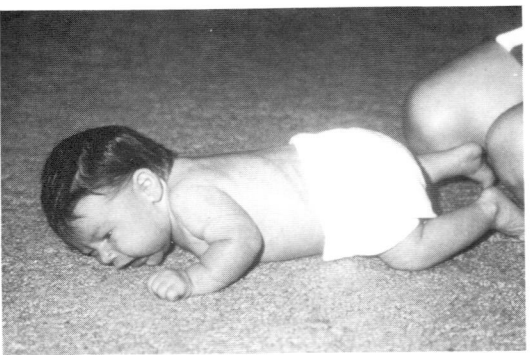

Figure 168

Neonate—One Month

Extension:

Momentary neck extension, a protective reaction (Fig. 168). Reflexive flexion posture, no functional muscle control has developed; hips are flexed with weight bearing on head and upper limbs.

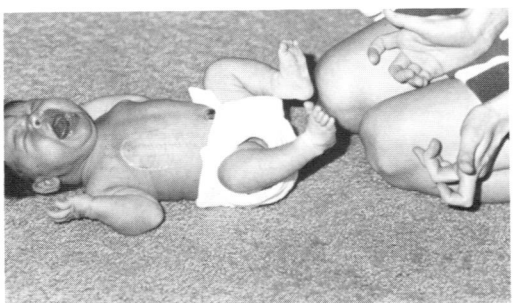

Figure 169

Flexion:

Symmetrical in supine (Fig. 169); limbs retracted assuming position of abduction and flexion.

Pronounced head lag; rounding of the back, no extensor tone (Fig. 170).

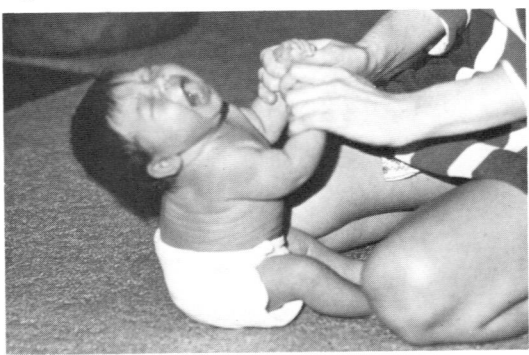

Figure 170

Rotation:

No rotation except for neck righting (rotation of head) (Fig. 171); rooting reflex stimulates rotation.

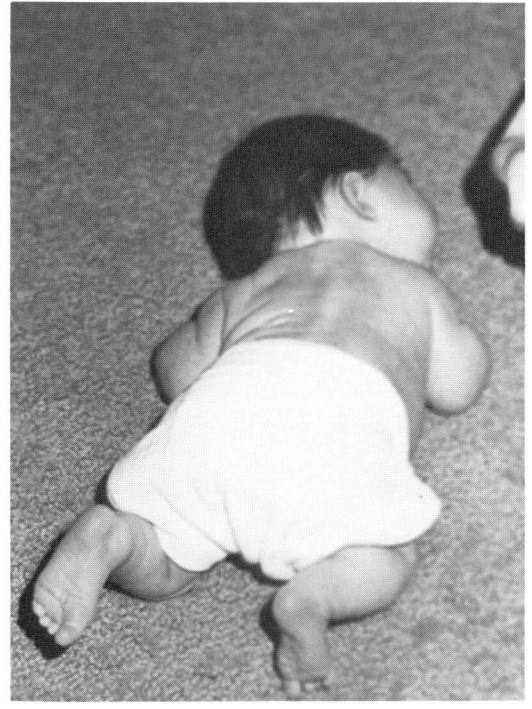

Figure 171

Hands:

Fisted mostly, grasp reflex (Fig. 172).

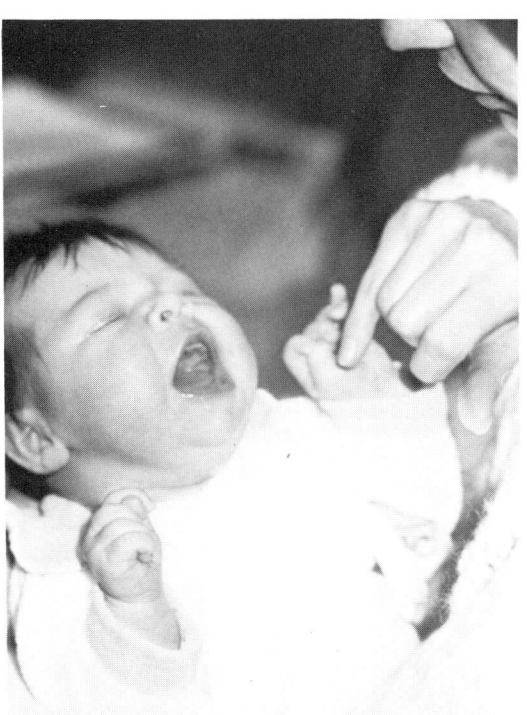

Figure 172

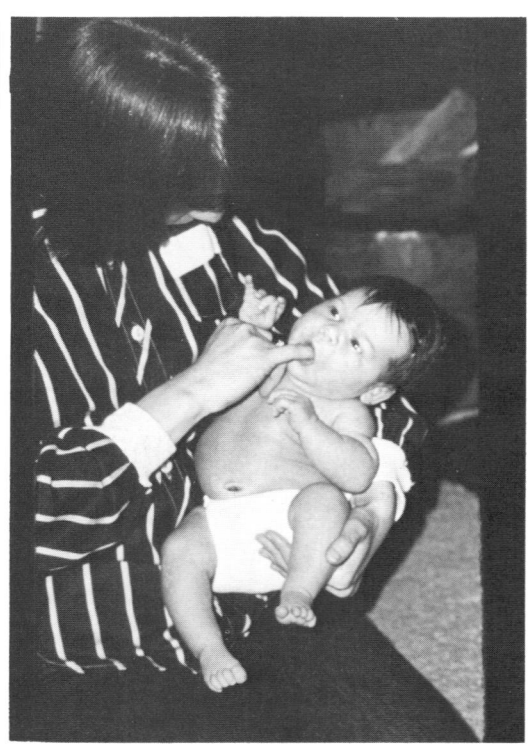

Figure 173

Eyes:

Able to focus within a limited range, nonconjugate vision common (Fig. 173).

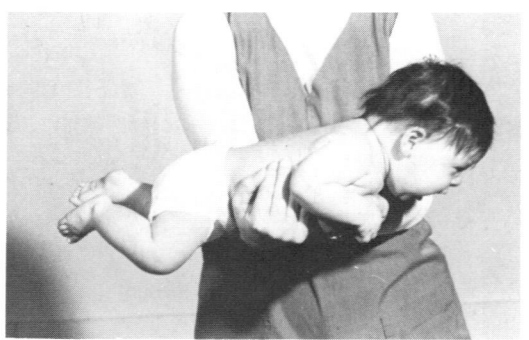

Figure 174

Two Months

Extension:

Neck extension developed to 45°; extension developing down trunk and upper limbs (STN); still no scapular stabilization (Fig. 174).

Back less rounded in sitting (due to extensor tone developing) (Fig. 175).

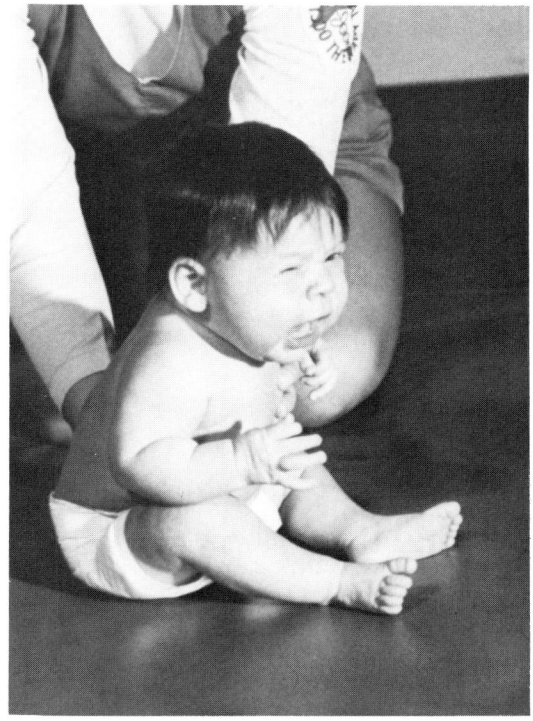

Figure 175

Flexion:

Lack of flexor control (Fig. 176).

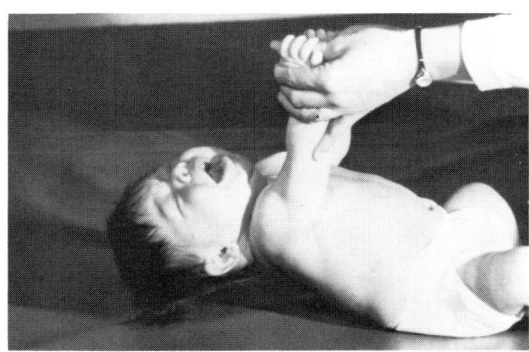

Figure 176

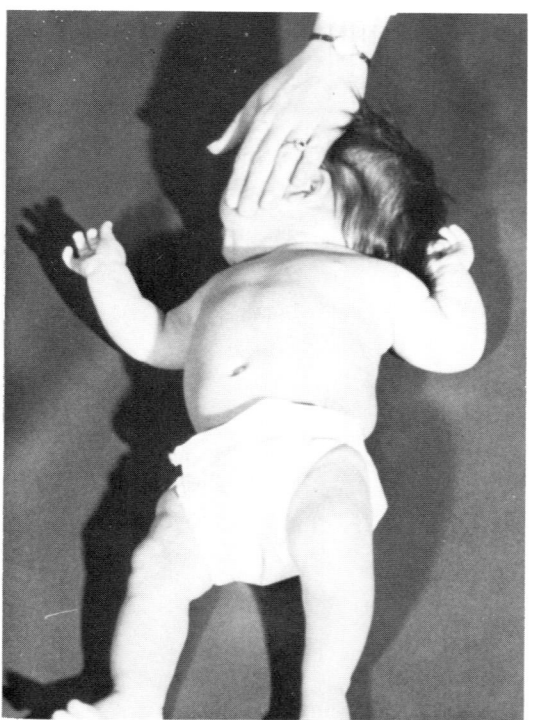

Figure 177

Patterns of flexion and extension with neck rotation from ASTN; weight bearing on face side (Fig. 177). Limbs retracted, away from body; flexor side may bring limb forward (ASTN).

Rotation:

Lateral flexion (Fig. 178), initial rotation influenced by the Galant and rooting reflexes.

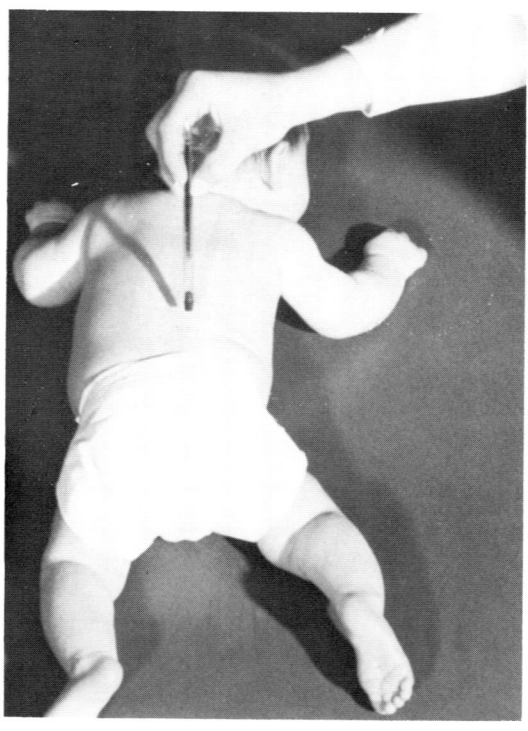

Figure 178

Hands:

Reflexive grasp (Fig. 179); hands maintain flexed position.
Involuntary release.

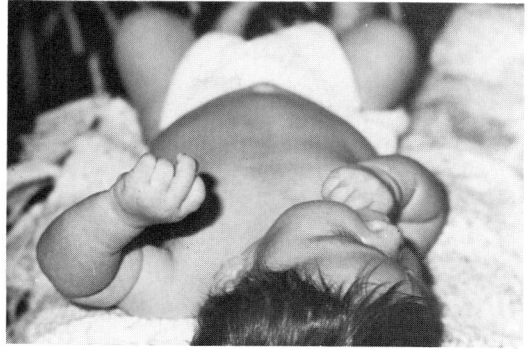

Figure 179

Eyes:

Focusing improved (Fig. 180); localization and coordination of hearing and vision.

Figure 180

Follows moving object to midline (neck rotation, disassociation of head from the trunk) (Fig. 181).

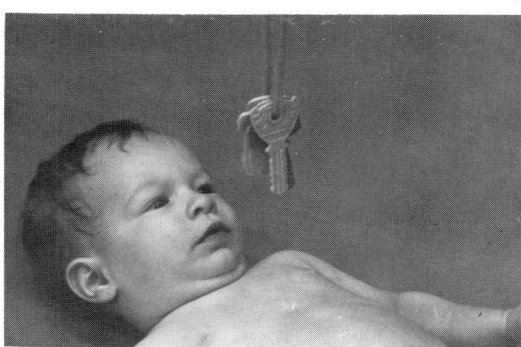

Figure 181

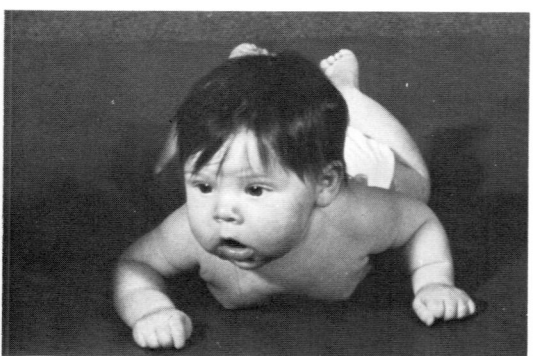

Figure 182

Three Months

Extension:

Neck extension, chin tucked (STN); increased extension in back and upper limbs (Landau); upper limbs move forward and bear weight; scapular stabilization; less flexion at hips but not full weight bearing as yet (Fig. 182).

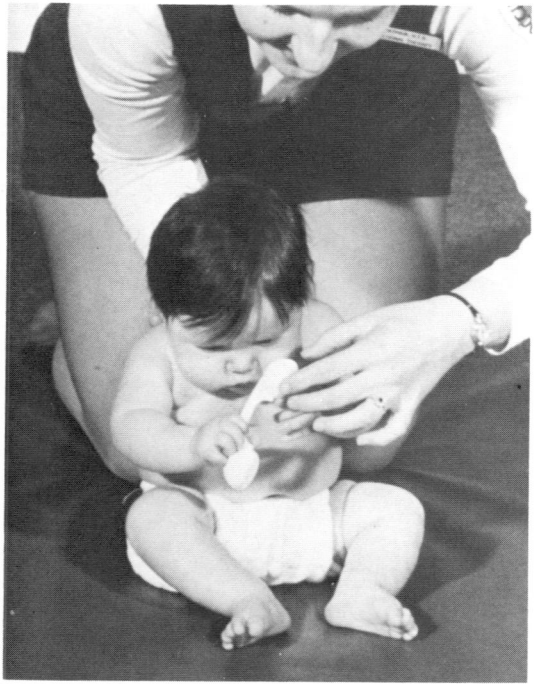

Figure 183

Flexion:

Increased flexion control; improved balance between flexors and extensors; head has a more midline orientation (Fig. 183).

Hands coming together to midline (STN), especially when holding a toy; eyes focus in midline.

Head in alignment with trunk.

Rotation:

Weight bearing on forearms; head turning creates weight shift; sensation of rotation beginning (Fig. 184); (if unable to shift weight, rotation may not develop).

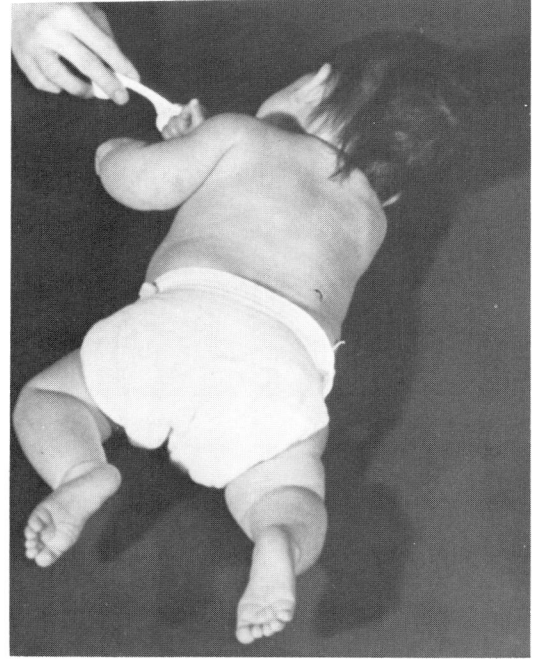

Figure 184

Hands:

Reaches out with both upper limbs (Fig. 185); lunges at object and can make contact; may or may not be able to grasp.

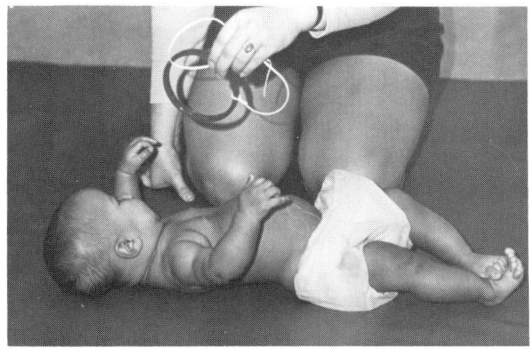

Figure 185

Brings hands together and looks at them (influence of STN); might suck fingers or fists or mouth object (Fig. 186).

Beginning to pull at clothing; continues to "scratch" surface, such as mother's breast when feeding (palmo-mandibular reflex).

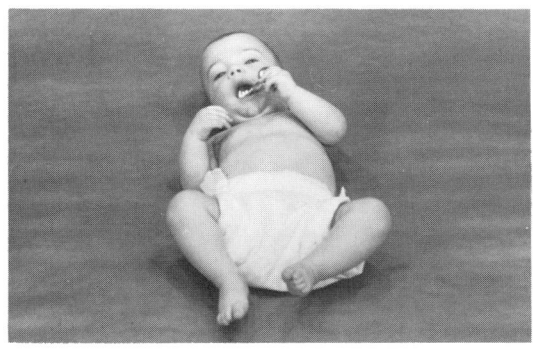

Figure 186

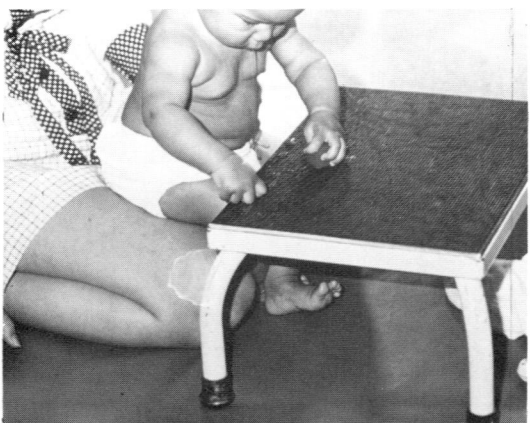

Figure 187

Retains object using an ulnar grasp as opposed to the palmar reflex grasp (Fig. 187).

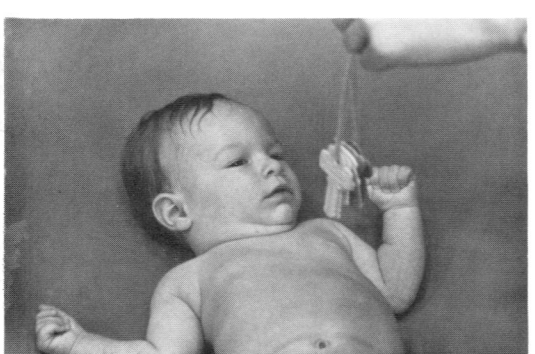

Figure 188

Eyes:

Follows slow moving object through 180°; may see head rotating with eyes (Fig. 188).

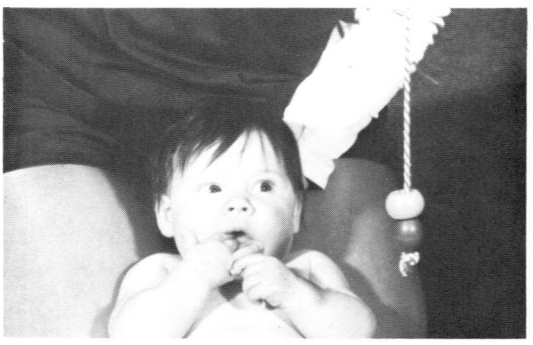

Figure 189

"Reaches" with eyes when held in sitting position (Fig. 189).

Four Months

Extension:

Increased extension at trunk (Landau reaction); neck and limbs extended (Fig. 190).

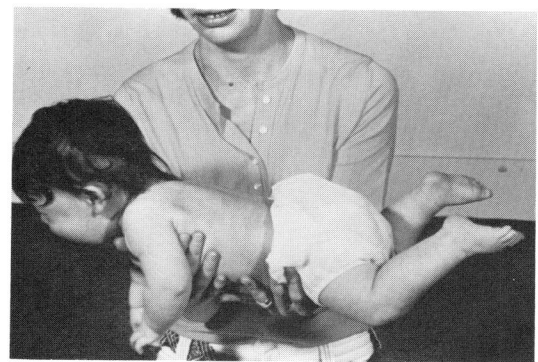

Figure 190

Hands to midline, increased adduction, elbows in line with shoulders (STN) (Fig. 191).

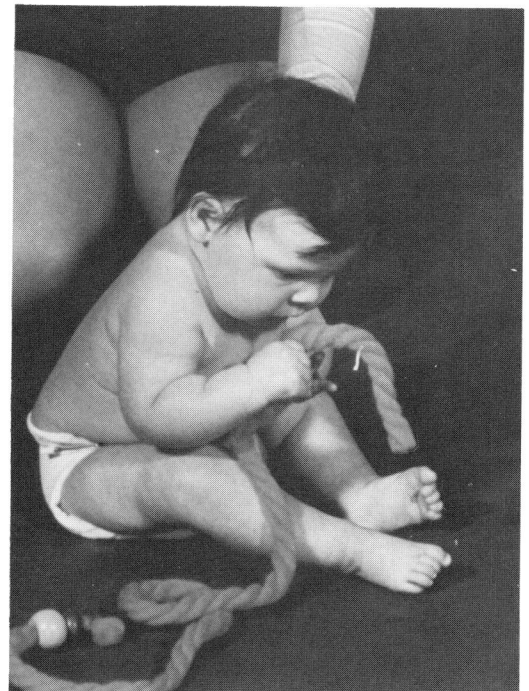

Figure 191

Able to arch back in supine (Fig. 192); this gives pelvic stability and mobility; weight bearing on heels, disassociation between upper and lower extremities has increased. (Need anterior and posterior mobility in pelvis before rotation develops in pelvic girdle. Children with cerebral palsy generally have no pelvic mobility, so lack alternate flexion and extension patterns and subsequently fail to have rotation).

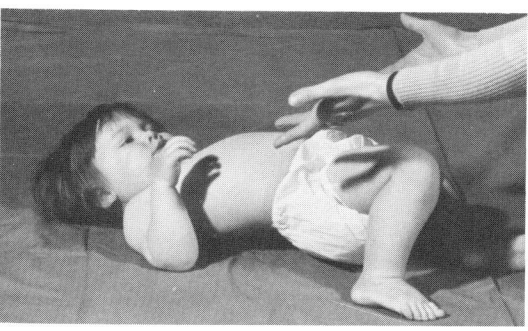

Figure 192

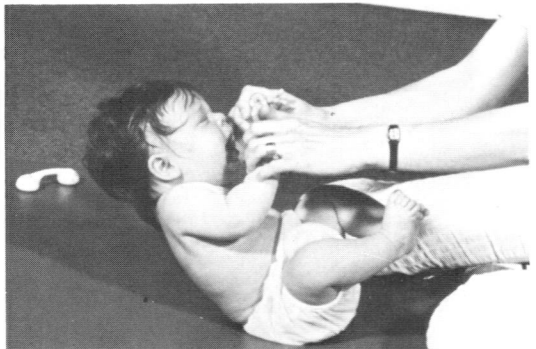

Figure 193

Flexion:

Increased flexor control; head in midline; lower limbs continue to be abducted; asymmetrical movement of these extremities crossing over (ASTN, crossed extension); increased weight shift (Fig. 193).

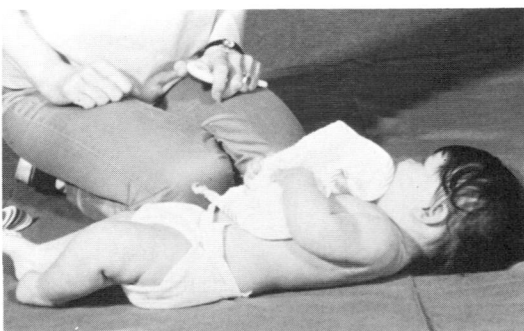

Figure 194

Hands and upper limbs more in the midline; scapular stability; increased extension in supine (Fig. 194).

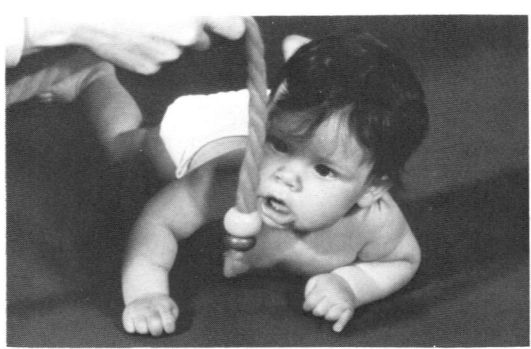

Figure 195

Rotation:

Increasing weight shift bilaterally; chin tucked in (Fig. 195).

Hands:

Gross grasp with emphasis continuing on ulnar side (Fig. 196).

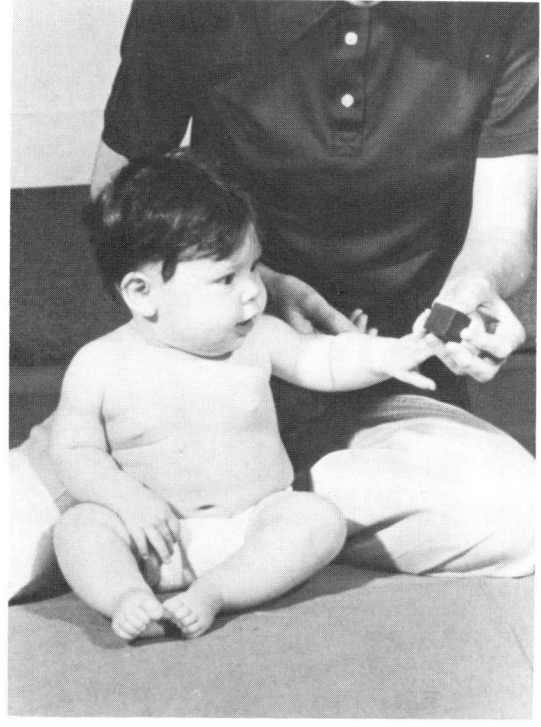

Figure 196

Upper limb and hand extend beyond body; will then press against opposite hand or body (Fig. 197).

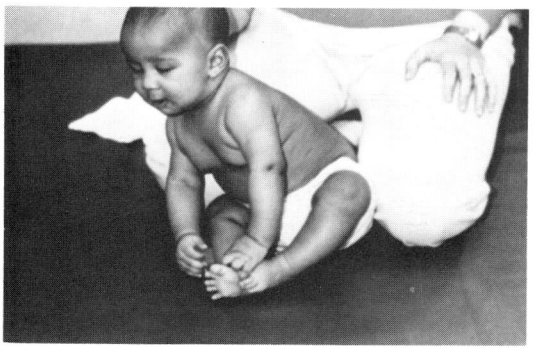

Figure 197

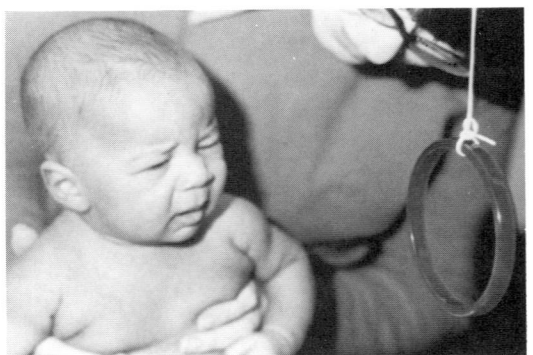

Figure 198

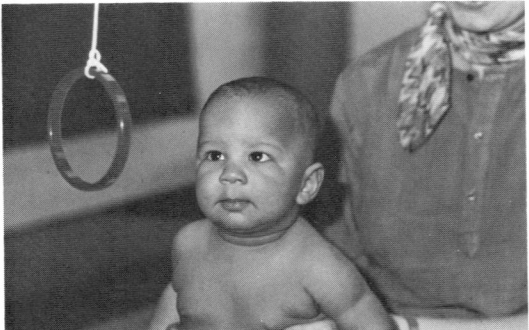

Figure 199

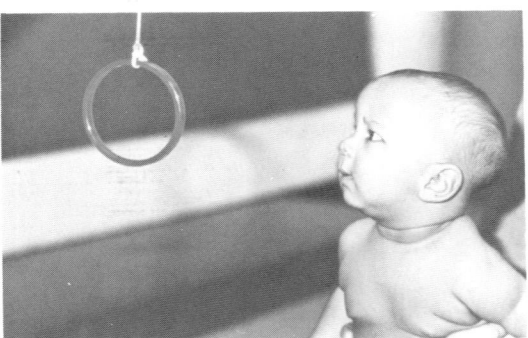

Figure 200

Eyes:

Eyes follow object smoothly (Fig. 198); can rotate neck (Fig. 199) freely (Fig. 200).

Five Months

Extension:

Sitting, less support, increased extension in lower back (Landau); increased stability of scapula with increased facility of limbs reaching forward (Fig. 201).

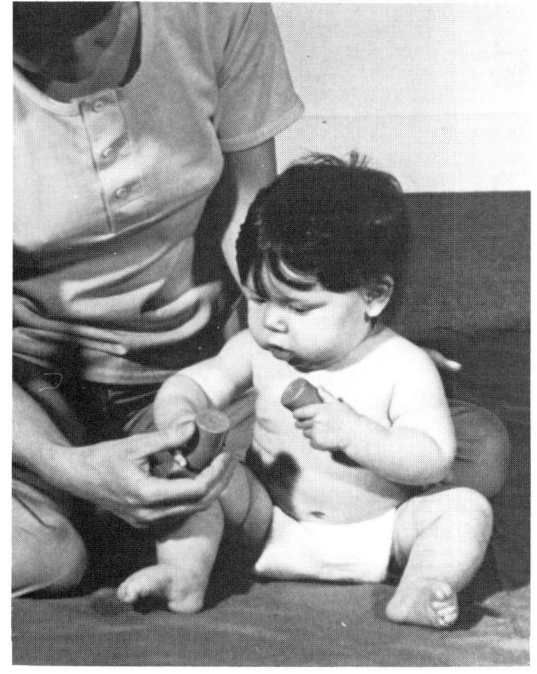

Figure 201

Shifting weight on forearms (positive support of arms, propping); reaching with hands open (ulnar release); lower extremities continue with abduction, external rotation; less flexion in hips, neck stabile; equilibrium reaction beginning in the prone position (Fig. 202).

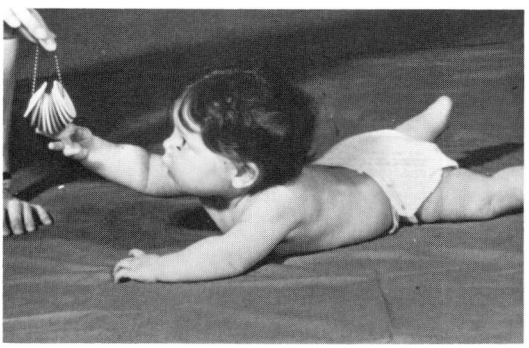

Figure 202

Foot to mouth causes elongation of lower spine and neck (Fig. 203); helps development of trunk extension and abdominal musculature, disassociation of pelvis to trunk.

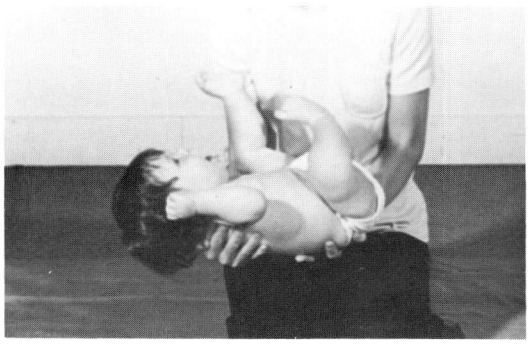

Figure 203

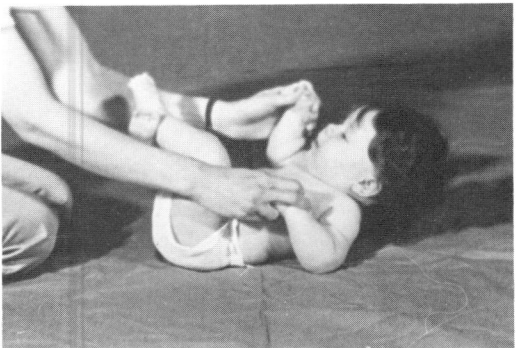

Figure 204

Flexion:

Pull to sit with no head lag (Fig. 204); starting to lift and flex lower extremities; abdominal control developing with pelvic mobility that begins with flexion of the lower extremities.

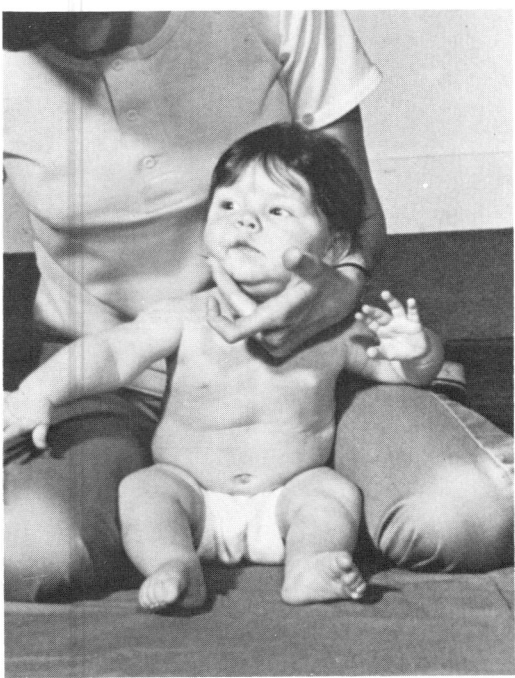

Figure 205

Continues to have a baby belly (Fig. 205), needs flexor control (abdominals).

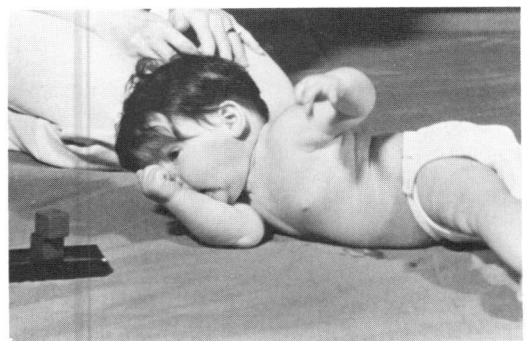

Figure 206

Rotation:

Weight shift-sidelying (Fig. 206); rotation in upper trunk, subtle movements; stability and mobility developing in shoulder girdle; in sidelying, shoulders retract; can roll back to supine. Rolling prone to supine:
a. neck extension initiates movement; weight shift; rotation; may lose balance and roll over (not sufficient control in flexors to catch balance).

Have neck flexion in supine to start roll.

b. use Landau to roll over, starting with neck extension; goes past midline; rolls over like a log.

Hands:

Grasps object dangled in front of face (Fig. 207).

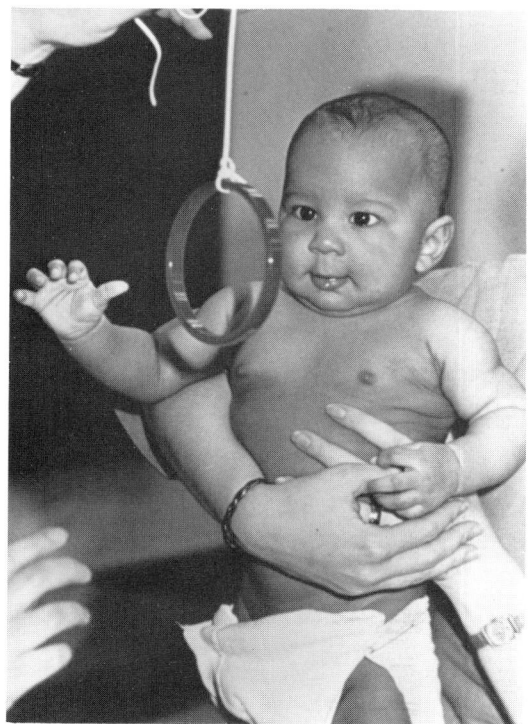

Figure 207

Uses palmar grasp with increased use of radial digits (Fig. 208).

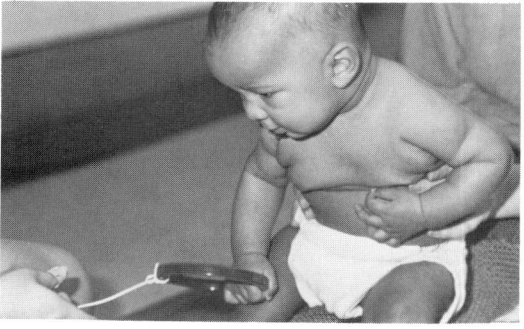

Figure 208

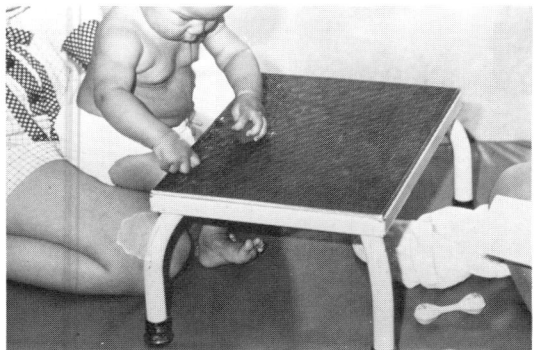

Figure 209

Forearm may be in neutral position (Fig. 209).

Figure 210

Can lift a cube, slap, pat, and do raking movement with fingers (Fig. 210).

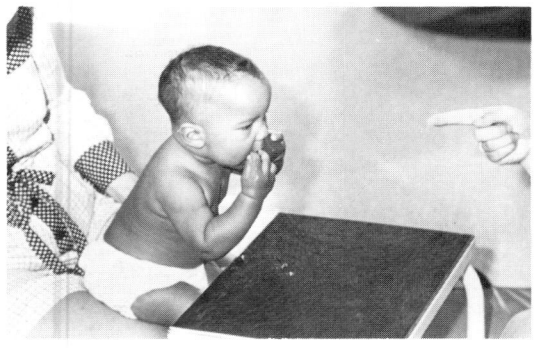

Figure 211

Continues to use a bilateral hand approach (Fig. 211). (All of these hand movements are due to development of ulnar and radial release reflexes.)

Eyes:

Maintains fixation on self (Fig. 212), although not necessarily on a stationary object if a distracting influence is present (Fig. 213).

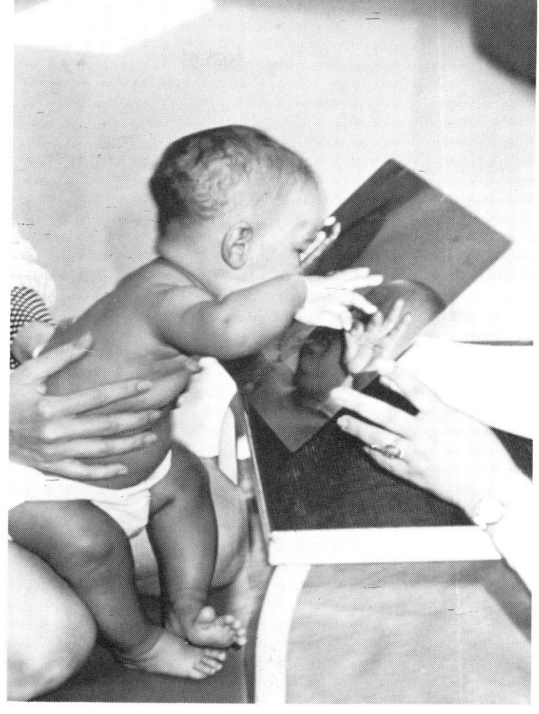

Figure 212

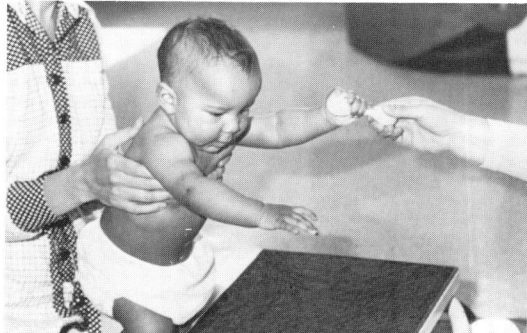

Figure 213

Six Months

Extension:

Influence of STN in the upper and lower extremities (Fig. 214). Landau is stronger with more scapular stability with the extension; must have trunk extension to have mobility in the upper extremities.

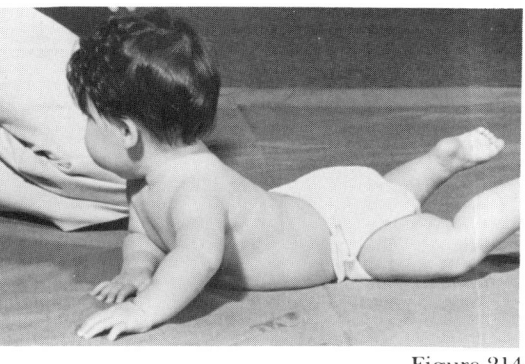

Figure 214

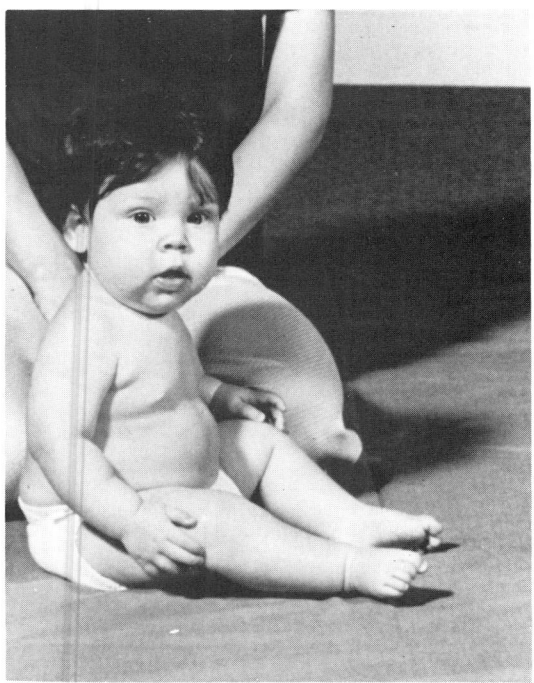

Figure 215

Sits with back straighter due to balance in flexion and extension increasing including the hips (Landau) (Fig. 215).

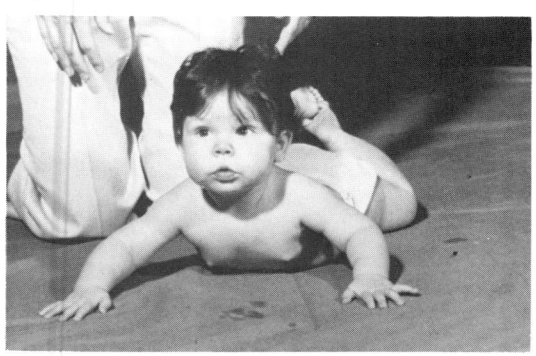

Figure 216

Elbow extension (STN) (Fig. 216); mobility of upper limbs in prone position enables pushing backwards; added scapular stability; pressure on palms gives added extensor tone to upper limbs for weight bearing.

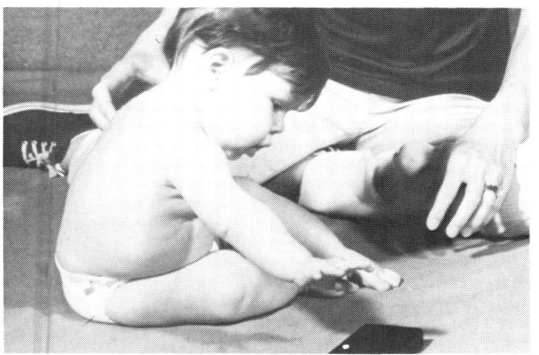

Figure 217

Protective extension in forward plane, propping, hands open (Fig. 217).

Stands weight bearing (positive supporting) (Fig. 218).

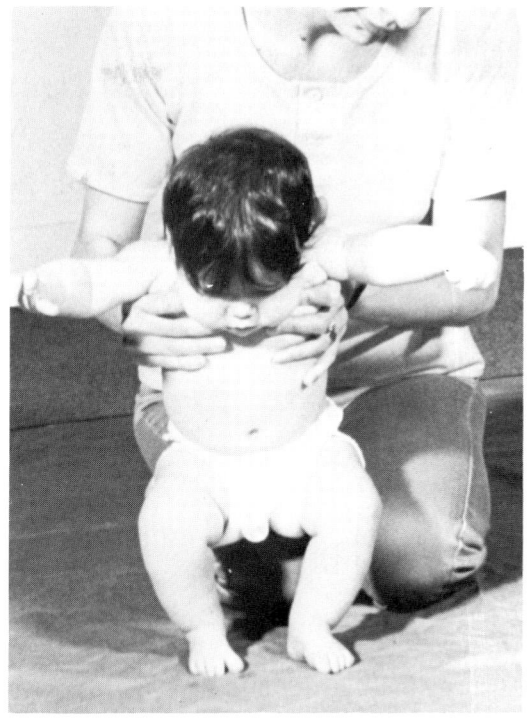

Figure 218

Flexion:

Pull to sit (Fig. 219); active flexion of the neck; pulling with upper limbs; raises lower limbs in extension; increased abdominal control.

Good balance between flexion and extension, righting reactions initiated.

Equilibrium reactions in supine.

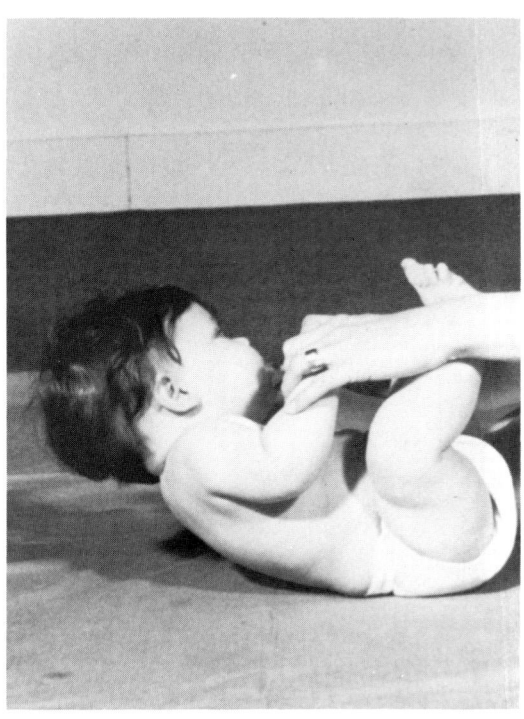

Figure 219

Figure 220

Rotation:

Weight shift on extended upper limbs; more control in shoulder and scapula (Fig. 220).

Figure 221

Roll from supine to prone using body righting on the body rotation (Fig. 221):
a. need increased neck flexion.
b. upper limb reaches out and across the midline of the body (ATNR, STN).
c. if initiates roll with lower limbs, needs increased flexion to get past the midline; abdominals, asymmetrical movement of lower limb to cross over the opposite leg (crossed extension).

Hands:

Radial-palmar grasp (Fig. 222).

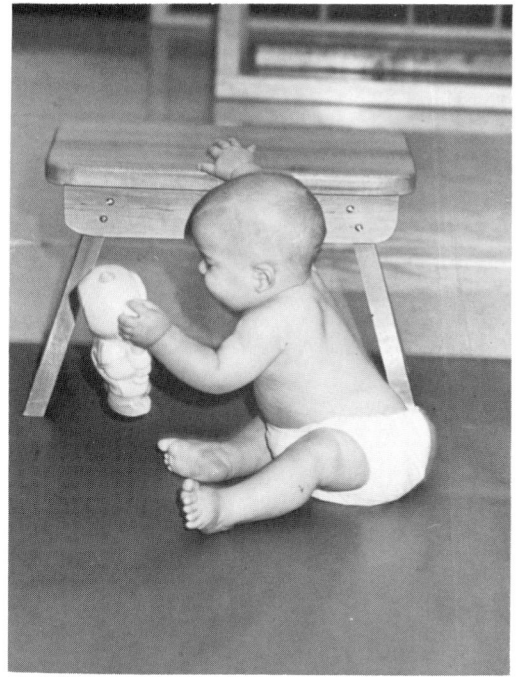

Figure 222

If drops object, may resecure it (Fig. 223).

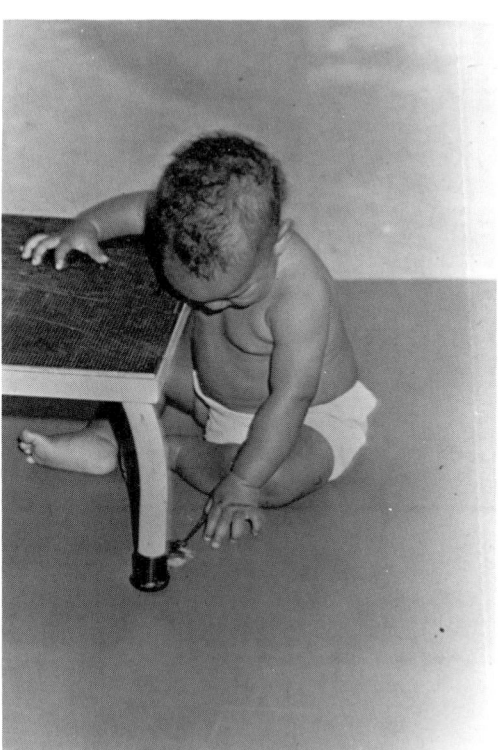

Figure 223

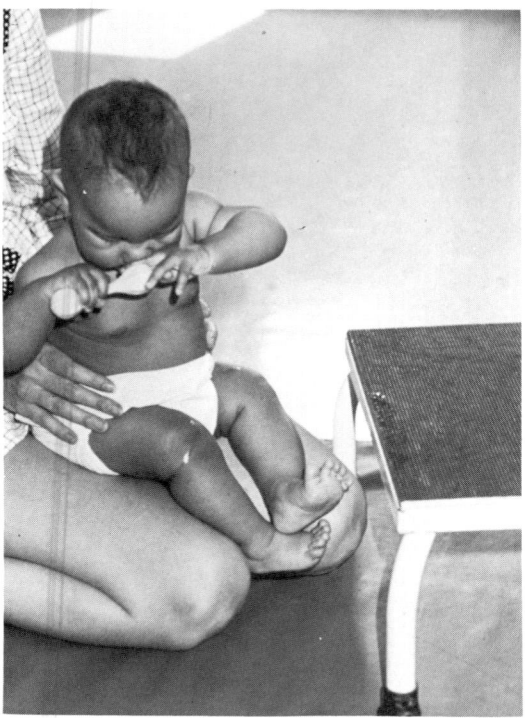

Figure 224

Transfers object from one hand to the other (Fig. 224).

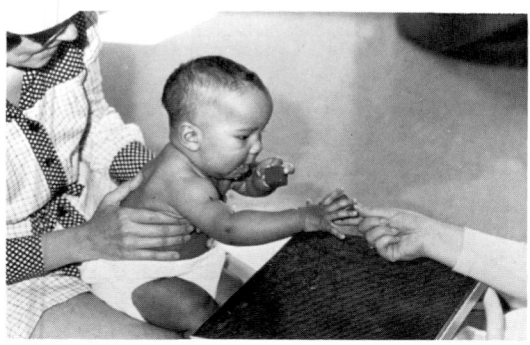

Figure 225

Reaches out with one limb while holding object with the other (asymmetrical movement, radial and ulnar release) (Fig. 225).

Pats image in a mirror (Fig. 226).

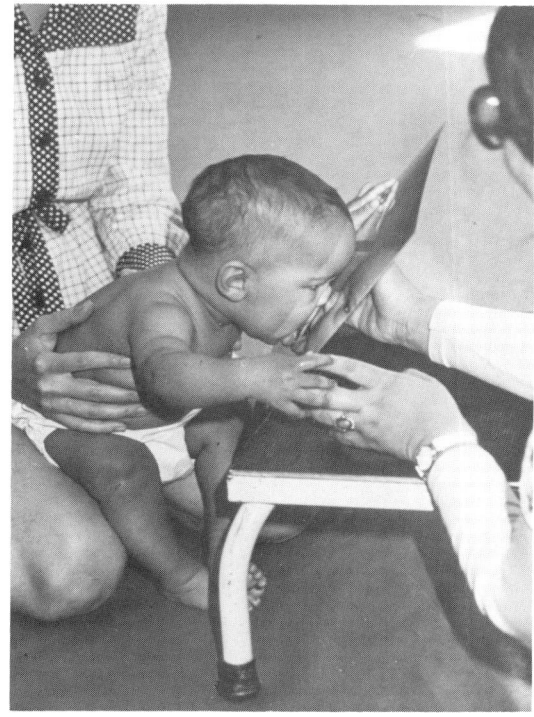

Figure 226

Eyes:

Refinement of all eye movements, accommodation reflexes, conjugate movements, depth perception (Fig. 227); required from this time on in their development.

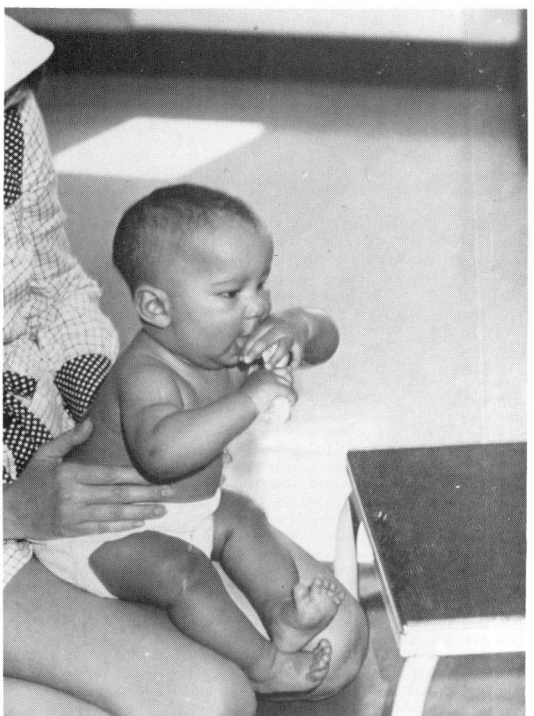

Figure 227

Eight Months

Extension:

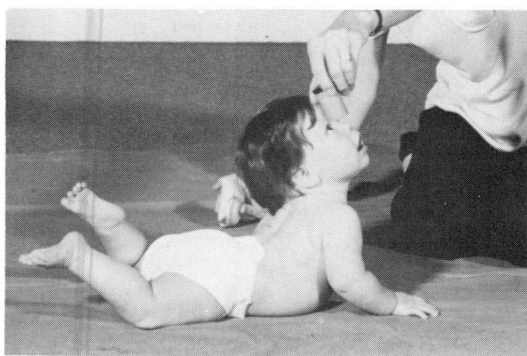

Figure 228

Pivot-prone-type position—hyperextension in lower back, stability in pelvis, weight bearing (Fig. 228).

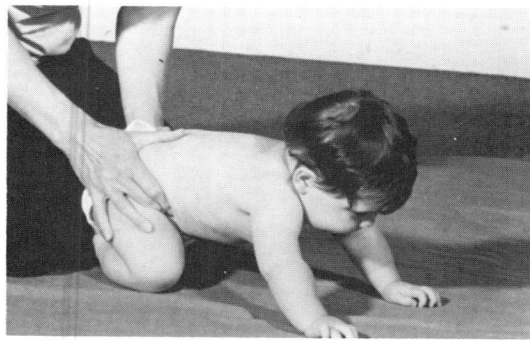

Figure 229

Able to push backward into the quadruped position (Fig. 229):

a. increased stability and mobility in the hips.
b. need neck and back extension, antigravity posture.
c. controlled extension in upper extremities.

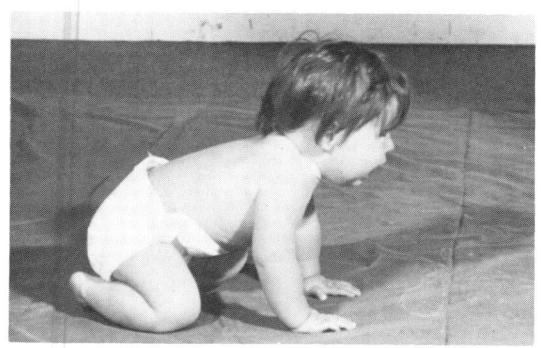

Figure 230

While in quadruped position (Fig. 230), begins to rock back and forth (weight shift-exteroceptive and proprioceptive stimulation; balanced hip flexion and extension; hip mobility).

Able to push back into sitting position, at first symmetrically, then develops a-symmetrical side sit position using pelvic rotation and stability in shoulders (Fig. 231).

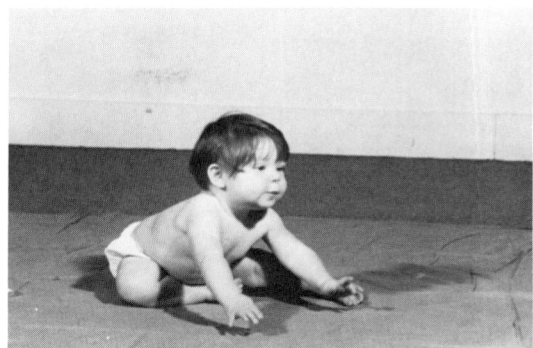

Figure 231

In sitting, lower extremities have more extension reaching to recover balance (equilibrium and righting reactions) (Fig. 232).

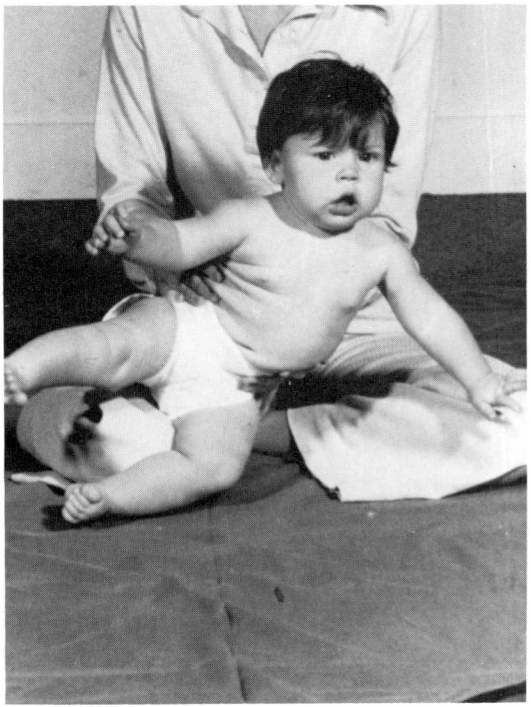

Figure 232

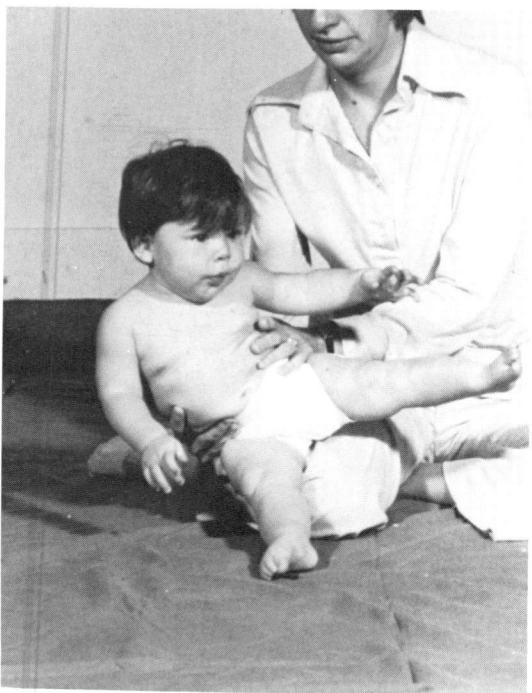

Figure 233

At this time all components of extension are available but need further refinement (Fig. 233).

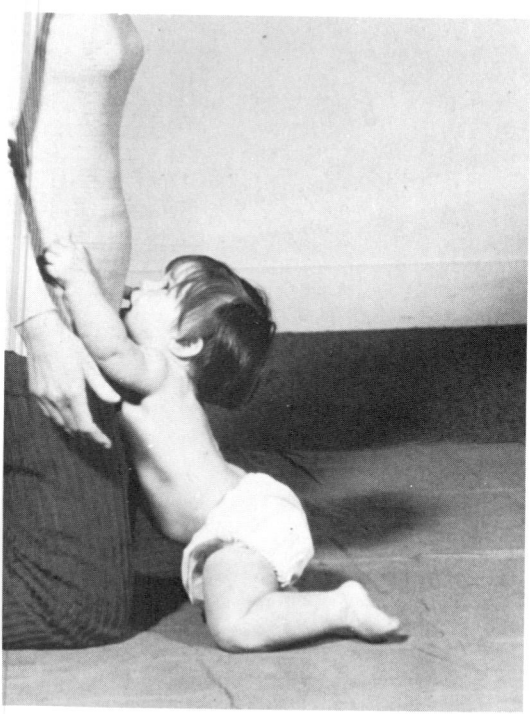

Figure 234

Able to pull to stand, with minimal abduction for standing (Fig. 234).

Able to kneel, with back and hip extension and knee flexion (disassociation)
(Fig. 235).

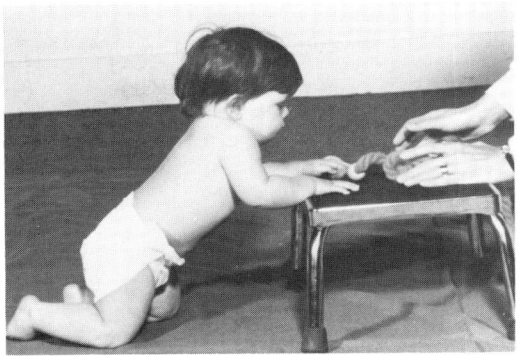

Figure 235

Standing with feet flat (positive and
negative supporting reflexes becoming
integrated) (Fig. 236).

Figure 236

Figure 237

Protective extension fully developed (Fig. 237).

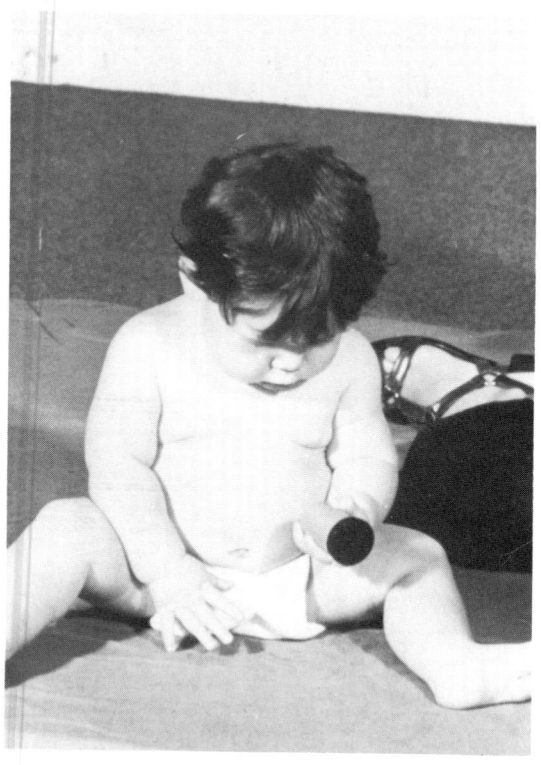

Figure 238

Flexion:

Sits with balance (Fig. 238). Most components of flexion developed by seven to eight months (has established balance between flexion and extension).

Rotation:

Pushes back into quadruped position, rotates pelvis into side sit (Fig. 239), brings lower extremities out in front for "long sit" position (Fig. 240) (righting reactions; equilibrium reactions; disassociation of body part movements now under voluntary control).

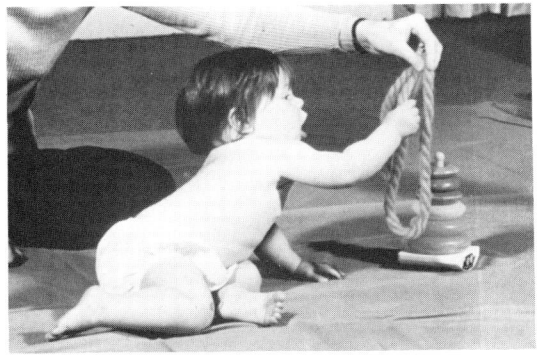

Figure 239

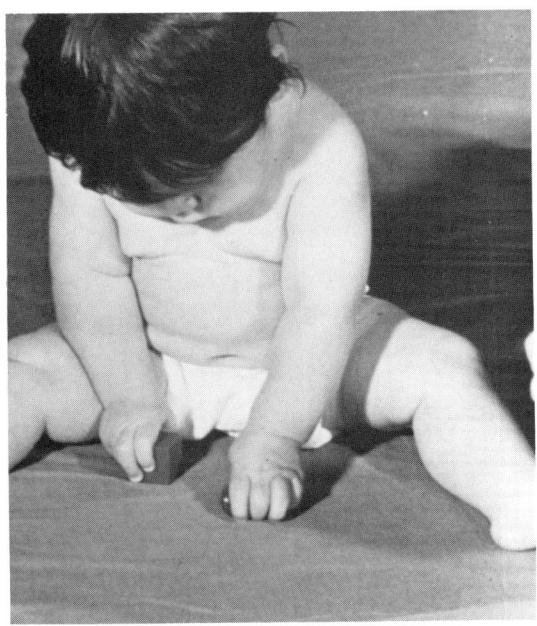

Figure 240

Crawling (on stomach) (Fig. 241) requires—
a. weight on one side of pelvis, shifting weight to other side.
b. proprioceptive input into the pelvis and shoulder.

Figure 241

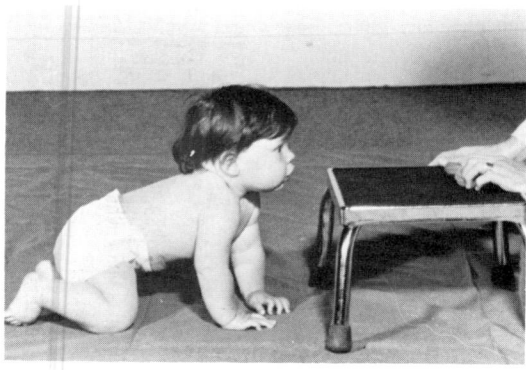

Figure 242

Creeping forward (Fig. 242)—
a. has sufficient trunk, shoulder, and pelvic girdle stability.
b. reciprocal movements, shifts weight, upper trunk stabilized, shifts weight, pelvis on opposite side stabilizes.

Half-kneels using rotation (Fig. 243).

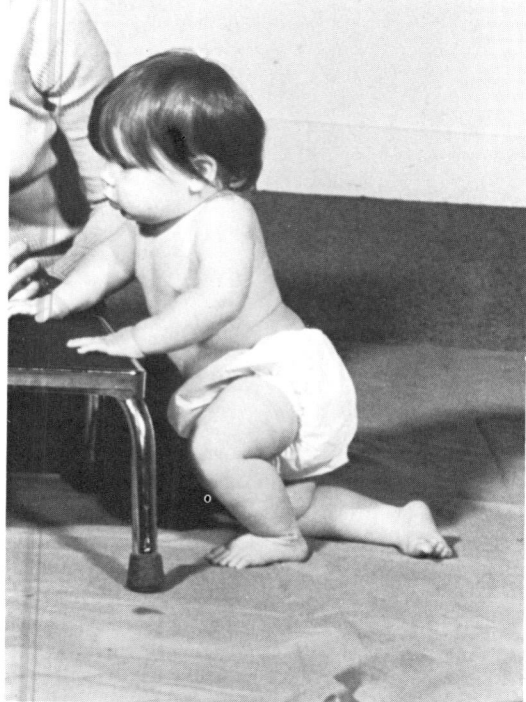

Figure 243

Hands:

Pincer grasp, bilateral (Fig. 244).
Pincer grasp, unilateral (Fig. 245);
transfer.

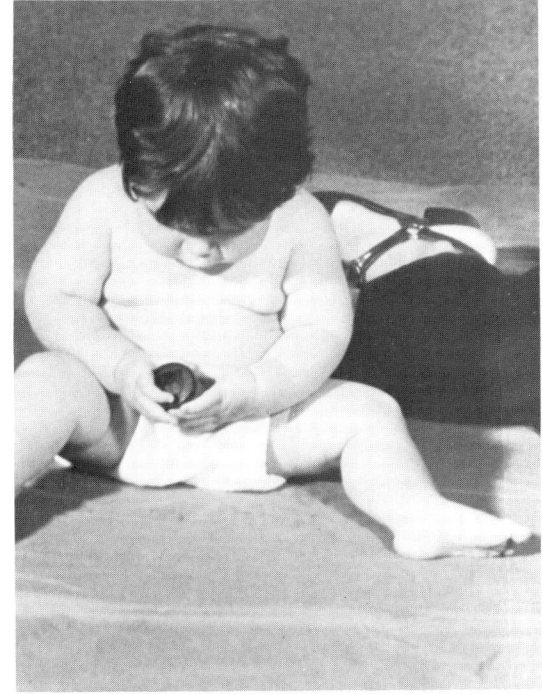

Figure 244

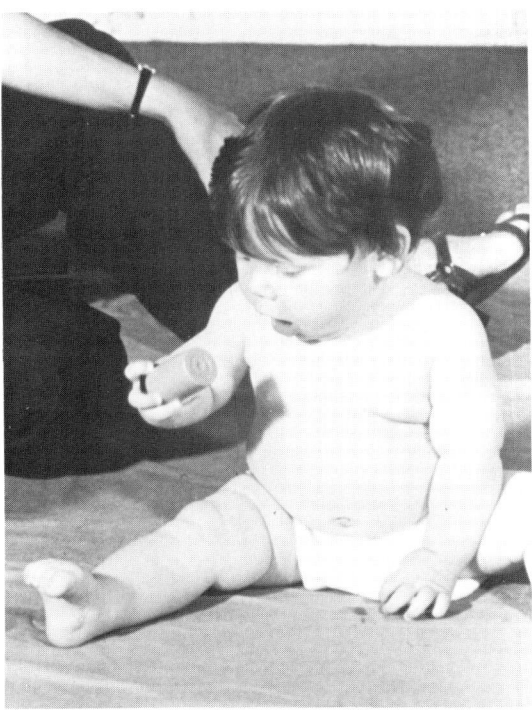

Figure 245

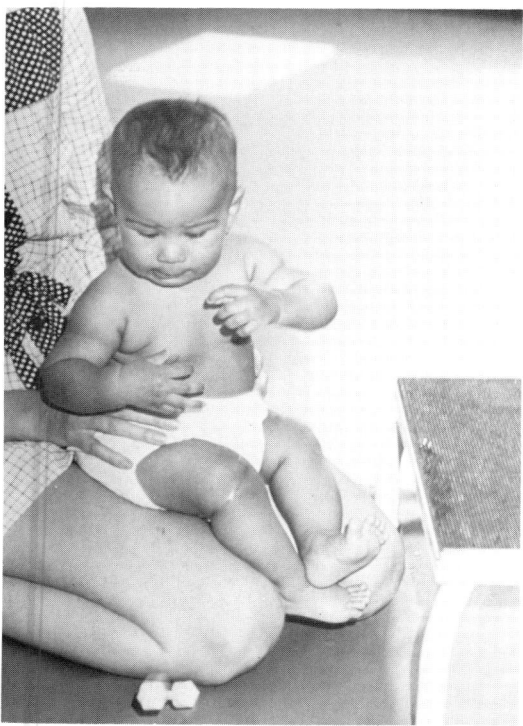

Increased maturity of neutral to supination patterns but not complete (Fig. 246).

Figure 246

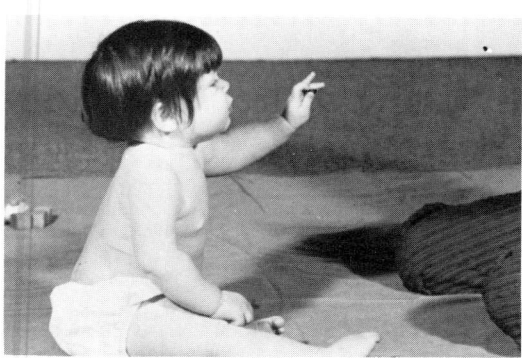

Crude voluntary release of objects (Fig. 247).

Figure 247

Ten Months

Extension and Flexion:

Independence in sitting, grasp and release functions, and pincer position (finger and thumb) is available voluntarily (Fig. 248).

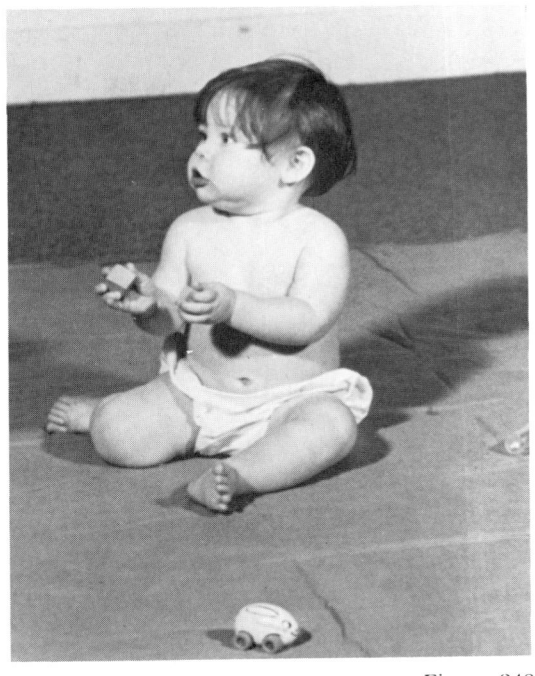

Figure 248

Can twist, turn, pivot, and regain sitting balance (Fig. 249).

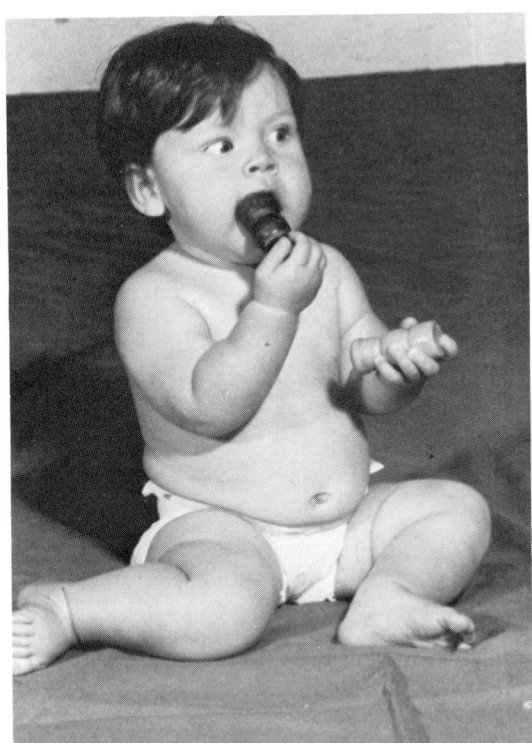

Figure 249

May be able to "bear walk" on the hands (Fig. 250).

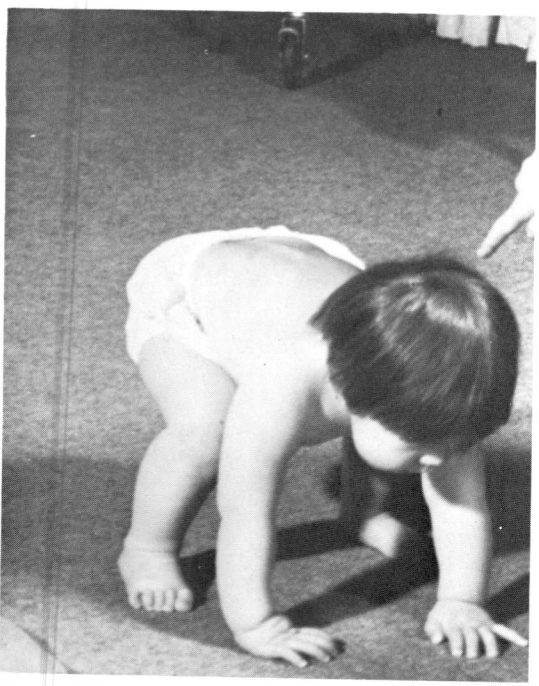

Figure 250

Controlled cruising sidewards (Fig. 251). (Full extension component present; flexion component complete when child can stand independently.)

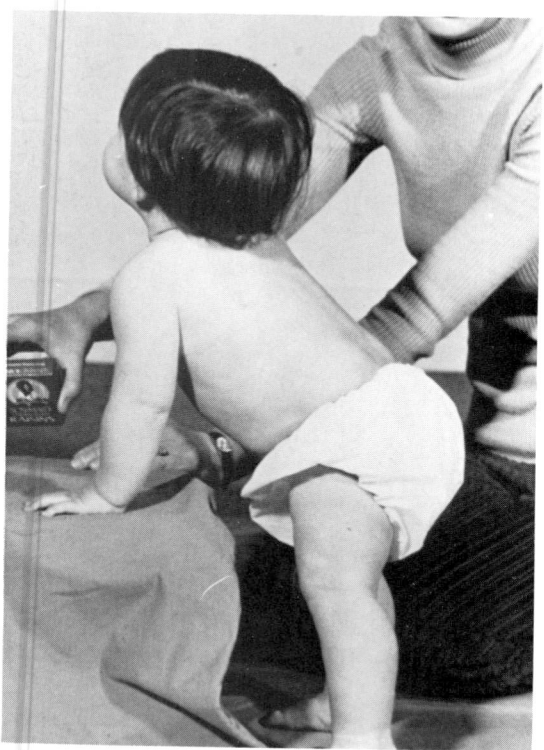

Figure 251

The crouched position (Fig. 252) requires weight bearing on the hands, which requires control of the shoulder girdle for complete internal and external rotation and supination of the upper limbs.

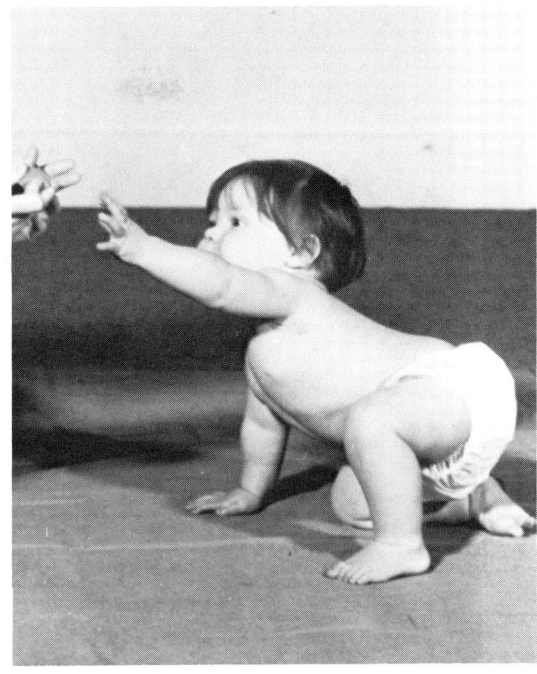

Figure 252

Walks with both hands held (lower extremities in abduction and external rotation) (Fig. 253).

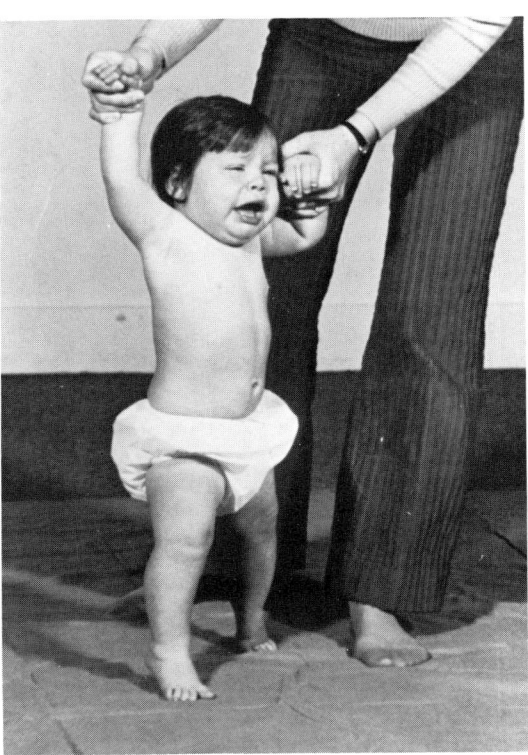

Figure 253

Initial standing (high "guard" of upper extremities, abduction and external rotation of lower extremities) (Fig. 254).

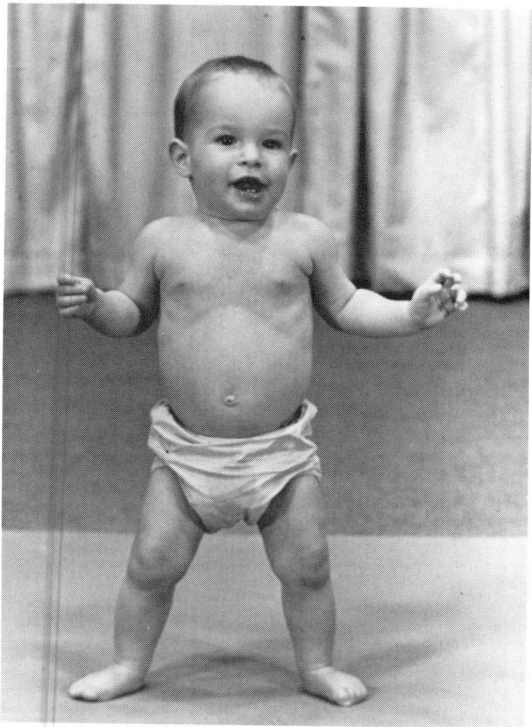

Figure 254

Hands:

Forefinger isolation; beginning to isolate fingers (Fig. 255).

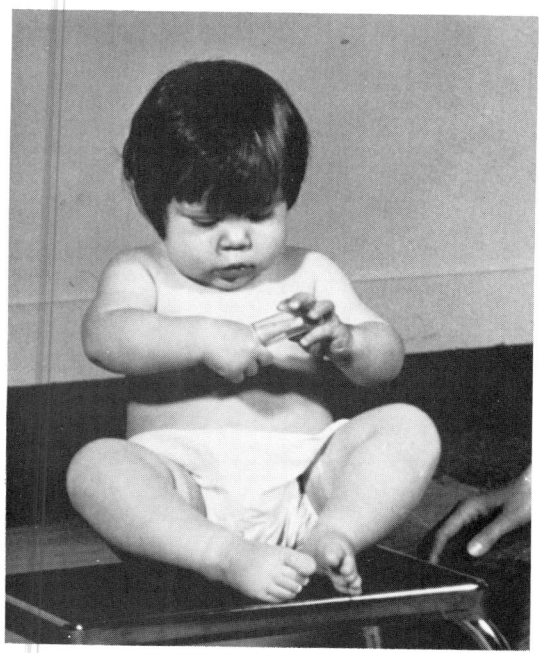

Figure 255

Picks up small objects with pincer
grasp (Fig. 256).

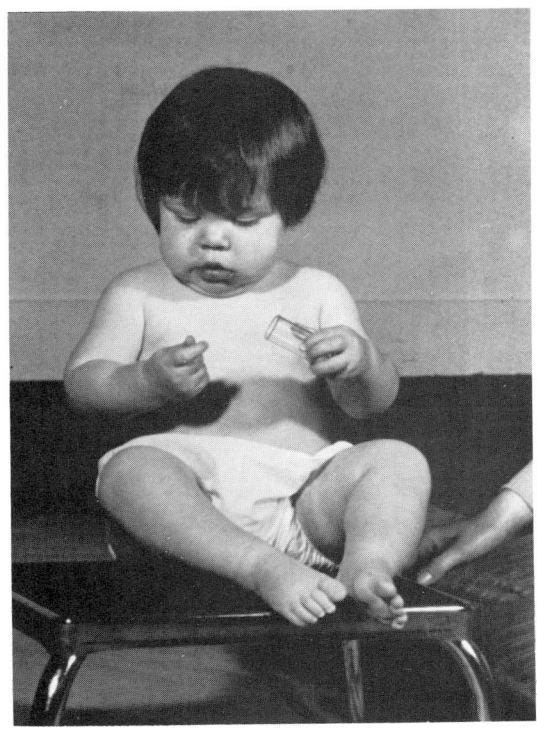

Figure 256

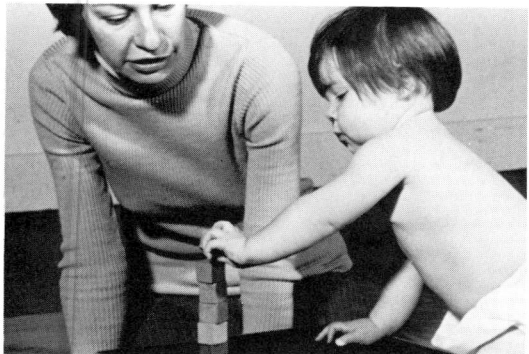

More advanced use of hands combined with wrist extension (Fig. 257) and supination (Fig. 258).

Figure 257

Figure 258

Twelve to Fifteen Months

Independence in standing, walking, and hand usage (Fig. 259).

Basic movements are available, but the child requires more stability for mobility and greater refinement for achieving skills.

Reflex cues were included in some of the descriptions. However, these were used mainly as a guide to demonstrate how they influence the different changes in sensorimotor development. It is important to keep in mind how tone develops, distributes, and thus influences bodily movement so that the components of movement can be analyzed and interpreted in both normal and abnormal sensorimotor development.

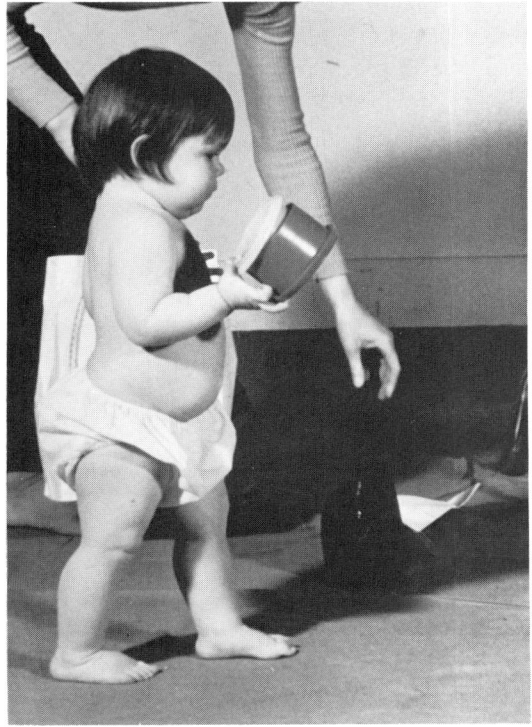

Figure 259

Chapter VI

ABNORMAL DEVELOPMENT

It has been stated that postural reflexes play a dominant role in the regulation of the degree, strength, balance, and distribution of muscle tone. They regulate muscle tone for the maintenance of posture and for the performance of movements. Without their full development and integration, normal activities might not be realized or, at the least, activities might be compromised. A review of these influences on normal development has been presented. This chapter presents an overview of these influences on the distribution of tone when there is a persistence of abnormal reflexes. This results in abnormal sensorimotor development.

Normal muscle tone should be viewed as an inherent ability of the body to adapt to varying positions. In this way automatic, spontaneous movements are available for rapid adjustments to environmental demands. Because cerebral palsy is a typical neurological disability that manifests abnormal tone and persistent reflexes, examples of this disability will be cited for discussing abnormal distribution of tone.

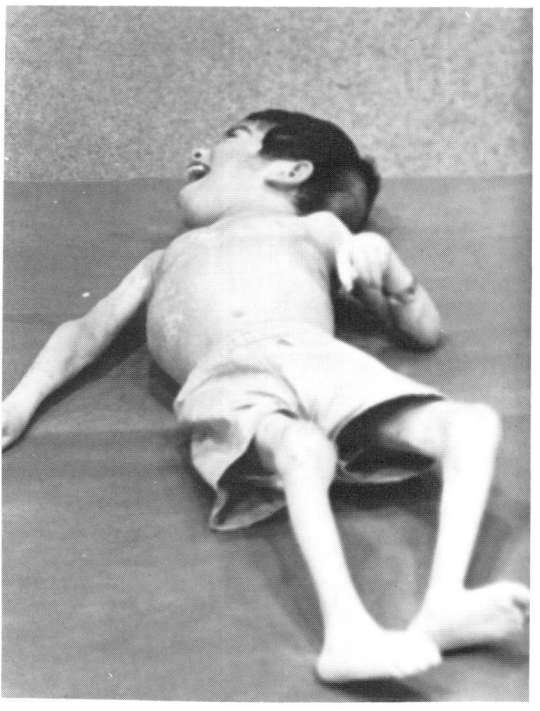

Figure 260

Spastics, in general, lack movement (Fig. 260). They are dominated by tonic patterns. They have too much stability and abnormal reciprocal innervation. If they have varying degrees of reciprocal cocontraction, they may acquire "fixed position" deformities. They tend to be fixed in progravity patterns because they lack normal antigravity movements. This results in postural fixations that are proximal in origin. These in turn result in an abnormal distribution of muscle tone in the rest of the body. The retention of these pathological tonic movement patterns results in maldevelopment of the righting and equilibrium reactions. Consequently, this may preclude the development of normal rotation patterns. Keep in mind that it is the combined influences of tone and reflexes that determine the patterns of posture and movement. In spastics voluntary movements are slow and they are limited in range. Usually just the effort of moving creates and/or reinforces abnormal tone and movement patterns.

The spastics, therefore, may demonstrate a strong tonic labyrinthine reflex, prone or supine (Fig. 261). This creates retraction of the shoulders and neck, extension at the hips, knees, and ankles, and inward rotation and adduction of the lower extremities and inversion of the feet.

Figure 261

The athetoid, in general, has too much uncontrolled mobility (Fig. 262). Movements lack proximal stability, postural tone fluctuates, and control of movements during the transitional stages is lacking. Also, they have abnormal reciprocal innervation with too much reciprocal inhibition. Primitive reflexes and/or patterns are retained, though not fixed. Righting reactions may be present, but they manifest an unpredictable sequence with unpredictable movements. Whenever possible, athetoids will attempt to stabilize their positions by distal fixing in the limbs and compensatory fixing in the trunk and use their head for balance stability.

Figure 262

The cerebral palsied child with hypotonicity has very little tone or minimal to moderate tone for controlled stability (Fig. 263). There is hyperextensibility at the joints and usually excessive extension with no counterbalance of flexion.

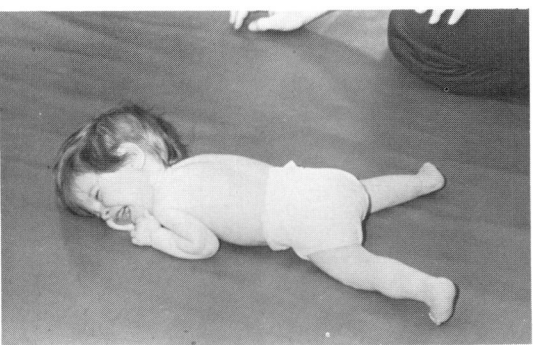

Figure 263

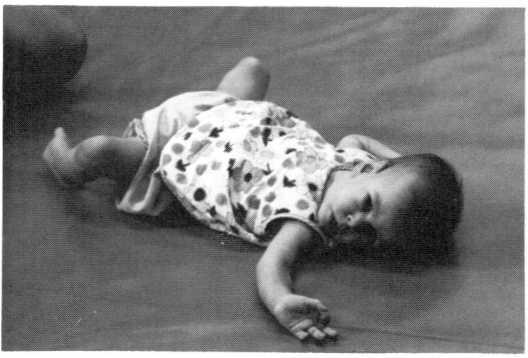

Figure 264

The opposite problem that may be seen with hyperextensibility at the joints is the "frog leg" position or flexed hips and knees with external rotation, and/or the "W" position of the upper limbs with flexed elbows and external rotation (Fig. 264). In order to gain stability, they fix the neck in hyperextension, adduct the scapulae and lock into this position in order to lift the head while supine.

Figure 265

This child does not develop controlled extension of the low back (Fig. 265). This biases the child and results in flexion at the hips. Also lack of extensor tone results in the child sitting with a rounded torso or kyphotic spine and protracted shoulders. The compensation is hyperextension of the neck and emphasis on flexor movements. Disassociation of the humerus and scapulae may not be present, thus the scapula moves with the humerus when the upper limb moves forward. Within one to two years, a child with this type of tone may become spastic but usually afflicted with an athetoid or ataxic type of cerebral palsy.

Chapter VII

CASE REVIEWS

This chapter presents the results of tests on two cerebral palsied children. Tests include reflexes, distribution of tone, CNS processing, and sensorimotor development. These tests will be reviewed to demonstrate a procedure that may be used to determine muscle tone, patterns of movement, positions, and development. It is not necessary at all times to include these tests as this is time consuming. Observation and manual manipulation coupled with the distribution of tone and CNS processing assessments are sufficient to designate the pertinent information. A medical history is not necessary to determine tone and development, thus is not included.

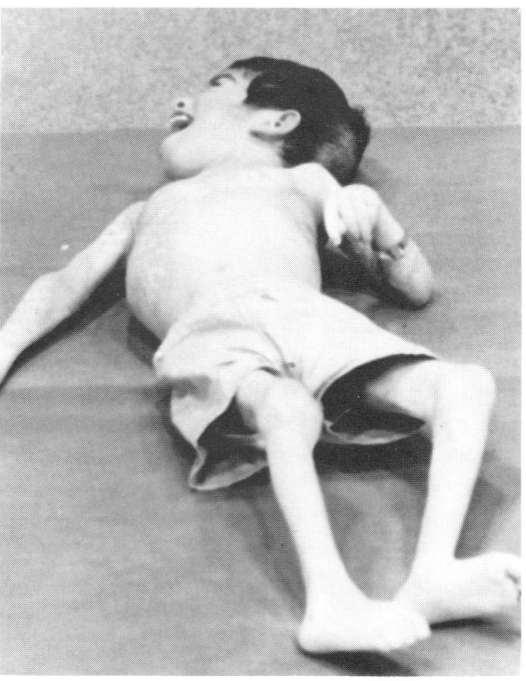

Figure 266

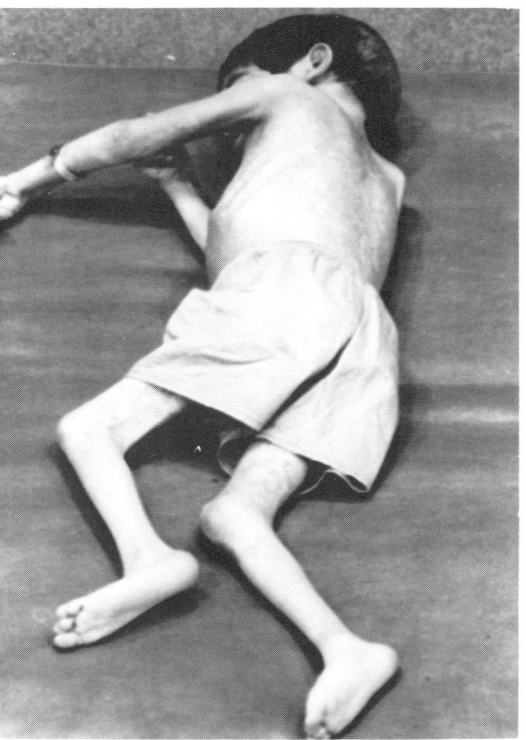

Figure 267

Figures 266 through 271 and Charts 3 through 7 (*see* Appendix) are test results of the first child to be reviewed. Chart 6 reveals an obvious predominance of extensor tone as noted by the reflex and movement columns as well as the photographs. Minimal influence from the tonic labyrinthine-prone reflex reinforces the predominance of extensor patterns. Limited flexion is indicated with the persistence of crossed extension and tonic neck reflexes (Fig. 266). The third column in Chart 6 indicates that the total body is involved. The trunk, which is the anchor point, is primarily influenced by extensor tone. The extremities are influenced by flexor and extensor tone, but extensor tone continues to predominate (Fig. 267). The fourth column reveals that distribution of tone is in both asymmetrical and symmetrical patterns of movement (*see* Fig. 266).

Chart 7 shows that lower level reflexes are dominating (the first four to six months) so that balance between flexor and extensor tone is insufficient to allow rotation (*see* Figs. 266, 271). Body righting on the body indicates some degree of rotatory components, but righting and equilibrium reactions are compromised or not developed as yet due to the abnormal lower level influences (*see* Fig. 267).

Head control in prone indicates that a degree of extensor tone has developed in the upper limbs due to symmetrical tonic neck reflex influence (Fig. 268) and in the trunk musculature due to the Landau reaction (*see* Figs. 268, 269). Absence from the parachute reaction and lack of stimulation from pressure on the palms of the hands (primitive grasp and positive support-upper limbs) reinforces insufficient extensor tone in the upper limbs at higher levels of activity (*see* Figs. 268, 269).

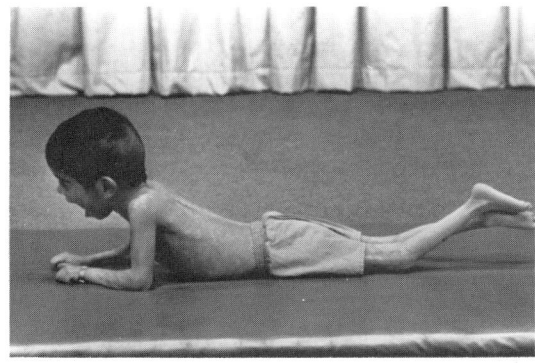

Figure 268

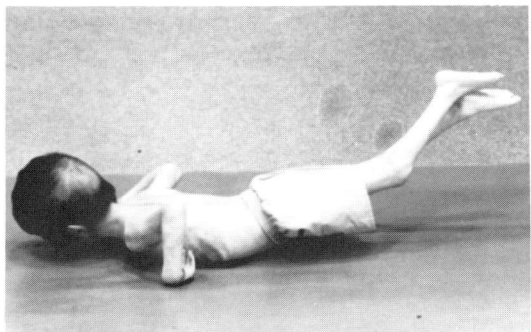

Figure 269

Presence of the Landau, though delayed, reveals some ability to sit with or without support (Fig. 270). Positive supporting reflex (Fig. 271) demonstrates that extensor tone is dominant, preventing any ability to stand or walk. Therefore, maintaining sitting position is the highest sensorimotor level of activity for this patient at this time.

Results from this degree of involvement are less difficult to determine. However, with the less involved cerebral palsied, the same procedure is used to determine which patterns of movement are influenced and compromised by abnormal tone and how this tone affects movement at the various levels of sensorimotor development.

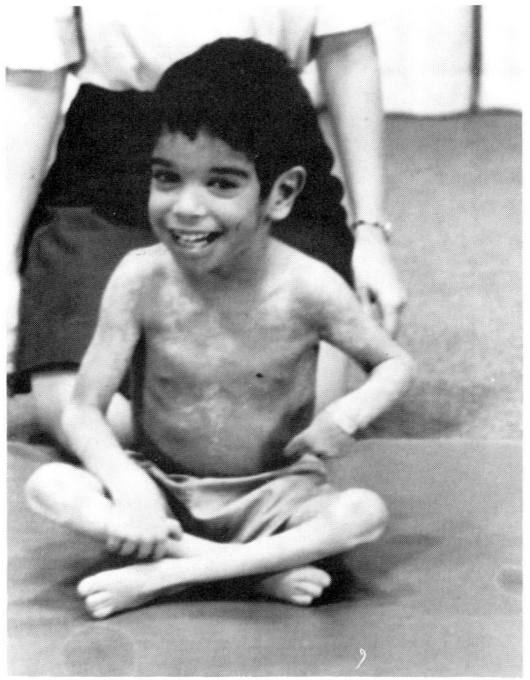

Figure 270

Figure 271

Follow a similar systematic review for the second child using Figures 272 through 276 and Charts 8 through 12 (*see* Appendix) to establish distribution of tone, patterns of movement, and levels of development as a self-assessment exercise.

Figure 272

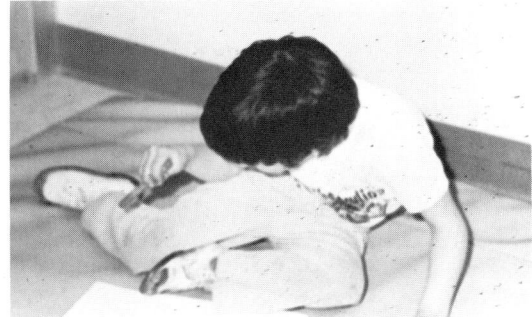

Figure 273

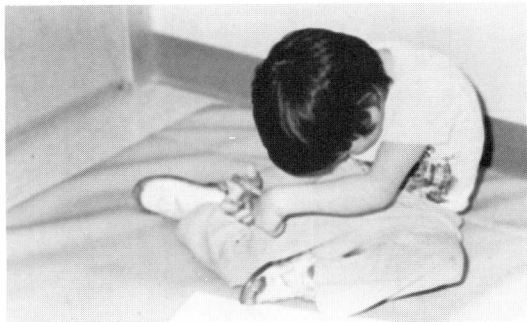

Figure 274

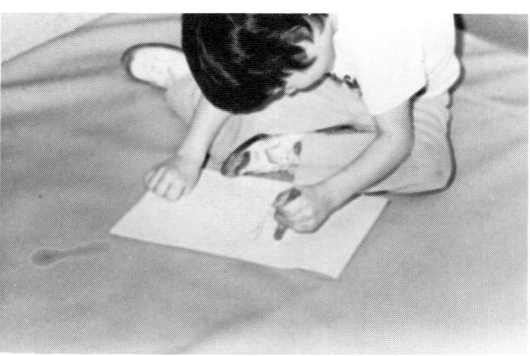

Figure 275

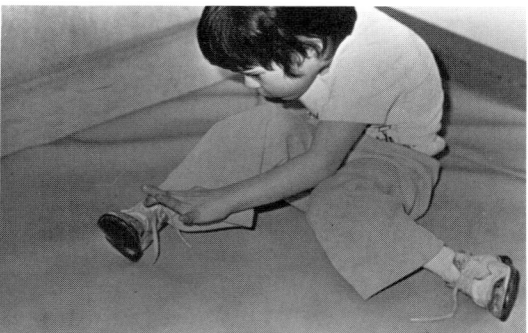

Figure 276

APPENDIX

Chart 3

M. S.

B. D.: 6-20-62

Name: Date: 2-24-69   Reflex Level:

REFLEXES	YES	NO	COMMENTS
1. LEVEL ONE — SPINAL			
a. Flexor Withdrawal		X	
b. Extensor Thrust		X	
c. Crossed Extension	X		Questionable
.2. LEVEL TWO — BRAIN STEM			
a. Asymmetrical Tonic Neck	X		
b. Symmetrical Tonic Neck	X		
c. Tonic Labyrinthine — supine	X		
prone	X		Mild
d. Associated Reactions	X		
e. Postive Supporting Reaction	X		Very Strong
f. Negative Supporting Reaction		X	
3. LEVEL THREE — MIDBRAIN			
a. Neck Righting		X	
b. Body-Righting-Acting-On-The-Body	X		
c. Labyrinthine-Righting-Acting-on-the-Head		X	
d. Optical Righting	X		Only In Prone
e. Amphibian	X		Beginning Bilaterally
4. AUTOMATIC MOVEMENT REACTIONS			
a. Moro Reflex		X	Startle
b. Landau · Reflex	X		Beginning
c. Protective Extensor Thrust		X	Beginning On Rt. Not Lt.
5. LEVEL FOUR — CORTICAL EQUILIBRIUM REACTIONS			
a. Prone-Lying		X	STN
b. Supine-lying		X	ASTN
c. Four-foot kneeling		X	
d. Sitting			
e. Kneel-Standing		X	
f. Standing — hopping		X	
dorsiflexion		X	
see-saw		X	
g. Simian Posture		X	

Chart 4

M. S.

B. D.: 6-20-62

NAME: DATE: 2-24-69

	YES	NO	COMMENTS
I. HEAD RAISING:			
1. Prone	X		
2. Supine		X	
3. Sidelying		X	
II. TURNING:			
1. Supine-sidelying	X		To both sides
2. Supine-prone		X	
3. Prone-supine	X		With difficulty
III. CRAWLING:			ASTN prominent; can assume
1. Puppy dog	X		and maintain temporarily.
2. Static — makes amphibian movements no forward motion of body	X		
3. Crawls — makes amphibian movements moves body forward		X	
4. Bunnyhops — assumes 3-point crawling using complete rotation		X	
5. Creeping — assumes 4-point crawling using complete rotation		X	
6. Creeping — uses partial rotation up to sitting then assumes 4 foot kneeling and creeps		X	
IV. SITTING:			When placed in tailor, can main-
1. Maintains		X	tain temporarily with rt. arm support.
2. Assumes using complete rotation		X	
3. Assumes using partial rotation		X	
4. Assumes symmetrically		X	
V. STANDING:			
1. Kneel stands		X	
2. Kneel walks		X	
3. Pulls up to standing		X	
4. Stands unassisted.		X	
5. Walks.		X	
VI. TRICYCLE:			

Chart 5

NAME: M.S.

ARM — HAND			
Reflexive grasp — no eye-hand coordination (0-4 mos.)			
Conscious grasp — pronation (4-8 mos.) a. crude			
b. between palmar and fingers — ulnar			
c. thumb adducted, not utilized			
Eye-hand coordination begins (6 mos.) a. arms used asymmetrically — control from shoulder and shoulder girdle			
b. Corralling reach			
Radial palmer grasp (7 mos.)			
Scissor grasp (8 mos.)			
Thumb envelopes object (8 mos.)			
Elbow flexible (8 mos.)			
Crude pinch — pincer grasp (9 mos.)			
Advertent release of grasp (9 mos.)			
Wrist flexibility (9 mos.)			
Use of forearm between mid-position and pronation (9 mos.)			
Pincer release (11 mos.)			
Supination more frequently (11 mos.)			
Opposition (12 mos.)			
Supination — cortically controlled (12 mos.)			

ADDITIONAL COMMENTS:

    Left hand fisted.
    Right side seems less involved and right hand is utilized in volar
        flexion - does have grasp and release.
    Thumb out of palm bilaterally.
    Utilizes ASTN for elbow extension.

Chart 6

DISTRIBUTION OF TONE   M.S.

REFLEX	MOVEMENT	PART	DISTRIBUTION
TONIC LABYRINTHINE-SUPINE	EXTENSION	BODY	TOTAL
LANDAU	EXTENSION	BODY	TOTAL
POSITIVE SUPPORTING	EXTENSION	LEGS-TRUNK	SYMMETRICAL
POSITIVE SUPPORTING-ARMS	EXTENSION	ARMS-HANDS	SYMMETRICAL
EXTENSOR THRUST	EXTENSION	LEGS	SYMMETRICAL
MAGNET	EXTENSION	LEGS	SYMMETRICAL
PRIMARY STEPPING	EXTENSION	LEGS	SYMMETRICAL
MORO	EXTENSION	ARMS-HANDS	SYMMETRICAL
PARACHUTE	EXTENSION	ARMS-HANDS	SYMMETRICAL
ULNAR RELEASE	EXTENSION-PRONATION	HANDS-FOREARMS	SYMMETRICAL
TONIC LABYRINTHINE-PRONE	FLEXION	BODY	TOTAL
FLEXOR WITHDRAWAL	FLEXION	LEGS	SYMMETRICAL
GALANT	FLEXION-LATERAL	LEG-TRUNK	SYMMETRICAL
PLACING	FLEXION	FEET-HANDS	SYMMETRICAL
GRASP	FLEXION	HANDS-ARMS	SYMMETRICAL
RADIAL RELEASE	FLEXION-SUPINATION	HANDS-FOREARMS	SYMMETRICAL
CROSSED EXTENSION	FLEXION-EXTENSION	LEGS	ASYMMETRICAL
SYMMETRICAL TONIC NECK	FLEXION-EXTENSION	LEGS-ARMS	ASYMMETRICAL
ASYMMETRICAL TONIC NECK	FLEXION-EXTENSION	LEGS-ARMS	ASYMMETRICAL

Chart 7

CNS PROCESSING
M.S.

REFLEXES	TONE	1	2	3	4	5	6	7	8	9	10	11	12
MAGNET	E	X											
GALANT	F R	X	X										
PRIMARY STEPPING	F E	X	X										
ROOTING	R	X	X	X									
SUCKING	F	X	X	X									
PRIMITIVE GRASP ⟨F E⟩	(F E)	X	X	X	X								
CROSSED EXTENSION ⟨F E⟩	(F E)	X	X	X	X								
FLEXOR WITHDRAWAL	F	X	X	X	X								
ULNAR RELEASE	E	X	X	X	X								
RADIAL RELEASE	F	X	X	X	X								
TONIC LABYRINTHINE–PRONE	F	X	X	X	X								
TONIC LABYRINTHINE–SUPINE ⟨E E⟩	(E E)	X	X	X	X								
SYMMETRICAL TONIC NECK ⟨F E⟩	(F E)	X	X	X	X								
ASYMMETRICAL TONIC NECK ⟨F E⟩	(F E)	X	X	X	X								
MORO	E	X	X	X	X	X	X						
PLACING	F E	X	X	X	X	X	X	X					
POSITIVE SUPPORTING ⟨E⟩	(E)	X	X	X	X	X	X	X	X				
POSITIVE SUPPORTING–ARMS	E			X	X	X	X	X	X				
LANDAU ⟨E⟩	(E)					X	X	X	X	X	X	X	X
PARACHUTE	E					X	X	X	X	X	X	X	X
NECK RIGHTING	R	X	X	X	X	X	X	X					
BODY RIGHTING ON THE BODY ⟨R⟩	(R)					X	X	X	X	X	X	X	X
BODY RIGHTING ON THE HEAD	R						X	X	X	X	X	X	X

Chart 8

T. D.
B. D.: 3-12-69

Name: _____   Date: 10-10-75   Reflex Level: _____

REFLEXES	YES	NO	COMMENTS
1. LEVEL ONE — SPINAL			
a. Flexor Withdrawal		X	
b. Extensor Thrust		X	
c. Crossed Extension		X	
.2. LEVEL TWO — BRAIN STEM			
a. Asymmetrical Tonic Neck	X		
b. Symmetrical Tonic Neck	X		
c. Tonic Labyrinthine — supine	X		
prone	X		
d. Associated Reactions	X		
e. Postive Supporting Reaction	X		
f. Negative Supporting Reaction	X		
3. LEVEL THREE — MIDBRAIN			
a. Neck Righting	X		
b. Body-Righting-Acting-On-The-Body		X	
c. Labyrinthine-Righting-Acting-on-the-Head			
d. Optical Righting	X		Prone only
e. Amphibian	X		
4. AUTOMATIC MOVEMENT REACTIONS			
a. Moro Reflex	X		Modified
b. Landau Reflex	X		
c. Protective Extensor Thrust		X	
5. LEVEL FOUR — CORTICAL EQUILIBRIUM REACTIONS			
a. Prone-Lying		X	
b. Supine-lying		X	
c. Four-foot kneeling		X	Poor
d. Sitting		X	Poor
e. Kneel-Standing		X	
f. Standing — hopping	X		
dorsiflexion	X		
see-saw		X	
g. Simian Posture		X	

ADDITIONAL COMMENTS:

Poor patterns of movement. Rt. side more involved.

Chart 9

T. D.

B. D.: 3-12-69

NAME: DATE: 10-10-75

	YES	NO	COMMENTS
I. HEAD RAISING:			
1. Prone	X		
2. Supine	X		Very poor
3. Sidelying		X	
II. TURNING:			
1. Supine-sidelying	X		
2. Supine-prone	X		
3. Prone-supine	X		
III. CRAWLING:			
1. Puppy dog	X		
2. Static — makes amphibian movements no forward motion of body			
3. Crawls — makes amphibian movements moves body forward			
4. Bunnyhops — assumes 3-point crawling using complete rotation	X		
5. Creeping — assumes 4-point crawling using complete rotation	X		Poor reciprocal creeping
6. Creeping — uses partial rotation up to sitting then assumes 4 foot kneeling and creeps			
IV. SITTING:			
1. Maintains	X		
2. Assumes using complete rotation	X		
3. Assumes using partial rotation	X		Poor patterns
4. Assumes symmetrically			
V. STANDING:			
1. Kneel stands	X		Poorly and with difficulty
2. Kneel walks	X		Minimal and with difficulty
3. Pulls up to standing	X		Minimal and with difficulty
4. Stands unassisted		X	
5. Walks		X	
VI. TRICYCLE:	X		Strapped foot pedals

Chart 10

NAME: ___T.D.___

ARM — HAND			
Reflexive grasp — no eye-hand coordination (0-4 mos.)			
Conscious grasp — pronation (4-8 mos.) a. crude _____	X		
b. between palmar and fingers — ulnar ___	X		
c. thumb adducted, not utilized _____			

Eye-hand coordination begins (6 mos.)
  a. arms used asymmetrically — control
    from shoulder and shoulder girdle ___			

b. Corralling reach _____	X		
Radial palmer grasp (7 mos.) _____			
Scissor grasp (8 mos.) _____			
Thumb envelopes object (8 mos.) _____			
Elbow flexible (8 mos.) _____	X		
Crude pinch — pincer grasp (9 mos.) _____			
Advertent release of grasp (9 mos.) _____	X		
Wrist flexibility (9 mos.) _____			
Use of forearm between mid-position and pronation (9 mos.) _____			
Pincer release (11 mos.) _____			
Supination more frequently (11 mos.) _____			
Opposition (12 mos.) _____			
Supination — cortically controlled (12 mos.) ___			

ADDITIONAL COMMENTS:

   Fluctuating tone throughout..
   Left hand use only.

Chart 11

DISTRIBUTION OF TONE   T.D.

REFLEX	MOVEMENT	PART	DISTRIBUTION
TONIC LABYRINTHINE-SUPINE	EXTENSION	BODY	TOTAL
LANDAU	EXTENSION	BODY	TOTAL
POSITIVE SUPPORTING	EXTENSION	LEGS-TRUNK	SYMMETRICAL
POSITIVE SUPPORTING-ARMS	EXTENSION	ARMS-HANDS	SYMMETRICAL
EXTENSOR THRUST	EXTENSION	LEGS	SYMMETRICAL
MAGNET	EXTENSION	LEGS	SYMMETRICAL
PRIMARY STEPPING	EXTENSION	LEGS	SYMMETRICAL
MORO	EXTENSION	ARMS-HANDS	SYMMETRICAL
PARACHUTE	EXTENSION	ARMS-HANDS	SYMMETRICAL
ULNAR RELEASE	EXTENSION-PRONATION	HANDS-FOREARMS	SYMMETRICAL
TONIC LABYRINTHINE-PRONE	FLEXION	BODY	TOTAL
FLEXOR WITHDRAWAL	FLEXION	LEGS	SYMMETRICAL
GALANT	FLEXION-LATERAL	LEG-TRUNK	SYMMETRICAL
PLACING	FLEXION	FEET-HANDS	SYMMETRICAL
GRASP	FLEXION	HANDS-ARMS	SYMMETRICAL
RADIAL RELEASE	FLEXION-SUPINATION	HANDS-FOREARMS	SYMMETRICAL
CROSSED EXTENSION	FLEXION-EXTENSION	LEGS	ASYMMETRICAL
SYMMETRICAL TONIC NECK	FLEXION-EXTENSION	LEGS-ARMS	ASYMMETRICAL
ASYMMETRICAL TONIC NECK	FLEXION-EXTENSION	LEGS-ARMS	ASYMMETRICAL

Chart 12

CNS PROCESSING

T.D.

REFLEXES	TONE			1	2	3	4	5	6	7	8	9	10	11	12
									MONTHS						
MAGNET	E			X											
GALANT	F	R		X	X										
PRIMARY STEPPING	F	E		X	X										
ROOTING		R		X	X	X									
SUCKING	F			X	X	X									
PRIMITIVE GRASP	(F)			X	X	X	X								
CROSSED EXTENSION	F	E		X	X	X	X								
FLEXOR WITHDRAWAL	F			X	X	X	X								
ULNAR RELEASE	E			X	X	X	X								
RADIAL RELEASE	F			X	X	X	X								
TONIC LABYRINTHINE-PRONE	(F)			X	X	X	X								
TONIC LABYRINTHINE-SUPINE	(E)			X	X	X	X								
SYMMETRICAL TONIC NECK	(F	E)		X	X	X	X								
ASYMMETRICAL TONIC NECK	(F	E)		X	X	X	X								
MORO	(E)			X	X	X	X								
PLACING	F	E		X	X	X	X	X	X						
POSITIVE SUPPORTING	(E)			X		X	X	X	X	X	X				
POSITIVE SUPPORTING-ARMS	E					X	X	X	X	X	X				
LANDAU	(E)							X	X	X	X	X	X	X	X
PARACHUTE	E							X	X	X	X	X	X	X	X
NECK RIGHTING	(R)			X	X	X	X	X	X	X					
BODY RIGHTING ON THE BODY	R							X	X	X	X	X	X	X	X
BODY RIGHTING ON THE HEAD	R								X	X	X	X	X	X	X

Chapter VIII
TREATMENT PRINCIPLES

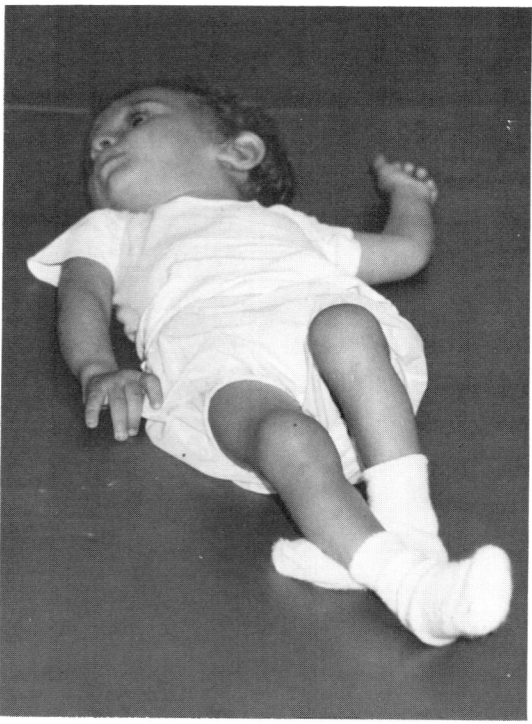

Figure 277

During and following completion of the reflex and sensorimotor evaluations, these factors should be observed and considered in determining the distribution of tone and its influence on the child's movement and development.

What is the basic tone (Fig. 277)?

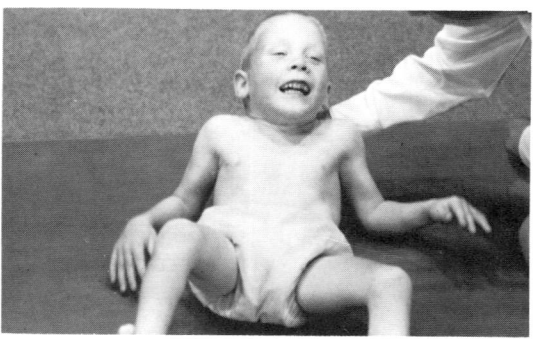

Figure 278

What is its reaction under various conditions (Fig. 278)?

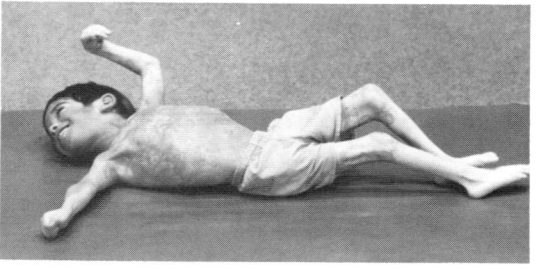

Figure 279

Are there primitive and/or postural reflexes persisting (Fig. 279)? How do these postural reactions interfere with balanced tone in the flexors and extensors? How do these postural reactions influence the distribution of tone?

How does this interfere with the development of higher reactions such as the righting and equilibrium reactions (Fig. 280)?

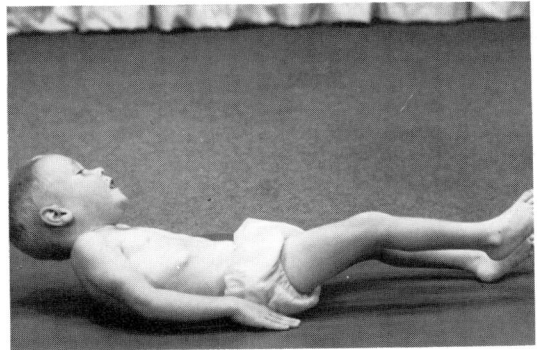

Figure 280

How does the total sum relate to skill and/or functional abilities (Fig. 281)?

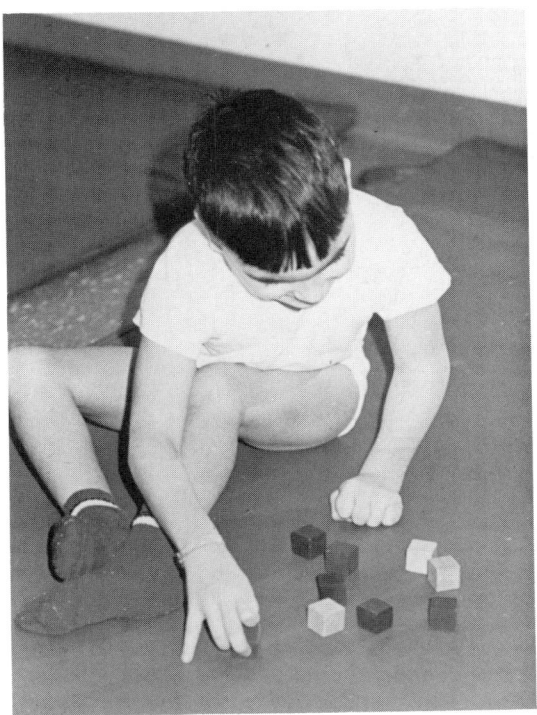

Figure 281

Having this basic information, a treatment program can be planned. One must realize that the persistence of certain reflexes may prevent flexor and/or extensor tone from being integrated and processed in order to allow normal movement to develop (Fig. 282).

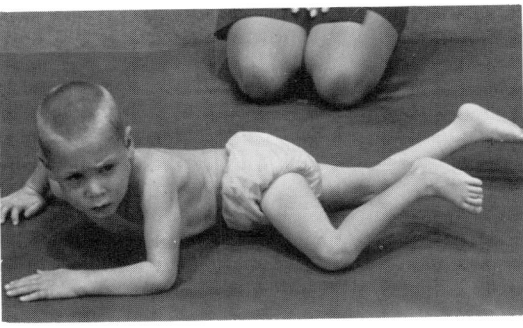

Figure 282

Figure 283

If there is failure of integration of postural reflexes (Fig. 283), how much will this prevent sensorimotor development.

Figure 284

To what degree will abnormal distribution of tone prevent or maintain asymmetry or symmetry of movement (Fig. 284)?

It must be determined how abnormal tone or lack of balance between agonist and antagonist will prevent balance in various positions (Fig. 285).

Figure 285

How are various parts of the body involved and how does the patient compensate (Fig. 286)?

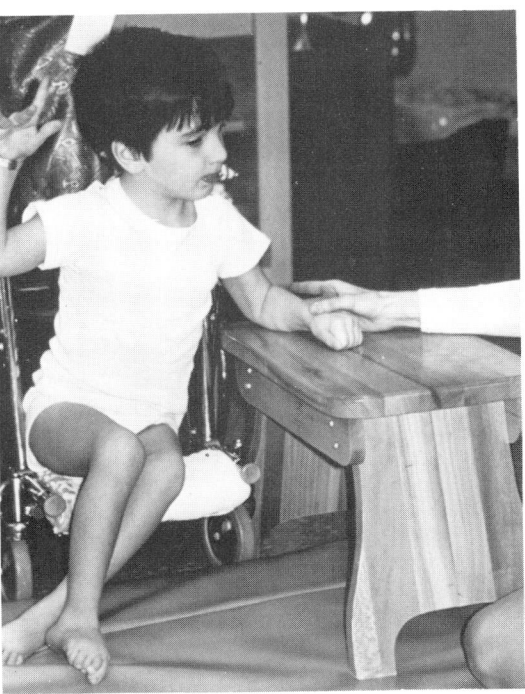

Figure 286

There are other considerations in planning a treatment program and in making a decision concerning its appropriateness, such as age and needs of the child and parents. Is treatment the highest priority, or should residual functional abilities be enhanced or maximized? Each therapist must add or include his or her own experience and plan a treatment program accordingly in order to obtain the maximum benefit for the patient.

The goal of treatment is not to inhibit specific reflexes *in toto* and then proceed to the next step. The goal is to think of the normal influence of these reflexes and how they eventually contribute to the distribution of tone leading to function. This should be accomplished through the reconstruction of patterns that follow the normal, developmental sequences. In this way, normalizing tone first and then reconstructing the patterns of movement for each developmental step just as the normal child does, is the treatment method of choice rather than inhibition of abnormal patterns of posture and movement. *It is absolutely necessary that one knows normal development and associated intricate movement patterns before treatment can be applied to the abnormal.*

Basic principles underlying a theoretical rationale that should be considered—

1. At birth, myelinization is incomplete and is known to continue in the CNS into the fourth decade of life.
2. Consequently, learning and change within the CNS has a great potential, with the possibility that learning occurs until the end of life.
3. The CNS is known to be a plastic system though learning is greatest during the early years of life.
4. Sensory deprivation alters, delays, and/or prevents learning. These facts have been proven through animal and human studies.

To establish learning and change within the CNS, the following criteria must be met—

1. Meaningful input.
2. Active participation.
3. Repetition with change (so the system does not habituate).

Therapy is based on—

1. Normalizing tone.
2. Changing abnormal patterns of movement, by—
   (a) integrating primitive responses,
   (b) enhancing higher reactions, and
   (c) facilitating sequential development.

Chapter IX
EARLY DIAGNOSTIC SIGNS

An infant who may show obligatory, persistent, and/or multiplicity of primitive reflexes; who demonstrates deviations in higher reactions and movement patterns; may be demonstrating diagnostic signs of neurological dysfunction. This, combined with prenatal and/or natal and/or postnatal difficulties is certainly considered at high risk. Without question these infants should be placed on an early management program to prevent abnormal influences in the development of tone, movement, and sensorimotor development. Parents, especially mothers, can be given suggestions on how to handle their infant during feeding, diapering, playing, sleeping positions, etc., depending on the child's needs. It is not necessary at all times to have a formal program designated at this early date. Infants who are questionable can be followed during clinic visits, and assistance can be given to the mother for specific problems. In this way the baby is followed closely by the physician, and the therapist and can be observed for any immediate changes that may occur or for discharge. In this way no excessive dysfunction or trauma is done to the baby or the parents, whether the problem is a major or minor one. Studies have been done that demonstrate that the majority of parents prefer early programming or management programs instead of a period of waiting or long delays before their child receives assistance.

Early evaluation and/or a management program and/or a treatment program are of the utmost importance. An attempt must be made to give these babies more normal sensorimotor experiences before more serious abnormal patterns are established. It is essential to capitalize on the flexibility and pliability of the young nervous system to influence its development into more normal, sequential, postural reactions and movements. It is necessary to develop the central nervous system to its fullest potential so that it is compromised to its minimum. This can be accomplished by *starting treatment in the early months of life.*

CONCLUSION

The child with a normal central nervous system develops in an orderly, sequential manner. He develops from a being with mass movements of symmetrical synergies dominated by lower centers of primitive reactions to a child with a highly complex, integrated nervous system under cortical control having volitional, postural, and refined patterns of movement.

Underlying this developmental sequence is the role that the primitive, postural reflexes play in developing necessary tone for the postural behavior that will be required for gross motor movements to fine motor skills. Reflexes play a dominant role in the regulation and distribution of muscle tone. Normal, balanced muscle tone is the result of the total integration of postural reflex activity at all levels of the CNS. Each reflex produces specific postural patterns, which in turn determines the strength and distribution of muscle tone throughout the body and utilizes this for regulating movement. Righting and equilibrium reactions blend and interact to create smooth, coordinated patterns of movement. Therefore, our total postural behavior is the result of the interaction and integration of postural reflexes, which forms the background of normal voluntary movement and skills.

A similar approach of the role of reflexes in the distribution of tone should be correlated in the management of the child with a neurological dysfunction, such as the cerebral palsied who does not have a normal nervous system and therefore does not have an orderly distribution of tone and an orderly developmental process. The patient with head trauma or a cerebral vascular accident should also be considered from this point of view.

As specified in Chapter IX, early assessment and/or treatment is of the utmost importance when attempting to regulate tone for its maximum use. In this way, the disorganized child may be able to reach his maximal functional ability.

"There is a wide range of ability among children with disabilities as there is among all children. You can provide a child an opportunity to discover for himself, and to achieve success—no matter how small. In this way, he can develop a feeling of competence and worth, helping him to lead as independent a life as possible" (author unknown).

BIBLIOGRAPHY

Amiel-Tison, C.: Neurological evaluation of the maturity of newborn infants. *Arch Dis Childh*, 43, 89, 1968.

Andre-Thomas, Y.C. and Dargassies, S.: *Clinics in Developmental Medicine*. Neurological Examination of the Infant, vol. 1. Philadelphia, J.B. Lippincott Co, 1960.

Ayres, A.J.: *Sensory Integration and Learning Disorders*. Los Angeles, Western Psychological Ser, 1972.

Barnes, M.R., Crutchfield, C.A., Heriza, C.B.: *The Neurophysiological Basis of Patient Treatment*, vol. I. Morgantown, W.Va., Stokesville Pub Co, 1973.

_____: *The Neurophysiological Basis of Patient Treatment*, vol. II. Morgantown, W.Va., Stokesville Pub Co, 1978.

Bayley, N.: Bayley Scales of Infant Development. New York, Psychological Corp, 1969.

Bergen, A.: *Selected Equipment for Pediatric Rehabilitation*. Valhalla, N.Y., Blythdale Children's Hosp, 1974.

Bleck, E.E.: Locomotion prognosis in cerebral palsy. *Dev Med Child Neurol*, 17:18-25, 1975.

Bobath, B.: The very early treatment of cerebral palsy. *Dev Med Child Neurol*, 9:373-90, 1967.

_____: *Abnormal Postural Reflex Activity Caused by Brain Lesions*. London, William Heinemann Med Books Ltd, 1971.

_____: Motor development, its effect on general development, and application to the treatment of cerebral palsy. *Physiotherapy*, 57, 526-31, 1971.

Bobath, B. and Bobath, K.: Motor Development in the Different Types of Cerebral Palsy. London, William Heinemann Med Books Ltd, 1971.

Bobath, K.: The normal postural reflex mechanism and its deviation in children with cerebral palsy. *Physiotherapy*, 57, 515-25, 1971.

Bobath, K. and Bobath, B.: Cerebral palsy. In P.H. Pearson and C.E. Williams (Eds.): *Physical Therapy Services in the Developmental Disabilities*. Springfield, Thomas, 1972.

Brazelton, T.B.: *Infants and Mothers*. New York, Delta Pub, 1969.

_____: *Neonatal Behavioral Assessment Scale*. Philadelphia, J.B. Lippincott, 1973.

Brazie, J.V. and Lubchenko, L.O.: The newborn infant. In C.H. Kempe, Silver, and O'Brien (Eds.): *Current Pediatric Diagnosis and Treatment*, 3rd ed. Los Altos, Calif., Lange Med Pub, 1973.

Brunnstrom, S.: *Movement Therapy in Hemiplegia*, New York, Harper and Row Pub, 1970.

Campbell, S.K.: Facilitation of cognitive and motor development in infants with central nervous system dysfunction. *Phys Ther*, 54: 346-53, 1974.

Caplan, F. and Caplan, T.: *The Second Twelve Months of Life. The Princeton Center for Infancy and Early Childhood*. New York, Grosset and Dunlap, A. Filmways Co, 1973.

Carter, R. and Campbell, S.: Early neuromuscular development of the premature infant. *Phy Ther*, 55: 1332-41, 1975.

Colangelo, C., Bergen, A., and Gottlieb, L.: *A Normal Baby: The Sensory-motor Processes of the First Year*. Valhalla, N.Y., Blythedale Children's Hosp, 1976.

Connor, F.P., Williamson, G.G. and Siepp, J.M. (Eds.): *Program Guide for Infants and Toddlers with Neuromotor and Other Developmental Disabilities*. New York, Teachers Coll Press, 1978.

Drillien, C.M.: School disposal and performance for children of different birthweights born 1953-1960. *Arch Dis Child, 44*: 562-70, 1969.

_____: Abnormal neurologic signs in the first year of life in low birthweight infants: possible prognostic significance. *Dev Med Child Neurol, 14*: 575-84, 1972.

Dubowitz, I.M.S., Dubowitz, V., and Goldberg, C.: Clinical assessment of gestational age in the newborn infant. *J Pediatr*, 77:1-10, 1970.

Easton, T.A.: On the normal use of reflexes. *Am Sci, 60*: 591-98, 1972.

Erickson, M.L.: *Assessment and Management of Developmental Changes in Children*. St. Louis, The C.V. Mosby Co, 1976.

Farber, S.D.: *Sensorimotor Evaluation and Treatment Procedures for Allied Health Personnel*, 2nd ed. Indianapolis, Indiana Univ. Foundation, 1974.

Finnie, N.: *Handling the Young Cerebral Palsied Child at Home*, 2nd ed. New York, E.P. Dutton & Co, 1975.

Fiorentino, M.R.: *Normal and Abnormal Development. The Influences of Primitive Reflexes on Motor Development*. Springfield, Thomas, 1972.

_____: *Reflex Testing Methods for Evaluating CNS Development*. Springfield, Thomas, 1979.

Flanagan, G.L.: *The First Nine Months of Life*. New

York, Simon & Schuster, 1970.

Frankenburg, W.K. and Dodds, J.B.: *Denver Developmental Screening Test*, rev. ed. Denver, La Doca Foundation, 1970.

Gilfoyle, E. and Grady, A.: *A Developmental Theory of Somatosensory Perception in the Body Senses and Perceptual Deficit*. Edited by A. Henderson and J. Coryell. Boston, Boston University, 1973.

Goff, B.: The application of recent advances in neurophysiology to Miss M. Rood's concept of neuromuscular facilitation. *Physiotherapy*, 58, 409-215, 1972.

Heriza, C.: *Reflex Developmental Evaluation and Treatment of Developmentally Disabled Children*. Lawrence, Children's Rehabilitation Unit, Univ of Kansas, 1976.

Hirt, S.: The tonic neck reflex mechanism in the normal human adult. *Am J Phys Med, 46:* 362-69, 1967.

Holt, K. (Ed.): *Clinics in Developmental Medicine. Movement and Child Development*, vol. 55. Philadelphia, J.B. Lippincott Co, 1976.

————: *Reflex activity in infancy. Dev Paed*, 1977.

Hooker, D.: *Prenatal Origin of Behavior*. Lawrence, Univ of Kansas Press, 1952.

Horton, M.C.: The development of movement in young children. *Physiotherapy, 57:* 149-58, 1971.

Hoskins, T.A. and Squibb, J.E.: Developmental assessment: a test for gross and reflex development. *Phys Ther, 53:*117-26, 1973.

Illingworth, R.S.: *The Development of the Infant and Young Child. Normal and Abnormal*, 6th ed. Edinburgh and London, E and S Livingstone Ltd, 1975.

Johnson and Mogarb: *Developmental Disorders: Assessment, Treatment, Education*. Baltimore, Univ Park Press, 1976.

Johnston, R.B.: Motor function: normal development and cerebral palsy. In Johnson and Mogarb: *Developmental Disorders: Assessment, Treatment, Education*. Baltimore, Univ Park Press, 1976.

Knott, M. and Voss, D.E.: *Proprioceptive Neuromuscular Facilitation*, 2nd ed. New York, Harper and Row, 1968.

Kong, E.: Very early treatment of cerebral palsy. *Dev Med and Child Neurol*, 8, 198-202, 1966.

Levine, B. and Salek, B.: An Approach to the Treatment of the Cerebral Palsied Children. Long Island, New York, Suffolk Rehab Ctr.

Levitt, S.: *Treatment of Cerebral Palsy and Motor Delay*. Philadelphia, J.B. Lippincott Co, 1977.

Lovell, K.E.: The effect of postmaturity on the developing child. *Med J Aust, 1:*13-17, 1973.

Lubchenco, L.O., Delivoria-Papadopoulos, M., and Searls, D.: Long-term follow-up studies of prematurely born infants. II. Influence of birth weight and gestational age on sequelae. *J Pediat, 80:* 509-12, 1972.

Manning, J.: Facilitation of movement—the Bobath approach. *Physiotherapy*, 58, 403-408, 1972.

McGraw, M.B.: *The Neuromuscular Maturation of the Human Infant*. New York, Hafner Pub Co, 1962.

Meier, J.H.: Screening, assessment, and intervention for young children at developmental risk. In T.D. Tiossen (Ed.): *Intervention Strategies for High Risk Infants and Young Children*. Baltimore, University Park Press, 1976.

Moore, J.C.: *Neuroanatomy Simplified*. Dubuque, Iowa, Kendall/Hunt, 1969.

————: *Concepts From the Neurobehavioral Sciences*. Dubuque, Iowa, Kendall/Hunt, 1973.

O'Connell, A.S. and Gardner, E.B.: *Understanding the Scientific Basis of Human Movement*. Baltimore, The Williams and Wilkins Co., 1972.

O'Doherty, N.J.: Neurological foundation of motor behavior in infancy. *Physiotherapy* 57:144-48, 1971.

Paine, R.: Evolutions of infantile postural reflexes. *Develop Med Child Neurol, 6:*345-61, 1964.

Parmelee, A.H.: The hand-mouth reflex of Babkin in premature infants. *Dev Med Child Neurol, 31:* 734-40, 1963.

————: The palmomental reflex in premature infants. *Dev Med Child Neurol, 5:*381-487, 1963.

————: A critical evaluation of the Moro reflex. *Pediatrics, 33:*773-88, 1964.

Parmenter, C.: The asymmetric tonic neck reflex in normal first and third grade children. *Am J Occup Ther, 29:*463-68, 1975.

Payton, O.D., Hirt, S., Newton, R.A. (Eds.): *Scientific Bases for Neurophysiologic Approaches to Therapeutic Exercise: An Anthology*. Philadelphia, F.A. Davis, 1977.

Pearson, P. and Williams, C. (Eds.): *Physical Therapy Services in Developmental Disabilities*. Springfield, Thomas, 1972.

Prechtl, H. and Beintema, D.: *Clinics in Developmental Medicine. The Neurological Examination of the Full Term Newborn Infant*, vol. 12. London, Spastics International Medical Publications. William Heinemann Medical Books Ltd, 1964.

Roberts, C.J.: Developmental and neurological sequelae of the common complications of pregnancy and birth. *Brit J Prev Soc Med*, 24, 33-38, 1970.

Rosenbloom, L. and Horton, M.E.: The maturation of fine prehension in young children. *Dev Med Child Neurol, 13:*3-8, 1971.

Rushworth, G.: On postural and righting reflexes. *C P Bull, 3:*535-43, 1961.

Saint-Anne Dargassies, S.: Neurodevelopmental symptoms during the first year of life. *Dev Med and Child Neurol*, 14, 235-46, 1972.

Samilson, R.L. (Ed.): *Clinics in Developmental Medicine*. Orthopedic Aspects of Cerebral Palsy, vols.

52 and 53. London, William Heinemann, 1975.

Scherzer, A.L.: Early diagnosis, management and treatment of cerebral palsy. *Rehab Lit*, 35:194-9, July, 1974.

Scientific American, vol. 241, No. 3, Sept., 1979, 45-240.

Stern, F.: The reflex development of the infant. *Am J Occup Ther*, 25:155-58, 1971.

Stockmeyer, S.A.: A sensorimotor approach to treatment. In P.H. Pearson and C.E. Williams (Eds.): *Physical Therapy Services in the Developmental Disabilities.* Springfield, Thomas, 1972.

Twitchell, T.E.: Reflex mechanism and the development of prehension. In K.J. Connally (Ed.): Mechanisms of Motor Skill Development. New York, Academic Press, 1970, pp 25-29.

Wilson, V.J.: The labyrinth, the brain and posture. *Am Sci, 63:* 395-404, 1975.

INDEX

Page numbers for charts are in italics.